WARFARE IN THE
NINETEENTH CENTURY

European History in Perspective

General Editor: Jeremy Black

Benjamin Arnold *Medieval Germany*
Ronald Asch *The Thirty Years' War*
Christopher Bartlett *Peace, War and the European Powers, 1814–1914*
Robert Bireley *The Refashioning of Catholicism, 1450–1700*
Patricia Clavin *The Great Depression, 1929–1939*
Mark Galeotti *Gorbachev and his Revolution*
David Gates *Warfare in the Nineteenth Century*
Martin P. Johnson *The Dreyfus Affair*
Peter Musgrave *The Early Modern European Economy*
J. L. Price *The Dutch Republic in the Seventeenth Century*
A. W. Purdue *The Second World War*
Christopher Read *The Making and Breaking of the Soviet System*
Francisco J. Romero-Salvado *Twentieth-Century Spain*
Matthew S. Seligmann and Roderick R. McLean
Germany from Reich to Republic, 1871–1918
Brendan Simms *The Struggle for Mastery in Germany, 1779–1850*
David Sturdy *Louis XIV*
Peter Waldron *The End of Imperial Russia, 1855–1917*
James D. White *Lenin*

European History in Perspective

Series Standing Order
ISBN 0–333–71694–9 hardcover
ISBN 0–333–69336–1 paperback
(*outside North America only*)

You can receive future titles in this series as they are published by placing a standing order. Please contact your bookseller or, in case of difficulty, write to us at the address below with your name and address, the title of the series and the ISBN quoted above.

Customer Services Department, Macmillan Distribution Ltd
Houndmills, Basingstoke, Hampshire RG21 6XS, England

WARFARE IN THE NINETEENTH CENTURY

David Gates

palgrave

First published 2001 by
PALGRAVE
Houndmills, Basingstoke, Hampshire RG21 6XS and
175 Fifth Avenue, New York, N.Y. 10010
Companies and representatives throughout the world

PALGRAVE was formerly Macmillan Press Ltd and St. Martin's Press
Scholarly and Reference Division.

ISBN 0–333–73533–1 hardback
ISBN 0–333–73534–X paperback

This book is printed on paper suitable for recycling and
made from fully managed and sustained forest sources.

A catalogue record for this book is available
from the British Library.

Library of Congress Cataloging-in-Publication Data
Gates, David.
    Warfare in the nineteenth century / David Gates.
    p. cm. – (European history in perspective)
    Includes bibliographical references and index.
    ISBN 0–333–73533–1 (cloth)   ISBN 0–333–73534–X (pbk.)
    1. Military history, Modern – 19th century. 2. Military art and science –
History – 19th century. I. Title: Warfare in the 19th century. II. Title.
III. Series.

U41 .G39 2000
355'.009'034–dc21   00–048340

10   9   8   7   6   5   4   3   2   1
10   09 08 07 06 05 04 03 02 01

Printed in China

In loving memory of my parents, Margaret and George Gates, whose lives were too often blighted by war

CONTENTS

PREFACE

Military history's boundaries are difficult to identify, for it is hard to think of anything that has not influenced, or been influenced by, war. This book seeks to place warfare in the Eurocentric world of the 1800s in its political, social, cultural, intellectual and technological context. At the end of the day, any such study must reconcile the extent of the author's vision with the number of words allocated by the publisher; and I can only regret not having had the space to explore certain issues more fully. What I have deliberately shunned, however, is the production of a collection of campaign narratives; reference to events on the battlefield is made only for illustrative purposes. Of this period's major wars there are in any case innumerable studies, many of which concern themselves with little other than marches and fighting, and go into far more detail than could conceivably be possible in a work of this size.

In any event, the scope of the subject posed documentation problems. No literary compilation could fully reflect the breadth of my own explorations over many years, still less pose as an exhaustive list of potential sources; so I have restricted myself to providing a select bibliography, essentially as a guide to further reading.

For similar reasons, it is impossible to do justice here to all those who, in one way or another, have assisted me in this book's production. However, I would like to reiterate my thanks to them and stress, as always, that any errors are mine alone.

D. G.

1

THE NAPOLEONIC ERA AND ITS LEGACY

In many regards, Napoleon's genius was more practical than theoretical. As a military reformer, he was not so much an innovator as someone who was obliged to build on or adapt existing concepts, largely because he was constrained by the technological possibilities of his time. Indeed, in this respect he lived during an era of such prolonged consistency that many of his contemporaries, notably the soldier and, later, celebrated military theorist Antoine-Henri de Jomini, persuaded themselves that the 'essential nature' of warfare could not change.[1]

Certainly, from around 1700 until the Crimean War 150 years later, armies continued to consist of three principal branches – infantry, cavalry and technical units such as artillery, engineers and sappers – and were, for the most part, dependent on smoothbore, muzzle-loading flintlocks and ordnance. These weapons had been, and continued to be, refined through incremental rather than revolutionary change. Detachable, socket bayonets, for instance, constituted a significant improvement on the old plug variety in that they afforded individual infantrymen a simultaneous capacity for both fire and shock action. Indeed, although military thinkers since the days of Niccolo Machiavelli had pondered on the implications that gunpowder would have for tactics in particular and warfare in general, despite the ultimate reliance on small and large firearms, at the end of the 1700s many of the features of ancient warfare still seemed to be present. Smoothbore guns had neither much more accuracy nor reach than the slings, bows and ballistae that they had superseded, while, for close fighting, manual weapons – swords, bayonets and lances – were commonly relied upon. And just as, for the infantry, movement on and between battlefields remained a matter of stamina, traction continued to be furnished by harnessing 'natural' forces, too: until the

1

introduction of primitive railways, horses remained the fastest means of land transport and not only served as mounts for the cavalry but also hauled guns and vehicles. Similarly, the movement of most shipping was still essentially reliant on air and water currents. No, too little, or an adverse wind could utterly paralyze any sailing vessel. Whilst this meant that, particularly in comparatively shallow, coastal waters, there was still some scope for the use of galleys, on the other hand banks of oars were a relatively inefficient, manpower-intensive way of propelling a ship of any size.

All of this suggested that much could still be gleaned from the writings of Thucydides, Xenophon, Polybius, Caesar, Tacitus, Vitruvius and other classical authors. Indubitably, all of the Enlightenment's military intellectuals were to some degree influenced by them, notably in the intense debate about the relative merits of the *ordre profond* and the *ordre mince*, of shock-action and firepower. The latter had come to predominate by the beginning of the 1800s and, through its ramifications for the deployment of forces, was, in time, to help transform the very concept of the battlefield; once apt, this term became something of a misnomer as improvements in the reach of weaponry and increases in the size of fighting units led to engagements being fought over ever larger tracts of territory.

During the initial decades of the 1800s, the essential constancy that prevailed in the means with which war could be waged dictated that innovation was confined to changes in how it was conducted. At this, Napoleon surpassed his predecessors and many of his contemporaries. Exploiting latent potential that had often been identified by others, he succeeded in making better use of what material and intellectual resources were at hand. So far as the recruitment, organization, tactics and sustenance of his armies are concerned, he drew heavily on eighteenth-century military thought, notably the works of the Duc de Broglie, Pierre de Bourcet, Jean Folard, François Mesnil-Durand, Henry Lloyd, Jean-Baptiste de Gribeauval, Jean Pierre du Teil and Jacques Antoine Hippolyte, Comte de Guibert. Developing and refining these theorists' embryonic concepts in the light of his own and others' experience in the French Revolutionary Wars, he carried them as far as was practical in the musket and horse era.

Guibert's *Essai général de Tactique* of 1770, for instance, formed the basis of the French Army's ordinance of 1791, which, with a few modifications, was followed throughout the Napoleonic Wars. In addition to the traditional linear formation, which enabled infantry, deployed two or three ranks deep, to maximize its firepower, this prescribed the use of columns, particularly at the regimental and battalion level, for rapid manoeuvre, The two might also be blended together in *l'ordre mixte*, while numerous skirmishers sheathed such close-order formations to protect them and to harass those of the enemy. Where possible, infantry formed hollow squares to resist cavalry attacks, which horsemen executed boot-to-boot in either line or column.

Battlefield tactics are – or at least should be – a function of the capabilities of the armaments employed. Throughout the Napoleonic Wars, the muzzle-loading smoothbore musket served as the universal infantry weapon. It underwent only slight refinement and there was little to distinguish one pattern from another.[2] The model initially used by the French, for instance, dated back to 1777. After 1803, it began to be superseded by a modified version. Even without its detachable bayonet, which was triangular in section and 40.6 centimetres long, this was all of 1.53 metres in length and weighed 4.65 kilograms. The calibre was 1.75 centimetres, though the soft lead balls used as ammunition did not fit tightly in the barrel, into which they were inserted with a ramrod and held in place with paper wadding. Indeed, Napoleonic manual exercises – the drills relating to the loading and firing of a musket – comprised upwards of ten distinct phases, which were regulated by drum taps or shouted orders. In brief, from a pouch on his right hip, the soldier would take a cartridge. Made from stiff paper, this contained a musket ball and its propellant charge. Tearing off the end containing the shot with his teeth, the musketeer would sprinkle a little of the gunpowder into the pan on the side of the lock; a fine touch-hole led from this into the interior of the barrel. He would then place the butt of his musket on the ground and tip the bulk of the charge into the barrel, spitting the ball down on top of it. The paper cartridge, screwed into a ball, would follow it. Drawing the ramrod from a slot within the stock, he would then push all of this to the bottom of the barrel. As there was no rifling to contend with, this was not too difficult. Indeed, without the wadding formed by the cartridge paper, there was a danger that the bullet would roll out, should the gun's muzzle be tilted downwards. After retrieving the ramrod – an action which panicky soldiers tended to forget in the heat of battle – and returning it to its housing, he would bring the musket up to the present position. When the trigger was pulled, a flint ignited the powder in the pan, the sparks from which, if all went well, detonated the main charge in the barrel.

Misfires, however, were common. Worn flints or damp powder might result in a complete failure of the firing mechanism, or a mere flash in the pan might leave the main charge unexploded at the bottom of the barrel. Although safety dictated that this had to be removed by one means or another, it was not unheard of for inexperienced, agitated or careless soldiers to repeat the entire loading procedure until, when it finally ignited, the disproportionately large charge blew the musket (and its owner's face) to pieces. Emitting flames and sparks, the lock and pan also posed a hazard which, albeit more unpleasant than life-threatening, could make musketeers shirk somewhat as they squeezed the trigger. This, coupled with the weapon's recoil, did little to promote accurate, aimed shooting.

In any event, the appreciable windage in the barrel, together with the variable aerodynamic properties of the bullets, made muskets of very limited reliability when it came to firing at individuals, though they were capable of throwing a ball up to 300 metres. As one contemporary observer averred:

> A soldier's musket, if not exceedingly badly bored, and *very crooked, as many are,* will strike the figure of a man at 80 yards, it may even at 100 yards; but a soldier *must be very unfortunate indeed* who shall be wounded by a *common musket* at 150 yards, PROVIDED HIS ANTAGONIST AIMS AT HIM; and as to firing at a man at 200 yards with a common musket, you may just as well fire at the moon and have the same hopes of hitting your object [my emphasis].[3]

In fact, it is generally far better to speak of reach rather than accuracy here; for, unassisted, the human eye can scarcely identify individual targets 800 metres away and, even today, using the most precise weapon and sophisticated sights available, it is improbable that the best of marksmen could, with a single shot, hit a fleeting target of this kind at a range in excess of 500 metres.[4]

In any case, during Napoleon's time muskets were primarily designed to maximize the rate of fire as opposed to its range or accuracy. The 'Brown Bess', used by the British infantry from the middle of the eighteenth century until the middle of the nineteenth, did not even have any sights; soldiers were simply told to 'Look along the barrel with the right eye from the breach pin to the muzzle and remain steady. Pull the trigger strong with the forefinger.'[5] Although, above all, the growth in the employment of skirmishers stimulated debate about the concept of aimed fire,[6] technological limitations dictated that targets would, ideally, be large, dense formations at relatively short range. Amongst these, it was probable that at least a percentage of incoming fire would find a victim; and, as the likelihood of this increased with the volume of fire, the deployment of troops in close-order continued to be emphasized for both attack and defence, though shallow, linear formations were clearly more advantageous than deep, columnar ones when it came to maximizing the number of troops who could see – and thus shoot at – a given target.

Then, as now, firepower was an amalgam of not just range but also the precision of a given weapon and its capacity to be consistently accurate. It also needs to be lethal. Most serious wounds were inflicted by smooth-bore muskets at ranges of under 100 metres; spent balls might bruise but were unlikely to cause debilitating injury, let alone death. Again, however, the degree of effectiveness was and remains dependent upon a range of interactive factors, namely the design of (including the materi-als utilized in) the construction of the firearm, the chemistry of the explosives employed as initiators and propellants, and the ballistic qual-ities of the projectile, both imparted to it on firing and in flight. Moreover, in devising a firearm, the relationship between its power and its strength and weight has to be kept in mind: just as the quantity of propellant required to hurl a projectile increases with the latter's weight, so too does the explosive force of the detonation. Increased strain on the chamber needs to be offset through a more robust construction. In the days before strong but lightweight metals were available, this implied a proportionate increase in the weight of the weapon, which affected its portability or, in the case of artillery, mobility. Further, the more violent the detonation, the heftier the gun's 'kick'. Napoleonic armaments could be troublesome in this regard. Prolonged bouts of firing commonly led to infantrymen suffering bruised shoulders, while cavalry preferred pis-tols and carbines – shorter, lighter versions of the musket – for shooting from the saddle lest they be unhorsed by the recoil of their own weapons. Such small arms were also somewhat easier to load on horse-back because of their shorter barrels, though this feature also led to a corresponding reduction in their range. Similarly, field artillery, which had to be drawn by horses and, lacking any recoil-absorption mecha-nism, manhandled back into position after each discharge, was perforce limited in weight and, thus, power.

During the First Empire, the French Army's ordnance, for example, comprised updated versions of the cannon and howitzers first designed by Gribeauval in 1776. They were mass-produced, being constructed from standardized parts, which, being interchangeable, also simplified their repair and maintenance. Classified by the weight of the projectile they fired, their bronze, brass or iron barrels had to be mounted on suitably sturdy carriages. This made for a very heavy object indeed.

Even the lightest version of the 12-pounder cannon – the largest field, as opposed to siege, gun – weighed some 818 kilograms. Of its crew of 15, eight were specialist personnel, the principal function of the rest being to help manhandle the piece in action. The barrel was elevated and depressed by means of a screw. Detachable levers were used to align the weapon with the target, and the carriage was fitted with front and rear housings for the barrel trunnions. Lifted into the first of these positions for firing, and into the second when the gun was to be moved any distance, this arrangement allowed the barrel's weight to be distributed more evenly, thereby keeping the gun as stable as possible. Nevertheless, despite this ingenious measure and the fact that Gribeauval's limbers were simplicity itself – essentially just an axle-tree, they were designed to carry neither ammunition stocks nor the gun's crew, who marched or, in the case of horse artillery, rode alongside their pieces – it still required no fewer than six draught horses, harnessed in pairs, to tow such a cannon.

As was the case with the overwhelming majority of the period's small arms, these guns had smooth bores and worked on the same principle as their more diminutive brethren. A lengthy ramrod was employed to insert munitions into the barrel, which had to be swabbed out between discharges with sponges affixed to poles. Once pushed to the bottom, the bag containing the propellant was pierced through a small vent, the touchhole, by means of which the crew, using a slow-burning cord, ignited the charge. They were direct-fire weapons; their shots flew in a straight line and could only be directed against visible targets. As muzzle-velocity determined the gun's reach, punch and precision, long barrels – which allowed the pressure generated by the combustion of the propellant to be optimized – were preferred. They fired two basic types of projectile: solid cast-iron shot – which did not explode and, consequently, had to be targeted precisely – and 'area', essentially anti-personnel, munitions in the form of grape and canister. The last of these, sometimes termed 'case', consisted of musket balls sheathed in a metal cylinder which disintegrated either on firing or on impact, showering the surrounding area with its contents. In land warfare, grape was a similar device, but, comprising bits of scrap metal, nails and pebbles, tended to excessively damage the bore of the gun and was reserved for use in emergencies, as was 'double loading' – the mixing of roundshot with canister. At sea, 'grape' denoted a form of heavy canister comprising nine balls, weighing between 200 and 500 grams, wired together round a central frame.

The reach of a gun varied according to the precise weight and type of projectile being used. Canister range for a 12-pounder extended up to 600 metres. Whilst it could throw roundshot up to three times this distance, targets were not normally engaged beyond 1000 metres. In either case, if the ground was sufficiently hard, the ball would ricochet, throwing up stones which might also inflict casualties, as would the shattered equipment and *disjecta membra* of the roundshot's victims. For such projectiles did not just kill; they smashed men and horses to pieces. Even when they had lost most of their kinetic energy and were slowly rolling along the ground, these chunks of cast iron were still quite capable of mangling one's foot.

For howitzers – which, in contrast to cannon, normally fired canister or exploding shells along a parabolic trajectory and, thus, might undertake indirect fire, *providing*, of course, that the target could be located[7] – the weapon's muzzle-velocity was of less importance than the size of the projectile. Accordingly, howitzer barrels were normally relatively short with wide bores, the French, for instance, employing six- and eight-inch calibres. The shells were hollow, cast-iron spheres filled with gunpowder and fitted with a fuse which could be adjusted in length. Ignited by the combustion of the propellant charge in the howitzer barrel, the fuse would burn as the projectile flew to its destination, detonating it, ideally, when it was directly overhead so as to rain splinters up to 25 metres in all directions. However, achieving consistency was problematic in that it took great skill on the part of gunners to judge the distance – and thus the appropriate length of fuse – to the target. Some shells exploded prematurely, while many others ploughed into their victims before bursting. Because their angle of descent was, unlike that of a cannon shot, quite steep, they were less likely to ricochet, and soft ground could swallow them entirely, smothering any explosion.

A variation on the common shell was spherical case shot, which had been devised by Lieutenant Henry Shrapnel of the Royal Artillery in 1784 and entered service with the British Army in 1804. Here, the charge was designed to do no more than fracture the shell's casing. Its contents – up to 170 musket balls – would then be released, continuing to travel in the same direction and at the same velocity. Spherical case was thus effectively a combination of the common shell and canister: it could be fired from either howitzers or guns and permitted even those targets lying at maximum range to be struck, the spread of bullets offsetting any imprecision in the initial targeting. Again, however, fuses needed to be expertly set to avoid untimely detonations, which frequently occurred. Indeed, it was not until as late as the 1850s that it was realized that, during the shell's flight, the bullets inside often jostled one another with sufficient violence to generate heat, which could detonate the charge prematurely. In any event, records of tests conducted in 1812 suggest that, at ranges of between 630 and 1370 metres, no more than 17 per cent of the bullets would ever prove effective.[8]

Even this degree of success would not be consistently attainable under campaign conditions, where the physical and psychological strains of battle would affect the gun crew's performance. Much would also depend upon the precise nature of the target and its immediate environment. Extended, linear and columnar formations had contrasting degrees of vulnerability that might also be varied by terrain features. Moreover, when burnt, the blackpowder that constituted the only explosive available during the Napoleonic era not only fouled barrels and touch-holes, but also produced hanging, thick clouds of acrid smoke which could soon obscure any target, either by enveloping it, the firing unit, or both.

This only accentuated the importance of maintaining control in the use of firepower. But if atmospheric and climatic conditions were significant considerations in the conduct of land battles, they were of paramount importance in engagements at sea. For here, in the age of sail and before the days of rotating turrets, training cannon on a target was as much a matter of bringing the whole vessel into a suitable position as it was of aiming the armament itself. Besides calling for great skill in the hoisting, lowering, reefing, letting-out and trimming of perhaps hundreds of square metres of billowing canvas, all of which had to be done by hand and with due regard for the prevailing winds and currents, this process was also affected by the roll and pitch of the ship and by the gun-ports' design, which determined the arc of fire; the reach of the ship's armament was often of more theoretical than practical value.

Since propelling a given mass across water was (and remains) a far more energy-efficient process than moving it over land or through the air, ships had the unique distinction of being able to shoulder enormous weights and yet remain mobile. Moreover, in a given period, soldiers and horses could only march a certain distance, which varied inversely with the weight of their burden and was also affected by other factors, notably their physical fitness, the nature of the terrain, atmospheric conditions and by the amount of nourishment the men and animals received. Once exhaustion set in, they had to rest. Although her speed was subject to prevailing weather conditions, providing there was sufficient exploitable wind, a ship, by contrast, could keep moving around the clock. Divided into watches, her crew members could alternate between operating her and eating and resting; only in times of real emergency need the entire vessel's company be activated.

Battle was obviously such an eventuality. Besides personnel whose primary responsibilities were those of sailing the vessel and manning her guns, a ship's complement would always include several artificers and, frequently, a small number of marines. These soldiers – drawn, in Britain's case, from six regiments placed under Admiralty control – helped officers keep order in an environment where tedium and harsh conditions were more likely to prove the solvent of discipline than fear. Specialists in close combat, marines also increased the punch of landing-parties, by means of which the effective reach of the vessel could be extended inland and beyond the range of its principal armament; for, although two-thirds of the Earth's surface is covered in water, vessels are perforce confined to the navigable stretches. In ship against ship actions, the marines would stiffen the hand-to-hand combat capabilities of the crew and, at close range, would supplement the vessel's firepower with their muskets. Aimed fire against enemy gun crews and personnel working in the rigging – particularly those courageous, agile sailors who, perched precariously high above the deck, were tasked with setting the topgallant and royal sails – had much to recommend it, but officers, on whom the control of the opposing vessel ultimately depended, were the prime target. Indeed, it was to such a sniper that Nelson himself fell victim at Trafalgar in 1805.

A ship's main firepower, however, comprised its cannon, which had to be of sufficiently large calibre to inflict damage on the structure as well as the crews of opposing vessels. Timber ships were sturdily constructed from large, often massive, pieces of wood. Not only did they have to be able to withstand the immense physical strains imposed by winds and waves, but also they had to be resistant to any chemical reactions that immersion in salt might result in. Oak and elm were found to be ideal for the building of large ships in particular, but, as demand often exceeded supply, other timber was experimented with. The vast Spanish galleon *Santissima-Trinidad*, which was lost at Trafalgar, was built from cedar, while many frigates, sloops and other small vessels were predominantly made from fir. Maple and teak were also tried, but were found to be less suitable, the latter because its splinters tended to cause septic wounds. This was an important consideration as, in maritime battles, flying fragments of timber were as likely to inflict casualties as the projectiles that shattered them.

If demolishing robust hulls, superstructures and masts called for heavy guns, then supporting such ordnance demanded a commensurably stout platform. The high load-bearing capacity of ships allowed tiers of cannon to be incorporated into their designs. The *Santissima-Trinidad* had all of 130 guns, nearly a third as many again as HMS *Victory*, one of the largest vessels in the Royal Navy. Moreover, although they worked on precisely the same principles as the pieces employed by armies, it was customary for naval guns to be of similar calibre to those reserved for sieges in land warfare. What Napoleon dubbed his 'most beautiful daughters', the awesome 12-pounder field guns of the *Grande Armée*, would have appeared puny alongside typical naval cannon, many of which fired shots weighing up to three or four times as much.

Clearly, such ordnance was incapable of moving very far or fast. Nor was it intended to. Carriages had small wheels and were designed with robustness in mind. They were secured in place by a web of ropes – a loose cannon was extremely dangerous because of its weight – and were hauled into their firing positions with the aid of pulleys. Run out through ports, the hatches of which were usually kept shut when the cannon were not in action in order to reduce the danger of water entering the hull, guns would, when discharged, bounce backwards and had to be restrained by a cradle of strong cables. Just as cannon were vulnerable to falling debris as well as to an adversary's direct fire, their primary target was often not so much the men on board an enemy vessel as the ship itself; disable or sink the latter and the former, providing hand-to-hand combat could be avoided, were rendered irrelevant. But whether achieved by inflicting casualties on the crew or through damage to its steering, rigging, yards, masts or hull, once control over a sailing vessel was lost or impaired, it might well prove impossible to bring its own ordnance to bear.

To enable naval guns to ravage hostile vessels, special projectiles were added to the varieties encountered in land warfare. We have already noted the use of a distinctive type of grape in maritime warfare, and there was also a number of special projectiles which were not dissimilar to the bolas in conception; fired from close range, these 'chain' shots shredded ropes, shrouds, sails and stays. During the Napoleonic era, French tactics placed great emphasis on the use of such weapons, whereas the British preferred to focus on firing at the hull and superstructure of enemy ships. This process could be commenced from a greater distance. Indeed, just as shot could ricochet on land, cannon balls could be made to skip over water if they struck the surface at the right angle and velocity. However, unlike their army counterparts, naval gunners were on a moving platform and had to make allowances for the effects that any swell might have on the frequency and angle of their fire. The shorter the range, the less serious this problem was likely to prove.

The British, above all, would brave an enemy's fire, seeking to engage him from ever-closer quarters. This, however, was a relatively new practice. During the eighteenth century, maritime rivalry had been dominated by, above all, the various conflicts between France and Britain, yet for the most part major clashes between their fleets had proved as inconclusive as they had intermittent. Just as French tactics – heavily influenced by the writings of Paul Hoste, a Jesuit professor of mathematics who had stressed the employment of geometric patterns as a means of transforming a group of ships into a controllable, disciplined entity – mirrored the linear structures employed in land warfare, so too did their naval strategy owe much to the reasoning that underpinned the conduct of war on land. Frequently, an indirect approach based on attrition or on manoeuvring for advantageous positions – neither of which necessarily called for the actual sinking of enemy vessels – was favoured. Indeed, French commanders normally shunned any thought of really coming to grips with the enemy and were very proficient at avoiding any such exigency. Instead, they preferred to slip away to fight another day after having inflicted as much damage as possible on the rigging of their adversary's ships.

For several decades, such policies had led to naval engagements invariably consisting of two opposing rows of ships-of-the-line (as they were revealingly known) sailing parallel to one another and exchanging broadsides. The results were predictably limited. However, the Battle of the Saints in 1782 had witnessed a departure from this established orthodoxy. Here, Admiral George Rodney had suddenly turned his squadrons towards the French line, piercing its centre. A vessel's cardinal weak spots were the stern and bows, where very few guns could be accommodated. If one ship succeeded in bringing itself alongside another at either of these points, it could rake its quarry with the great bulk of its own ordnance and with relative impunity. Indeed, from this position, it might achieve the most efficient use of its own firepower by engaging two ships simultaneously. So much is self-evident. Nevertheless, achieving and then maintaining such a situation was as dependent upon initiative, good seamanship and discipline as it was upon anything else. Ships do not have brakes and, if collisions were to be avoided, penetrating a line of hostile vessels called for appreciable navigational skills and a keen sense of timing. Above all, cutting across an opponent's bow or stern ineluctably involved exposing one's own vessel to his broadsides for a time at least.

This was to invite catastrophe, but, in war as in so many other areas of human activity, it is more often than not impossible to achieve significant results without running risks – and the more spectacular the outcome one desires, the greater the risks are liable to be. Like all great commanders, Rodney recognized this unpalatable fact and concentrated on minimizing the odds against success so far as was possible. On this occasion, he triumphed. However, war is a matter of probabilities, not certainties. In the age of sail, it was all too easy for even a badly mauled adversary to evade decisive defeat. Not only were the sturdy wooden ships capable of absorbing a lot of punishment without actually sinking, as a glance at the list of losses on both sides at Trafalgar confirms, but also a beaten opponent who had not had his ships secured by his adversary might slip away under cover of a storm or darkness or battle smoke, or might simply be better placed to exploit the prevailing wind. Engaging him as closely as possible was the best way to reduce his chances of escape. Besides promising to maximize the damage inflicted on his vessels, this tactic opened up the possibility of ensnaring them with grappling hooks, forcibly boarding them, defeating their crews in mêlée and actually taking possession of them.

The aggressive manoeuvre tactics that increased the likelihood of decisive success and were first employed by Rodney in 1782 were evidently inspired by a theoretical work that had appeared earlier that same year. Composed by John Clerk of Elden, this *Essay On Naval Tactics* formed the basis of a new doctrine that the Royal Navy steadily refined during the 1790s, applying it with particularly striking results in 1797 against the Spanish in the Battle of Cape St Vincent and against the Dutch at Camperdown. In these engagements, Admirals Jervis and Duncan, respectively, attained local superiority by making a perpendicular intersection of a key segment of their opponents' formations with the bulk of their own fleets. After defeating the isolated part of the hostile force in detail before the rest could hasten to its aid, the British ships, divided into sub-units and allowed to act on their own initiative within a stipulated operational framework, then concentrated against their adversaries' remaining vessels.

The Royal Navy's run of significant victories culminated with Trafalgar in 1805. Nelson himself evidently found Clerk's *Essay* so inspirational that he liked to have it read to him in his free time. Certainly, at Trafalgar he applied its message with his customary *élan* and boldness, famously urging his outnumbered fleet to 'engage the enemy more closely'. As he had correctly anticipated, this rapidly led to the suppression of the French and Spaniards' more numerous guns as damage, confusion and demoralization spread throughout the bowels of their ships. The last of these factors was, as always in war, the single most important one in determining the outcome. Confronted by an adversary who defied their best efforts and pressed ever closer, many of the Allied gun crews seem to have faltered at the mere thought of the enfilading fire that would soon be focused upon them; after letting off a few rounds, they abandoned their cannon for the relative safety of the far side of their vessels. Pierced by two columns of hostile ships, their mighty armada was defeated piecemeal; 18 of its 33 capital ships were pounded into submission or boarded.

Impressive though this was, as late as 1813 Britain continued to be haunted by doubts about the durability of her hard-won maritime supremacy. In the event, her fears of a resurgent naval threat proved unfounded, but this became a source of some disappointment and frustration to a generation of officers who, whilst encouraged to employ nautical power offensively, encountered few opportunities to do so. Apart from a handful of relatively insignificant engagements between individual squadrons or small flotillas, operations during the Napoleonic Wars after 1805 were essentially defensive and were dominated by the unglamorous mission of blockading continental ports. This called for an ability to stay at sea for lengthy periods and in all weather conditions, which could place great strains on both ships and crews. Operating a sailing ship was hard manual labour. This, together with the need to keep the vessel's company fighting fit – that is, in reasonable spirits and free of diseases like scurvy – called for a generous, varied diet, with a high protein and vitamin content. The Royal Navy proved particularly adept at satisfying these basic requirements and, consequently, its sailors tended to be that much healthier and more content than those of its principal opponents. Prize money – which was distributed to crews whenever they captured enemy vessels or cargoes and could amount to very substantial sums indeed – was another important factor in maintaining morale and gave men an incentive to seek out hostile shipping. Again, this put a premium on securing major engagements, where the chances of seizing one or more enemy ships were that much greater. (Nelson himself not only acquired fame, promotion and a peerage but also immense wealth through his victories.) Yet, though many must have expected a very different turn of events as the turbulent history of the nineteenth century unfolded, the Royal Navy would have to wait over a hundred years to fight a sea battle comparable in scale and importance to Trafalgar.

In addition to any human enemy, all mariners had three common foes: the sea, adverse weather and fire. In the Royal Navy, at least, the harshest disciplinary measures were normally reserved for those who behaved in a fashion that might jeopardize the vessel or its company. Fire posed an immense threat to ships constructed from timber, topped off with canvas sails and packed with gunpowder. Occasionally, red-hot shot – which had to be separated from the propellant charge by a wet sponge in order to avoid premature detonations – was employed to set ships ablaze, but this was as risky an undertaking for the practitioner as it was for the intended victim and was best done from the comparative safety of dry land. Fire ships, too, could prove dangerously intractable and, belching smoke, could make the process of command and control that much more difficult; apart from any other considerations, manoeuvres were, as we shall see, orchestrated by means of flag signals from vessel to vessel.

Indeed, the degree of visibility could have significant ramifications for the conduct of engagements. Ranks of musketeers were often engulfed in the smoke generated by their own weapons. This, like the fall of darkness, could obscure the enemy to such a degree that firing at him or discerning his movements might become impossible. For artillery, whether used at sea or on land, matters could be more complex still, for, unlike small arms, it generated smoke and threw up dust both in its immediate vicinity and around its quarry. This could complicate the process of target acquisition and fire control, reducing the rate of discharge well below the theoretical maximum of, in field artillery's case, two to three rounds per minute.

In any event, ammunition stocks were finite; field artillery's sustainability was determined by the number and capacity of the limbers and supply wagons in the army's train, while ships had nothing but their organic stocks to fall back on. In both cases, the precise blend of ammunition of different calibres, the ratio of one type of projectile to another and the size of the reserves of gunpowder were also important considerations. Whereas just a few dozen projectiles might exhaust the load-bearing capabilities of a given vehicle, voluminous but comparatively light cargoes like propellant charges would quickly fill it to capacity.

Similarly, accommodation allotted to, say, canister was not available for the storage of round shot, which had very different performance characteristics. On the other hand, both of these would be useless if the supply of propellant charges were to be exhausted, or if the guns in need of replenishment were of smaller calibre than the available ammunition. Furthermore, operating guns was always hard work and, as fatigue began to tell on the crew, their performance would tail off. The endurance of their pieces, too, had its limits. Although they resisted wear and tear quite well, withstanding up to 7000 consecutive discharges, metal barrels were ineluctably prone to overheating, especially during prolonged periods of frequent use. This could lead to them drooping, or to charges detonating prematurely. Because of all of these considerations, the speed of fire tended to vary, largely in accordance with operational priorities; artillery would redouble its efforts at crucial points in an engagement, while maintaining a more leisurely rate of fire at other times. Moreover, most commanders liked to keep at least some ordnance in reserve until the climax of a battle. Napoleon himself normally held back several batteries, including the numerous and powerful artillery of his Imperial Guard. This enabled him to commit as many as 120 guns, many with fresh, élite crews, in support of the *coup de grâce*.

Any attempt to refine the weaponry of this era and, thereby, loosen the tactical shackles it imposed was itself subject to technological constraints and to considerations regarding its cost-effectiveness. For example, rifling – grooves cut in the barrel – imparts spin to a gun's projectiles. This torque produces a more stable trajectory, making rifled armaments that much more accurate than those with smooth bores. However, whereas loading the latter through the muzzle was a comparatively easy matter because of the windage, in the case of the former it involved forcing the shot into the grooves of the rifling. Although, if wrapped in a greased leather patch, the soft metal bullets could be driven to the bottom of the barrel, it was a relatively slow, laborious task which became harder with every shot, since burnt powder would progressively foul the turnings. In fact, many riflemen carried a small mallet with which they tapped the ramrod down the bore. Consequently, rifles had a rate of fire that was far slower than that of muskets. Moreover, although the latter were not as precise, neither was their effective range so very much less. This meant that the rifleman retained the upper hand only so long as he could remain beyond the reach of his opponents – something he did best when released from the ranks and permitted to act on his own initiative. However, should his adversaries get close enough to employ their own armaments efficaciously, then the rifleman was in danger of being overwhelmed, if only in terms of the volume of his opponents' fire. It should be remembered that, whilst, ideally, one would want every shot from every weapon to prove lethal, in practice this does not occur. Nor is it strictly necessary; the demoralizing effects of near-misses can often prove destructive enough. If intimidated into keeping his head down, it made no difference what type of gun a marksman was armed with; and, once musketeers had penetrated sufficiently close to render the superior accuracy of rifles irrelevant, then their faster rate of fire could prove decisive.

The precise nature of the terrain and the formations employed were clearly important factors here; they helped determine the opposing sides' respective vulnerability. Certainly, riflemen were seen as having an Achilles' heel and, accordingly, special attention was paid to the formulation of their doctrine and tactics. The alternative – improvements to their weapons which were technically feasible, affordable and would not have disproportionate logistical and maintenance requirements – remained elusive until the mid-1830s, as we shall see. As early as the 1740s, however, breech-loading rifles, for instance, had been developed in Britain. Formed by a series of converging plates that screwed together, the breech obviated the time-consuming task of ramming the bullets down the barrel. This was hard to do in any position except standing, which often exacerbated the soldier's vulnerability. On the other hand, such delicate technology suffered badly as a result of the prolonged use and rough treatment it was ineluctably subjected to in the field. A weapon of this type saw some service with a small unit of sharpshooters in the American Revolutionary War, but, after proving difficult to keep in good working order, it had been virtually withdrawn by 1780. All of 40 years later attempts to devise a breech-loading rifle using this approach were still encountering problems, as even the eminent British gunsmith Ezekiel Baker was forced to concede:

> I have tried various ways of loading rifles at the breech, by means of screws placed in different positions; but after a few rounds firing, the screws have become so clogged by the filth of the powder working round them as to be very difficult to move, and will in time be eaten away with rust, which will render them dangerous to use.[9]

A pioneer who had encountered these difficulties as early as 1780, Bartholomew Girandoni had sought to overcome them by turning to compressed air as a propellant. The gas was stored in a small flask ingeniously accommodated in the rifle stock, while a magazine held all of 20 rounds of ammunition, allowing Girandoni's *Repetierwindbüchse* to achieve a rate of fire that hitherto had been unimaginable. The gun was, moreover, virtually silent, did not generate smoke and was highly accurate up to 250 metres, a range at which few marksmen employing traditional rifled muskets would be at all likely to hit an individual target. Impressive though all of this sounds, the very sophistication of the *Repetierwindbüchse* compromised its operational utility. As was discovered with subsequent generations of weapons that possessed this quality, its capacity for rapid fire too frequently led to ammunition being squandered. It also required bullets of a distinctive design, which created logistical complexities, as did its need for compressed air. Furnishing this was particularly demanding under battlefield conditions. The bottles were bulky and emptied at least as fast as the magazine, while, two metres high and made of cast iron, the compressor used to recharge them was barely portable, particularly in the wooded, hilly and otherwise broken terrain that skirmishers were best suited to. Last, but by no means least, the intricacy of the air rifle's design made manufacture and maintenance technically problematic and financially costly; in 20 years, no more than 1100 were produced. After seeing sporadic service with the Austrian Army during the French Revolutionary Wars, the gun was withdrawn in 1800.

If the problems encountered in the quest for dependable breech-loading small arms proved daunting at this juncture, then those involved in the production of artillery pieces were quite insurmountable; guns and howitzers continued to be muzzle-loading designs until the middle of the 1800s. Similarly, rockets – which had been in use in Asia for hundreds of years – might have offered a viable alternative to the more familiar artillery projectiles had it proved possible to perfect some way of guiding and detonating them. At the siege of Seringapatam in India in 1799, their employment by the natives against the British was noted by William Congreve, the eldest son of a general who, while working at the Woolwich Royal Laboratory, had designed a new carriage for artillery that reduced the weight on the trail, and thus made the piece easier to manhandle in general and to aim in particular. Attached to – and subsequently Controller of – the laboratory's staff, William, himself a gunner by training, was no less inventive than his father and, seeking to improve on the Indian model, eventually devised an explosive rocket that first saw service with the British armed forces in raids on Boulogne in 1804 and 1805, during which 'catamarans' – crosses between mines and torpedoes – also played a part. Congreve's rockets fell into light, medium or heavy categories, with warheads of up to 32 pounds comprising a thin perforated case filled with explosives and either a shell or a roundshot. Secured to a stick with iron bands that screwed into place, the rockets were launched from a wheeled cradle or portable tripod, the length and height of the trajectory being proportionate to the length of the stick. They could reach as far as 1800 metres, but aiming them was a haphazard affair and so they were best employed as indiscriminate, area weapons against sprawling targets. Indeed, they seem to have been at their best when used as incendiary devices. In this capacity they inflicted substantial damage on Copenhagen in 1807, and on various American towns and settlements in the Anglo-American War of 1812–15, but attempts to use them against troops in the field only highlighted their shortcomings. As an observer at one test in 1814 records:

> They certainly made a most tremendous noise, and were formidable spitfires; no cavalry could stand if they came near them. ... [B]ut in that seemed the difficulty, for none went within half a mile of the intended object, and the direction seemed extremely uncertain. ... [O]n a flat, ... where they would ricochet or bound along straight, they might do very well, but in the ... experiment they went bang into the ground, sometimes ... one way and sometimes another. Some, ... instead of going fourteen hundred yards as intended, were off in a hundred, and some pieces of the shell came back even amongst us spectators. ... [T]he wind at times carried [these rockets] ... three hundred or four hundred yards [off course] .... [10]

Besides this appalling inaccuracy, Congreve rockets also posed similar operational and logistical dilemmas to those encountered with the *Repetierwindbüchse*. The portable version might fire up to four times a minute, but, already encumbered with the tripod and sticks, a bombardier could not carry more than two or three rockets at a time, despite being provided with a special quiver to accommodate them in. They were also too inconsistent and inflexible a weapon when set against good old-fashioned artillery. Although they could do appreciable damage, on the few occasions that they did manage to strike hostile troop formations, they appear to have made an impact that was more psychological than physical. One of the few units of the Royal Artillery that were equipped with these exotic armaments participated in the Battle of Leipzig in 1813 and evidently had some success in terrorising some French infantry, who 'did not seem familiar with this new weapon ... and stood up against it; but when they saw in what a ghastly manner the victims died, even if only a drop of the fuel came too near, ... ran away'.[11] Among the casualties who were later found at this spot, testifies one soldier, were several who had been 'completely burnt on their faces and uniforms in a most uncommon way, so that one could readily understand how the enemy's morale had been shaken by this extraordinary operation'.[12]

By the time of the Waterloo campaign in 1815, however, the novelty was wearing off. One British officer chronicled what might well have been the rocket troop's only success – and even that proved ephemeral. He recalls seeing them, during the Anglo-Dutch-German army's retreat from Quatre Bras, placing a little iron triangle in the road with a rocket lying on it. The 'fidgety missile' he continues,

> begins to sputter out sparks and wriggle its tail, ... then darts forth straight up the chausée. A gun stands right in its way, between the wheels of which the ... rocket bursts, the gunners fall right and left, and, those of the other guns taking to their heels, the battery is deserted in an instant. ... [O]ur rocketeers kept shooting off rockets, none of which ever followed the course of the first; ... some actually turned back upon ourselves – and one of these, following me like a squib, actually put me in more danger than all the fire of the enemy.... Meanwhile, the French artillerymen, seeing how the land lay, returned to their guns and opened a fire of caseshot on us....[13]

Thereafter, Wellington, who had stipulated that the rocket troop bring light artillery pieces with them as well as their pyrotechnics, insisted that the latter be accorded less prominence than the former, even if this order did break the heart of Major Whinyates, the rocketeers' leading enthusiast. Nevertheless, Whinyates did seize his chance to launch a few rockets while at Waterloo; they disappeared into a field of tall crops and landed who knows where. Twenty years later, a wounded British dragoon, who had fallen amidst the enemy's lines, was able to tell him that he had 'heard the rockets passing and the French swearing... at them and the English for wishing to burn them alive ...'. Again, however, it is unclear whether these projectiles did any real physical harm. Actual damage was difficult to assess, and Whinyates was not alone in entertaining expectations that Congreve's rockets rarely fulfilled.[14]

Semaphores and flight by means of hot-air balloons were two other innovations which, by the 1790s, were being adapted for military purposes. The latter, pioneered by the Montgolfier brothers, caught the imagination of various military theorists, notably Britain's John Money. It was the French Revolutionary authorities, however, who first utilized balloons operationally. The garrisons of Valenciennes and Condé employed them as observation platforms when they came under siege in 1793, the crews communicating with the beleaguered towns by carrier pigeon. In April 1794, the French Army created the first of several official units of *aerostatiers*. Equipped with a silk balloon filled with hydrogen, within weeks it saw service at Fleurus, where its occupants relayed messages to the ground either with signal flags or by notes dropped in weighted bags.

Promising though this appeared, balloons were very much at the mercy of the prevailing winds. Money's second ride in one almost cost him his life – he was blown off course, descended into the sea and almost drowned – while at least one French balloon crew came down amidst hostile troops and, in addition to being taken prisoner, had to suffer the further indignity of watching their captors eat their carrier pigeon.[15] Moreover, like the gas bottles of the *Repetierwindbüchse*, balloons needed a compressor to fill them – a process which, in any case, took 36–48 hours. Such equipment was cumbersome and, together with the gondola and the envelope when deflated, required several vehicles to transport it. Above all, however, if the collation of useful intelligence from a floating balloon was easier said than done, then turning it into something that was comprehensible and disseminating it in a timely fashion to commanders on the ground was extremely difficult. Although Napoleon made some use of balloons as observation platforms in Italy in 1796 and was accompanied by a squad of *aerostatiers* during the Egyptian campaign of 1798, the loss of most of their equipment off Alexandria only underscored their inflexibility and helped persuade him to abolish this fledgling air arm when he came to power.

Visual telegraph systems, notably that devised for the French Army by Claude Chappe, proved a more successful venture, but, again, their utility was constrained by the human eye's limitations. Relay stations had to be prominently situated and, depending upon local weather and topographical conditions, at intervals of about ten kilometres. These nodes comprised a small tower on which stood a ten-metre cross. By means of a web of counterpoises and pulleys, which were controlled by levers mounted inside the tower, the horizontal beam, the 'regulator', could be swung through angles of 45°. At each of its ends was a hinged 'indicator', which could also be swivelled into different positions, giving a total of 196 contrasting patterns, or 'signs'. These could represent either single letters of the alphabet, enabling words to be spelt out one at a time, or whole words or phrases. Indeed, just as ship-to-ship communication was revolutionized by bunting systems, notably that perfected by Captain Home Popham in 1803, which enabled Nelson, for example, to send his famous Trafalgar message, so too did the Chappe and other semaphores permit the encoding of very complex missives. Not only did this mean that, if necessary, messages could be sent in a form that was incomprehensible to an adversary, but also that large volumes of information could be transmitted comparatively swiftly. A good operator could send up to three signs per minute, enabling messages to be transmitted at speeds as high as 200 kilometres an hour in clear weather conditions.

On the other hand, although the indicators and regulators were illuminated with lanterns, darkness, fog or storms too often prevented the next link in the chain from discerning them. Similarly, coupled with the need to maintain visibility between relay stations, the inherent limitations of any portable system constrained attempts to utilize such semaphores in mobile warfare. Miniature, wagon-mounted versions of the Chappe telegraph were experimented with, but, cumbersome though they were, they lacked the range of their bigger brethren. Above all, as line-of-sight devices they were too dependent upon geography to be employed in some areas; in very flat or heavily wooded terrain, suitable sites for the nodes could prove impossible to find.

In 1809, the Bisamberg, which overlooked so much of the Wagram battlefield and its surroundings, served an Austrian telegraph unit well in this regard, but such coincidences were rare. The principal means of disseminating orders and information remained the mounted courier for both Napoleon and his adversaries, though the former did employ teams of flag-waving soldiers to improvise a few communication links between his field forces and the distant termini of the French semaphore network. This mirrored established maritime practice, but was too manpower intensive an approach to be viable everywhere, particularly on the steppes of Russia, the venue for Napoleon's next campaign. Nor could any messages match the sophistication of those of the Chappe towers without large stocks of bunting and correspondingly comprehensive signal manuals being provided. Semaphores had more to recommend them, but, like flag systems, were effectively confined to the realm of fixed, rather than mobile, and strategic, as opposed to tactical, communication – a situation which, as we shall see, neither electric telegraphs nor telephones were to improve on very much.

Historians and economists remain divided over the wider benefits of military spending. As all weapons exist for one purpose, their general utility is ineluctably limited, and switching production from meeting the demands of consumers into satisfying those of armed forces can often prove inflationary. Moreover, since different types of military units have contrasting capabilities, besides complementing they can also compete with one another, if only to a degree.

All of this poses dilemmas for those concerned with the allocation of resources, which, in turn, has critical repercussions for military planning, since, in the final analysis, the availability of certain assets dictates whether a particular strategy is viable or not. Given the nature of their responsibilities, the military can be pardoned for a tendency to seek to over-insure; it is rare for them to be entirely satisfied with the personnel, equipment and supporting infrastructure at their command, for the case for some qualitative or quantitative improvement, if only to cope with contingencies, can always be made. However, not only are means inevitably finite, necessitating the balancing of military against other investments, but also priorities have to be identified within procurement and maintenance programmes. Just as maritime power might be judged to be of more importance than armies, infantry, say, might be of more use for a particular mission than artillery, or vice versa. Similarly, the topographical, climatic and other conditions prevailing in one theatre of war might be very different from another, necessitating adjustments to the ratios of regular to reservist personnel, and to a force's structures, equipment and clothing. During the nineteenth century, this consideration was particularly important for the great colonial powers, which, besides having to plan for the defence of their homelands, also had to take into account the demands imposed by their overseas possessions. It was one thing to raise, train and accoutre an army which, like the Prussians', was destined to be based within Central Europe's temperate climes and used exclusively to combat fairly predictable threats in that selfsame region; but recruiting, retaining, attiring and equipping soldiers who, like those of Britain, confronted a great variety of opponents and, frequently for prolonged periods, were scattered in sedentary garrisons from Canada to Africa or were performing constabulary operations on the frontiers of India, was another.

Prosperity and stability remain elusive without security, yet any investment in military capabilities has opportunity costs attached to it. Further, whilst all armed forces' *raison d'être* is to persuade any would-be adversary that a resort to violence as an instrument of policy, including defence policy, would be counterproductive, the failure of deterrence is self-evident, whereas its success is not. In preparing for wars that might never actually materialize, states run the risk of engaging in an expenditure of effort and resources which might well prove not merely wasteful but futile, too. On the other hand, to fail to take precautions can, if only with the benefit of hindsight, look like reckless negligence. So much depends upon the perception of threats, which, if discernible at all, can prove real or imaginary.

The term 'total war' has often been employed, yet it is essentially vacuous. At best, one can conclude that the totality of some conflicts has been greater than that of others. Indubitably, by the standards of the time, the Napoleonic War appeared to surpass its predecessors, at least those within living memory. Indeed, it was widely known as 'The Great War' until the contest of 1914–18 transcended it. Even the latter conflict, however, could fairly be depicted as limited in all sorts of respects. Many perceptions of a conflict's 'totality' largely turn on the extent to which the belligerents' human and material resources are committed to the struggle. But even this line of analysis is not very satisfactory, for many contests have been asymmetrical from the outset and have thus imposed far heavier burdens on one side than on the other, while still more conflicts have been waged with something less than the utter annihilation of the enemy in mind. It is little wonder that the difficulties in distinguishing total from limited wars troubled even that great doyen of military theorists Carl von Clausewitz, who, writing in the wake of the Napoleonic conflict, was to observe:

> A review of actual cases shows a whole category of wars in which the very idea of *defeating the enemy* is unreal: those in which the enemy is substantially the stronger power.... Wars have...been fought between states of *very unequal strength, for actual war is often far removed from the pure concept postulated by theory*. Inability to carry on the struggle can, in practice, be replaced by two other grounds for making peace: the first is the improbability of victory; the second is its unacceptable cost. ...Not every war need be fought until one side collapses.... Since war is not an act of senseless passion but is controlled by its political object, the value of this object must determine the sacrifices to be made for it in *magnitude* and also in *duration*.[16]

Although, relative to what had gone before them, some of the nineteenth century's wars were more intense, had ramifications for greater numbers of people and witnessed state intrusion into the lives of individuals in, frequently, unprecedented ways, this is true of neither every case of conflict nor of their various facets. It is, for example, often difficult to distinguish cause from effect when exploring the relationship between war and economic activity in what were essentially free markets, often very diverse economies and dynamic commercial systems. Violent conflict might, say, lead to the restructuring of labour forces or patterns of trade, just as it might result in the redistribution of wealth, altered priorities, and changes to supply and demand. However, none of these developments need necessarily affect overall growth rates or other putative indicators of economic health. Whilst some sectors of an economy might palpably suffer as a result of war, others might prosper or seem to be quite unaffected either way. For heavy industry, for instance, military requirements, even in wartime, often represented but a marginal increase in markets; there was nothing comparable to the boom this sector was to experience in the two world wars. After all, none of the major powers except Britain began the 1800s with anything other than inchoate capacities in this regard, and increasingly important though such assets became for the production of certain types of military equipment, most others could be, and largely were, manufactured on a cottage-industry basis in innumerable little workshops and foundries, all of which functioned with minimal, if any, state interference; if governments were the customers of manufacturers, it was the latter who essentially retained control over production and other decisions. Any requirements that could not be satisfied indigenously in whole or part could normally be met by imports, as the Boer Republics in South Africa found as late as the very end of the century. They not only equipped themselves with French and German artillery pieces purchased from Creusot and Krupps, respectively, but also British Maxim-Nordenfeld pom-pom guns. All of these were subsequently employed against the British in the war of 1899–1902, while both sides were to improvise shells and cannon in railway workshops.[17]

Indeed, in endeavouring to reconcile the competing demands of security with those of prosperity, throughout our period states frequently turned to private enterprise to share the burden, with the firms concerned being granted subsidies, monopolies or other privileges in return for their services. Britain's East India Company (EIC) was the very embodiment of this approach. Through a royal charter bestowed in 1600, it obtained the exclusive right to trade with any country east of the Cape of Good Hope and west of the Straits of Magellan. Seeking to carve out new markets and sources of supply in this region, and with the delegated prerogatives of a sovereign state, including those of declaring war and concluding peace with any non-Christian nation, it rapidly became as much of a military machine as it was a commercial organization. Its forces grew in proportion to its territorial acquisitions and, by 1820, totalled 300 000 men, of whom perhaps just 40 000 were Europeans. For political reasons, the officer corps comprised Britons. Nevertheless, their homeland did not have to finance the EIC's army, which was paid for purely through taxes levied by the company within its domains, notably India, with which the EIC retained its monopoly on trade until 1813. Acting either single-handedly or in collaboration with the forces of the Crown, EIC units were to participate in several major conflicts. Among these were the Egyptian campaign of 1801, the Anglo-Burmese Wars of 1824–26 and 1852, the struggle of 1838–42 for Afghanistan, which included the disastrous retreat to Peshawar, and the so-called 'Opium Wars' of 1839–42 and 1856–60.

If the loss of its monopoly on Chinese trade in 1833 underscored the growing challenge to the EIC's activities from its commercial competitors, the rivalry with Russia over Afghanistan highlighted a danger that was as perennial as it was worrying: the possibility that the company might embroil Britain in a war not just with some obscure Maratha, but with one of the other great powers. This had long threatened to render mercantilism counterproductive; indeed, as early as 1784, William Pitt the Younger, the then Prime Minister, had endeavoured to bolster governmental supervision of the EIC with the India Act, which established a Board of Control, the president of which was to be a member of the Cabinet. As it was, the Indian Mutiny of 1857–58, which so imperilled the Raj and caused Britain so much international embarrassment, had many of its roots in the EIC's policies. Indeed, no sooner had the rebellion been suppressed than the EIC had to relinquish the government of India to the British Crown.

The EIC was by no means the only corporation which raised its own regular or paramilitary units to supplement, or substitute for, those of its parent state, but most private enterprises that ventured into the military sphere at all contented themselves with providing other people's armed forces with *matériel* and services. Though largely cyclical, this trade was as varied as it was potentially lucrative. Rations, ordnance and small arms, together with supplies of powder and ammunition, were indispensable to both armies and fleets. The former, however, also needed massive quantities of, among other things, horses, manual weapons, footwear, clothing and accoutrements, while the building and maintenance of ships called for such items as canvas, pitch and rope, as well as technical specialists like naval architects, dockyard workers and makers of navigational instruments. Above all, huge amounts of mature timber were required for the construction and repair of vessels, necessitating long-term and timely investment in suitable forests. Since consumption tended to increase in wartime and yet neither the incidence of conflict nor the scale of the spurt in demand could be predicted with any accuracy, calculations invariably went awry. For instance, not the least of the many problems that the protracted contest with Revolutionary and Napoleonic France posed the Royal Navy was that of getting lumber merchants to furnish supplies of high-quality timber at peacetime rates.

Like all commercial activities, the trade in arms tends to flourish best in peacetime when conditions are relatively stable. Although conflict, or the threat of it, ineluctably generates a surge in demand for war materials, it can also expose companies to a range of dangers. Outstanding debts for services or equipment received; payments in a currency which might lose its value substantially or completely as a result of inflation, or political or strategic developments; the confiscation or destruction of merchandise while it is still in transit by either the belligerent powers or neighbouring polities that are anxious to preserve their neutrality: all of these can spell ruination for private enterprises conducting relations with warring factions. As in the case of the EIC, not the least of the eventualities they face, however, is that of interference in their activities by their own governments. This might even culminate in the company being taken temporarily or permanently into state ownership, with little, if any, compensation for its shareholders. As, in the course of the 1800s, European states made their bureaucracies more professional and their political systems more collective if not necessarily more democratic, the propensity for governmental regulation, and the scope and depth of such intervention, ineluctably grew.

Although this was particularly so in war, the very nature of their products, services and assets made certain companies a focus of governmental interest in peacetime, too. States are, after all, the principal customers of arms firms, the economic viability of which depends upon them finding markets for their products just like any other private enterprise. Their activities also call for raw materials, skilled labour, an industrial base, however primitive, and investment capital. The last of these can be difficult to generate internally if the companies' activities are not sufficiently profitable, whereas finding them externally depends upon the existence and willingness of banks which, in turn, rely on savers for the provision of their funds.

In a world dominated by the creeds and practice of free enterprise, where innumerable small firms and individual artisans and merchants pursued wealth however they felt was appropriate, it was as difficult for companies to try to protect themselves through the creation of cartels as it was for rulers to interfere in their activities and those of the population as a whole. In any case, state interest was defined in political and strategic, rather than economic, terms. Whereas, during the 1900s, rationing and bids to contain profits, wages and prices were a frequent feature of armed conflicts, in the 1800s tariffs and taxes were the main instruments with which a government might strive to control the market in both war and peace. Even cameralism, however, sought to promote certain forms of economic endeavour because they were seen as essential for the preservation of state power.

The closely related activities of mining, chemical production and the manufacture of armaments were among them. For example, gunpowder was indispensable in wartime, yet was far less in demand during peace. Had the timely provision of adequate supplies been left to the free market, disaster could all too easily have ensued. By the start of the 1800s, state-owned powder mills were to be found in most European countries, and the production of the ingredients of gunpowder – saltpetre (potassium nitrate), charcoal and sulphur – had also been fostered. Of these, saltpetre, which is formed by the decomposition of organic matter, proved the most difficult to procure in adequate quantities. Relatively abundant in tropical climes, it had to be produced artificially in *nitrières* – essentially compost heaps in walled enclosures – by many European states. Seeking to increase its availability, in the early 1780s the French government, for instance, offered a prize for the invention of an industrial manufacturing technique, which was won, some ten years later, by Nicolas Leblanc, who established a plant at St Denis.

Just as Britain had the Woolwich Arsenal and Laboratory for the manufacture of ordnance and propellants, at this juncture, the production of gunpowder in France was entrusted to the *Service des Poudres et Saltpêtres*. Its antecedents stretched back as far as 1354, but the *Service* itself had been established in 1775 as an agency of the Finance Ministry. Indeed, it exemplified the close links found in this era between states and private enterprise so far as the provision of *matériel* and services to armed forces was concerned; in 1787, its personnel were even issued with simple uniforms, giving them a paramilitary appearance. Under Napoleon, it was transferred to the purview of the War Ministry and the army's inspector-general of artillery, but it still enjoyed a good deal of autonomy and its staff were civilians.

If supplies of propellants and ammunition failed to keep pace, the manufacture of weapons would prove pointless. Indeed, the timely production of adequate quantities of gunpowder was one of several paramount concerns for any polity engaging in war. However, like so much else, this demanded careful preparation and investment in peacetime, which was not always undertaken even when it was practicable. On other occasions, the level of consumption was simply not foreseen or, indeed, foreseeable. This could lead to all manner of shortfalls which intruded into, and often transformed, people's daily lives. So it was that, at the outbreak of the American Civil War, the Confederacy found itself struggling with shortages of every kind, including a dearth of powder. Accordingly, new enterprises were set up and established ones expanded in order to satisfy the huge demand. Among the former was a Nitre Bureau, which laid down *nitrières* to generate saltpetre. Much of the raw material came from stables, but, in imploring households to conserve and donate the contents of their chamber-pots, the bureau also unintentionally inspired many a piece of ribald verse or prose. Nevertheless, in this regard, as with so much else, the Confederacy succeeded in eking out its relatively scant resources to the point where its troops in the field rarely lacked sufficient munitions.

Transport was another area where the state and entrepreneurs often worked hand in glove. Maintaining wagon trains, without which no army of the horse-and-musket period could take the field, was a costly business at the best of times, but during peace, especially, it was tempting to regard them as an extravagant luxury which could be foregone.[18] If done away with, however, whenever hostilities broke out, civilian contractors had to be induced to furnish horse teams and drivers, including those for artillery batteries, as well as transport vehicles.

Whilst such policies sometimes yielded financial savings – though private hauliers, particularly those faced with a desperate government, might demand exorbitant fees for their services – they had serious drawbacks in other respects. Civilians were essentially concerned with making money rather than with serving the state. They were not subject to military discipline and, too often, either absconded, stealing horses and valuable cargoes into the bargain, or abandoned their charges at the first sign of danger. In the course of lengthy conflicts especially, such problems encouraged belligerents to create train units which were manned by military personnel. In the French Army, for instance, whereas supply and transport under the Bourbon and Revolutionary regimes had largely been the preserve of private contractors, by 1804 a *Train d'Artillerie* had been formed which expanded to 15 battalions of 76 men each during the First Empire. After the campaigns of 1805/7 had revealed the shortcomings of the Breidt Company, which had been contracted to provide *La Grande Armée* with transport services, alongside these artillery drivers a *Train des Equipages Militaires* was also created which, by 1812, had swollen to 23 battalions. One of these was assigned to the medical corps, while each of the remainder was configured so as to be capable of supporting a large *corps d'armée*.

Wellington, summarizing both the fundamental importance of the commissariat to any army and the need for meticulous planning in the provision of its services, once observed that it was necessary 'to trace a biscuit…into a man's mouth on the frontier, and to provide for its removal from place to place, by land and water, or no military operations can be carried on.'[19] However, the more logistical backing given to the teeth of a force in the field, the greater the logistical demands imposed by its own tail. Supply wagons, their drivers and teams had their own requirements in terms of forage, rations, maintenance and so on. This created the need for yet more transport and personnel which, in turn, bred further demands and problems. Then, as now, not the least of these was that of finding routes which convoys could utilize at all. But, even in the best of circumstances, columns of vehicles tend to be ponderous, slender and vulnerable; if they do not actually impede an army, they are likely to slow it down.

Eager to maximize his forces' strategic mobility, Napoleon trimmed their tail to minimal dimensions. While standardization and interchangeable parts, as applied in the design of Gribeauval's artillery pieces, kept the range of spares and varieties of ammunition required to a minimum, thereby easing the logistical burden, his soldiers were expected to look to their own devices, supplementing their issued rations by living off the land wherever possible. Although Europe's growing affluence and the proliferation of root crops – notably potatoes and turnips – from the closing decades of the 1700s onwards made such an approach far more viable than before, it still meant that his troops usually had to keep moving to avoid exhausting a given locality's resources. That, however, was all part of Napoleon's thinking. Whereas armies in the eighteenth century, plodding methodically within a carefully constructed web of depots, had tended to seek not so much battle as advantageous positions, often with a negotiated peace in mind, Napoleon rejected this interminable, essentially attritional style of warfare in favour of lightning campaigns, in which the sole purpose of manoeuvre was to secure an engagement on favourable terms and, thereby, end the fighting. Aware that disease and exhaustion claimed the lives of far more soldiers than most pitched battles, and that the likelihood of demoralization – the greatest single threat to any army and one which was always aggravated and frequently caused by shortages of quotidian necessities – could only be increased by protracted operations, he strove to maximize his army's speed and mobility at the expense of its sustainability.

Nevertheless, it was Napoleon, after all, who famously observed that armies 'march on their stomachs'. He recognized that adequate logistical backing was of overriding importance in military operations and that his attempts to save his soldiers' heads with their legs could backfire. As the 1812 campaign in Russia and so many episodes of the conflict in the Iberian Peninsula were to highlight, Napoleon's doctrine was a calculated gamble. Yet this was and is the nature of war. (Indeed, among others, Robert E. Lee, in his campaigns of 1862/3, and Field Marshal Roberts, in pursuing his 'tiger spring' strategy during the Boer War, were to run much the same risks in their quests for decisive victory.) That it paid off more often than not is to be explained at least partly by the acute sense of the relationship between time and space with which Napoleon executed his operations, and the care he took in ensuring that his army's need for ammunition and other vital commodities could be adequately met.

To this end, a typical battalion of the *Train des Equipage Militaires* comprised a staff and four companies, each of which had over 150 draught animals with 34 wagons of various designs (but, again, with standardized, interchangeable parts wherever possible), a mobile field forge and 93 personnel, including blacksmiths, harness makers and wheelwrights, all of whom were officially soldiers. Nevertheless, civilians, employed on either renewable or fixed-term contracts, also had to be used to supplement the burgeoning staff of the *Intendance*, which subdivided into five *Services*, each of which discharged particular functions: the *Vivres-pain* supplied pulses and bread; the *Vivres-viande* furnished meat rations; the *Fourrages* provided hay, straw and grain; while the *Habillement* and *Chauffage* took responsibility for clothing and fuel, respectively. Whereas military organizations could provide many of the services required more efficiently, even with conscription or requisitions, or both, finding sufficient resources, including suitably trained and experienced personnel, from within the armed forces could prove very difficult. As armies grew ever larger and their demands for rations, forage and ammunition – together with the transport to move all of this, the bureaucracy to organize it and the taxes to pay for it – increased commensurably, states had no alternative other than to mobilize more and more of their resources and to do so with greater efficiency than their putative foes.

However, ideological and practical difficulties often conspired to render governments unable or unwilling to tamper with market forces and the liberties of companies and individuals. State-regulated mercantilism ran foul of the doctrines of Adam Smith and other advocates of *laissez-faire*, who reasoned that citizens were the best judges of their own interests and, if left to pursue them, would promote the wellbeing of a community in its entirety. As the possession of property was widely regarded as sacrosanct and was frequently the foremost indicator of people's position in the social hierarchy, the very notion of graduated taxation was politically controversial and, until after the French Revolution, was something that no European government could contemplate, still less levy. For much of our period, slaves were a common form of property, too; and the fate of Pitt's respective attempts to do away with them and bring in progressive taxation is revealing. Though matters turned out very differently in practice, his introduction of an income tax had to be presented – and was certainly intended – as a temporary, wartime measure, while his 1791 bid to abolish slavery failed completely. Whereas free labour could be dispensed with in hard times, slaves constituted capital investment, which could be difficult to liquidate. Only when the French wars had disrupted normal patterns of commercial activity, leading to, among other things, gluts in the cotton and sugar markets, was it politically possible for the USA and European powers to begin to abolish the slave trade.

In Britain's case, this was achieved in 1807, but the possession of slaves remained legal throughout her empire until 1833 and, in many other countries, for much longer. This was tragically true of the USA, where slavery injected prejudice, idealism and moral passion into the growing sectional argument that culminated in civil war. Nevertheless, initially at least, few people evinced any interest in stamping out slavery *per se*; they were far more concerned with preventing it spreading into the vast new territories acquired by the USA in the first half of the 1800s. If slavery became the bone of contention, it did so because, in addition to being a discrete political issue, it had a broader symbolism: it helped distinguish two societies, cultures and economies from one another in a struggle that was primarily about the relationships between individuals and their states, and between those states and the Federal government.

The cardinal possession of any individual is his or her life; and for a government to take it over is the greatest intrusion imaginable, particularly if the process culminates in the state sacrificing that life in pursuit of its perceived interests. Although, by the end of the 1800s, America and the Eurocentric world had officially divested themselves of slavery and its cousin, serfdom, this process of liberalization was more apparent than real in many regards. Certainly, in the course of the century, most states asserted an ever-greater claim to the lives of their citizens so far as preparation for and the waging of hostilities were concerned.

Just as its armed forces embody the ultimate power of any state, going to war was, and remains, its supreme prerogative. As early as the 1790s, most European polities already had contingency powers for the mobilization of their male populations in the event of an emergency. The enforcement of such rights was, however, subject to various tangible constraints, among others. In practice, no state had either the resources to identify and mobilize all its able-bodied men, or those necessary to train, equip, clothe and sustain them in the field. A mixture of political expediency and altruism also dictated that there be exemptions from military service for those who, on paper at any rate, merited special consideration. These included married men, those divorced or widowed with dependants, and those wealthy enough to purchase a substitute. Even where military service could not be avoided entirely, it was often possible for men to discharge their obligations by joining a local militia or garrison unit of some description, rather than the front-line regular forces.

It was not until the middle of the Napoleonic Wars that the concept of the *levée en masse*, first proclaimed by the French Assembly in 1793, became anything like a reality. Lazare Carnot might have been eulogized as the 'organizer of victory', but Napoleon and his Imperial bureaucrats and military officials succeeded in mobilizing a far greater percentage of France's manpower and other resources for their war effort than their Revolutionary predecessors, thereby exploiting thoroughly the intertwined notions of conscription and *guerre à l'outrance*. If, amounting to 200 000 men, the *Grande Armée* which he led into Germany in 1805 was probably the largest single field force Europe had ever seen, the host he amassed for the invasion of Russia was three times the size. While both of these campaigns were underway, moreover, he had scores of thousands of other troops protecting or consolidating what was to become the most expansive empire since Roman times. This situation persisted even after the disastrous retreat from Moscow, when, in Germany alone, Napoleon was still able to raise no fewer than 575 000 fresh soldiers, mostly conscripts, to supplement the veteran cadres he withdrew from Spain and Italy and the dregs of the old *Grande Armée*. Faced with such quantitative strength, his adversaries had no alternative other than to activate their own manpower on a similar scale. They eventually rose to the challenge, however, with the result that battles became ever grander affairs. Wagram in 1809, in which 161 000 Austrians backed by 534 guns were pitted against 180 000 French and allied troops with 488 guns, was the largest battle the gunpowder age had witnessed. But even this was surpassed four years later, when, over three days, all of 520 000 soldiers with some 2070 guns clashed around Leipzig along a front which at times extended for up to 42 kilometres.

How were Napoleonic forces organized? The backbone of any army during this period was its line infantry regiments, each of which comprised one or more battalions made up of several companies, the smallest tactical units. The precise strength of a regiment and the number of sub-units within it varied over time and from one state to another, but the French stipulations enacted half way through the Napoleonic Wars illustrate the basic structure that, by this time, was commonly employed by the armies of European powers. According to an imperial decree of February 1808, an infantry regiment was to comprise a staff of 50 – including adjutants and other administrators, medical personnel, eagle-bearers, musicians, a tailor, a cobbler and armourers – and four *battalions de guerre* and one *de dépôt*. At just four companies, the latter was smaller than the field battalions and was primarily concerned with the induction and training of new recruits. This was often undertaken by commissioned and non-commissioned officers who either had an evident talent for it or who, because of age or injury, were no longer really fit enough to participate in campaigns. Once he had learnt the manual exercise and the other complex drills of the Napoleonic battlefield, the novice would fill a vacancy in one of the *battalions de guerre*, each of which had 840 personnel divided into six companies of 140 officers and men.

On paper, an entire regiment of this pattern would thus comprise 3970 soldiers, of whom 108 would be commissioned officers. The French 1808 establishment of five battalions to a regiment was uncommonly large – most of the other European powers favoured a structure of two or three battalions – and reflected the burgeoning scale of both the First Empire's armed forces as a whole and its military commitments. Although it was unusual for more than two battalions of a given regiment to be present in the same theatre, the colossal *Grande Armée* that invaded Russia in 1812 included many regiments with no less than five *battalions de guerre*, which made them as large as an entire division had been in the Austerlitz campaign.

After completing their training with the depot battalion, new recruits would initially join one of the four 'centre' or fusilier companies that made up the bulk of any *battalion de guerre*. They normally manoeuvred in close-order lines and columns, or a mixture of the two, the soldiers firing in volleys rather than individually. To act in unison like this, particularly in the heat of battle, called for a high degree of discipline and training on their part, and for their officers to have effective command and control mechanisms. As we shall see, movements were choreographed, with drums and other musical instruments being used to both regulate and stimulate.

The battalion's two 'flank' companies – so called because they were deployed at the line's extremities on ceremonial occasions, if not always on the battlefield – were regarded as élite units and ideally comprised seasoned troops. The grenadier company was composed of men who were not only veterans, but also the biggest and strongest soldiers available; they were used as shock-troops, for particularly demanding assignments and as an ultimate reserve. The other flank company constituted the battalion's specialist light infantry, the *voltigeurs*. It was also made up of experienced troops, namely those whose physical stature was too small for them to qualify as grenadiers, but who were nimble, fit men who could sustain a rapid rate of movement for long periods, particularly across broken terrain. Trained as marksmen, they were primarily used for the *petite guerre* of reconnaissance, raids and outpost duties, as well as acting as skirmishers in set-piece engagements.

By the beginning of the 1800s, the last of these roles was acquiring greater prominence as the effects of the agricultural revolution that had first begun in Britain rippled across Europe. Enclosure; innovative farming techniques and crude machinery; new crops and livestock: all of this led to a dramatic increase in the production of food by a diminishing percentage of the total workforce. Much of the labour thereby released migrated into the towns and cities, swelling their populations and intensifying the growth of industry and commerce. Besides making the creation and support of larger military establishment feasible, aspects of this process had implications for battlefield operations. As urbanization, enclosure and afforestation progressively transformed the European countryside, tactics and units had to become more flexible, with skirmishers and columnar formations supplementing the linear ones that had been pre-eminent in the 1700s. No longer confined to the periphery of engagements, *petite guerre* operations became an integral part of major battles.

The French led the way in adapting their army to this change. In addition to the *voltigeur* companies attached to every *ligne* battalion, units composed exclusively of light infantry steadily grew in numbers until, by 1814, there were all of 36 such regiments – roughly one for every five *ligne*. The *infanterie légère* battalions had essentially the same architecture as those of the *ligne*, with 'flank' and 'centre' companies, though the latter were known as *chasseurs* and the grenadiers as *carabineers*. Capable of acting either in close or extended order, these troops were, by the standards of the day, not only tactically versatile, but also embodied an idea that was politically disturbing. The notion of encouraging common soldiers to use their initiative by releasing them from the constraints of cohesive formations and the close supervision of their officers ran contrary to the very ethos of Europe's feudal societies. It called for more mental preparation than it did tactical training, with some nationalities evidently proving more adaptable to it than others. Although experience in the campaigns against Revolutionary France and in the triad of crushing defeats inflicted on them by the eponymous emperor in the early stages of the Napoleonic Wars persuaded the great European powers of the importance of, among other things, light troops, their efforts to emulate the French in this regard were unsuccessful, qualitatively if not quantitatively speaking. By 1808, light infantry, usually organized along the very lines used by the French, formed a prominent feature of most European armies. However, conscripted Russian serfs and Austrian and Prussian peasants were at a grave psychological disadvantage when pitted against the children of the French Revolution. Further, the skirmisher's *modus operandi* clashed with the prevailing values of the time. Hit and run tactics struck many people as cowardly, as did the exploitation of cover on the battlefield. This, in many instances, was facilitated by uniforms that, in stark contrast to those of line troops, were dominated by drab, camouflage shades of green, grey and brown. Whilst this sort of garb might have been very practical, it was also as unappealing to aspiring heroes as it was to those females, especially, who expected soldiers to look chivalrous and dashing. (Indeed, few light infantry units were able to resist the temptation to adorn themselves with cords, braid and plumes, at least when they were off the battlefield, as well as taking pains to cultivate the debonair spirit traditionally associated with light horsemen.) More generally, too, military reformers in the feudal polities had to strike a balance between, on the one hand, undermining the social fabric and, on the other, improving their armed forces' operational efficiency; too often, measures that seemed necessary to protect the state from one kind of threat entailed risking its destruction by another. Cavalry was divided into two principal types, heavy and light. The former, comprising big men on large horses, relied upon straight, heavy swords as their primary armament, but they also had pistols and, sometimes, short muskets. Besides a sturdy helmet, in many instances they wore partial armour, notably a metal cuirass or breastplate, gauntlets and thick, knee-length leather boots. Such cuirassiers were as expensive as they were hefty, and few states could afford many, if any of them.[20] Their principal function was shock-action, whereas light cavalry, such as hussars and lancers, were chiefly designed with *petite guerre* missions in mind, notably rear, van and flank guards, screening, reconnaissance and the molestation of hostile troops, particularly fleeing, broken units. Originally infantry who used horses as a means of transport, dragoons were classified as either light or heavy, the latter version offering a cheaper if more vulnerable alternative to armoured cavalry. Indeed, more often than not, dragoons fought from the saddle during Napoleon's time, but continued to be equipped and trained to act as foot troops if and when required to do so. Indeed, their connections with light infantry, in particular, were often underscored by the use of titles redolent of the hunt, namely, among the Germanic powers, *Jäger zu Pferd*. At a time when few polities had any sort of police force, such troops were also to the fore in supporting the civil authorities in the maintenance of law and order – hence the expression, to dragoon.

Napoleonic cavalry regiments were made up of several squadrons, the precise size of both varying according to whether the unit was heavy or light. In the French Army, for example, *cuirassier* and *carabinier* squadrons averaged 90 officers and men, whereas those of *chasseur* regiments mustered around 145 personnel. Light regiments might also have as many as nine squadrons, compared with the four normally found in a heavy cavalry unit. A common feature of European armies by the early 1800s, horse artillery, comprising light cannon and howitzers served by mounted gunners, was ideal for providing such forces with close supporting fire. However, as with light forces in general, the degree to which such innovations were successfully exploited varied from one state to another. In Austria, for instance, where cavalry was regarded not as an arm which was capable of functioning *en masse* as an independent strike force, but as something to be scattered in support of the infantry, as late as 1809 *Kavallerie Batterien* were still being treated as nothing more than a particularly mobile form of positional artillery.

More generally, although it was eroded somewhat as his adversaries gradually copied his techniques, the superior doctrine followed by Napoleon's forces often proved enough of an advantage to offset any numerical inferiority. Thus, at Halle, in 1806, where the opposing sides were roughly equal in infantry and horsemen, the Prussians failed to extract any real benefit from having almost five times as much artillery as the French.[21] Whilst this can partly be accounted for in terms of how the various arms were employed discretely, the explanation is principally to be found in the supremacy of the French at closely coordinating units of cavalry, skirmishers, line infantry and guns.

From these component parts, Napoleon assembled a formidable killing machine. In 1800, he implemented something first envisioned by Bourcet and Broglie: whereas armies in the past had been cobbled together in an *ad hoc* fashion, with horse and foot regiments acting as the bricks in a unitary architecture, he reorganized the entire French Army, dividing it into several *corps d'armée* which, in turn, were composed of divisions that subdivided into brigades comprising two or more regiments. To this day, armies are modelled on this pattern. A typical *corps* in Napoleon's time, however, would consist of around 30 000 personnel, who were mostly divided between two or three infantry divisions and a cavalry division or brigade, each of which would have its own organic artillery and engineering units. The *corps* would also have additional artillery and other specialist reserves attached to its headquarters. By combining the three principal arms in these pyramid-like structures, Napoleon created a number of self-contained miniature armies that were capable of independent or semi-autonomous manoeuvre along, if desired, several axes.

This contrasted starkly with the type of operations that had prevailed in the 1700s. Sustained by an umbilical cord of depots, ideally protected by strongholds, the unitary armies of that period were ineluctably restricted in their size and capacity for manoeuvre. Encumbered with convoys and usually confined to a single axis of operations, they were obliged to move slowly – 16 kilometres would be considered a long day's march – and methodically, seeking marginal advantages in a war of positions that was effectively suspended during the winter months, when fresh fodder was unavailable and the movement of supplies and troops was complicated by road and weather conditions. Indeed, because of the pivotal function of fortresses, sieges were regular occurrences in this type of conflict, which, generally attritional, could prove very protracted, as in the case of the Seven Years' War and the American

Revolution. Although they did, of course, happen, even large engagements did not directly terminate conflicts. Whilst it is true that Frederick the Great once insisted that 'Battles determine the destiny of states. When you go to war, you must seek to bring on a rapid decision,'[22] this remark needs to be seen in perspective. A relatively small, thinly populated country, the Prussia of '*Alter* Fritz' seemed poorly placed to sustain a lengthy, attritional contest; she lacked the requisite resources and strategic depth. Frederick was thus obliged to fight pitched battles occasionally, not so much with the intention of annihilating the enemy and ending the conflict, but rather in a bid to gain the necessary time and liberty to redress a deteriorating position elsewhere in the theatre of operations. For him, battle was an 'emetic' that was prescribed when no other remedy was available; he took the view that even a defeat could not make his overall situation much worse. Consequently, even his two stunning victories of 1757 – Rossbach and Leuthen, in both of which he launched brilliant tactical offensives – were less the deliberate objective of preceding manoeuvres than the result of opportunistic decisions, while his very last war, that of the Bavarian succession, the so-called 'Plum and Potato' campaign of 1778/9, fizzled out without a single major clash having occurred.

This was largely because battle was immensely difficult to impose on an opponent and tended to take place by mutual consent. 'He who has an understanding of these things', asserted the veteran general and military theorist Henry Lloyd (*c.* 1718–83), 'can constantly wage war without ever finding it necessary to be forced to fight.'[23] Further limitations were imposed by command and control problems that were rooted in the armies' tactical doctrines and essentially monolithic nature. Without the devolution of power that a structure comprising *corps d'armée* and their sub-units permitted, marshalling a force of more than 70 000 men predominantly deployed in linear formations was largely impracticable, regardless of whether more troops were to hand or not. Consequently, even the largest battles of the 1700s, such as Blenheim (1704), Leuthen (1757) and Minden (1759) never involved more than 140 000 combatants and usually far fewer. Even the French Revolutionaries' *levée en masse* did not significantly change matters, the size of forces utilized on the battlefield remaining well within the parameters established earlier in the century.

The doctrine, structure and logistical arrangements of Napoleon's armies transformed all of this. Colossal swathes of Europe became theatres of war as his forces, usually distributed along several axes, manoeuvred in search of an opportunity to annihilate their opponents in decisive encounters. Although he claimed that '*Je n'ai jamais eu un plan d'operations*,' for Napoleon, strategy had no other purpose than to secure battles; these were the culmination of preceding operations and it was through them that he strove to destroy an adversary's means and will to resist. Whilst, like an accomplished chess player, he had favourite gambits, which will be outlined presently, he evidently preferred them precisely because they did not depend too much on preconceived notions and lent themselves to adaptation and variation. He saw battle as a matter of probabilities, not certainties, and was extraordinarily successful at maximizing the odds in his favour, emerging triumphant from nearly all of the 50 major engagements that he fought, against a variety of opponents, in his career. As Wellington, the victor of the 'close-run thing' at Waterloo, remarked, 'I have had experience enough to know how very exact a man must be in his calculations and how very skilful in his manoeuvres to be able to do that.'[24]

As Napoleonic weaponry had such limited reach, securing a battle involved the manoeuvring of forces, often over tremendous distances, to within a few metres of their quarry. At this, Napoleon excelled. His operations fell into three discernible phases: the move into contact, battle and the exploitation of its outcome. Protected and masked by cavalry, and loosely assembled in what he termed a '*battalion carré*', his *corps d'armée* would march within supporting distance of one another yet sufficiently dispersed to live off the land and engage in distributed manoeuvre. Once contact was made with the enemy's forces, the *carré* would begin wrapping itself around them like some immense bolas; unless they could evade being ensnared, they would be compelled to fight engagements which grew in intensity and scale. Finally, for the climactic confrontation, Napoleon would concentrate every available soldier, usually securing, if only on a local basis, enough of a qualitative or quantitative superiority to overwhelm his quarry. Any forces that escaped destruction on the main battlefield would be exterminated in a relentless pursuit which, as in the case of the 1806 campaign against Prussia, might last weeks and continue for hundreds of kilometres.

Strategically, Napoleon utilized three basic tools, either separately or in combination, according to circumstances. The first, *la manoeuvre sur les derrières*, was employed to destroy an opposing force which had been isolated by manoeuvre or had ventured out on a limb. A prime illustration of it is seen in Napoleon's 1805 campaign; after approaching the Austrian army at Ulm indirectly, he encircled and captured it. Through the exploitation of a central position and interior lines, which made it possible to achieve a local superiority on each battlefield in turn, his second *modus operandi* enabled him to defeat numerically stronger forces in detail, as he did in his first Italian and 1814 campaigns especially. He also used it, if only with initial success, in the Waterloo campaign, which, like his invasion of Russia, Napoleon opened with a strategical penetration, his third rudimentary device.

His forces' flexibility on the strategic plane was matched by their tactical sophistication; adapting their formations to changing circumstances, individual units might perform a whole sequence of operations within a given action. Moreover, by replacing unitary structures with combined forces of infantry, cavalry and artillery, Napoleon maximized the scope for synergy. Indeed, the key to tactical success in Napoleonic battles was the close coordination of the three arms. Where this failed to occur, as at Waterloo, disaster could easily ensue.

Music and War

Music fulfilled two important functions in all of this. Firstly, it served as a unit's clock by marking the various phases in its daily life; a distinctive bugle-call or drum-beat would signal the beginning of the soldiers' day and its end, or that it was time to, for instance, 'fall in' for duty or to 'fall out'. Musical instruments also had a crucial operational role in that, besides sounding such temporal calls as reveille, they were used to supplement gestures and the human voice in disseminating basic tactical instructions on the battlefield. Even units that were either sufficiently small or arrayed in a formation that was compact enough for all the troops to be in sight, if not earshot, of their officers could be rendered quite unwieldy by the pandemonium of battle. Brass and woodwind instruments, especially, could produce shrill, penetrating sounds which could be heard both over the roar of gunfire and from afar, while percussion, notably metallic-framed drums, which steadily superseded wooden ones, were prized for their fine sonorous qualities.

Moreover, travelling at the speed of sound, fanfares and drumbeats could cover considerable distances far faster than orderlies, however swift their horses. This permitted simple directives, at least, to be communicated almost instantaneously to forces spread across a swathe of countryside. Without this capability, effective command would have been all but impossible. Indeed, just as armies and, correspondingly, the engagements they fought grew in size, so too did the demand for some means of timely communication over ever-greater distances.

An early indication of this spiralling problem came with the widespread introduction of light infantry into European armies around the turn of the eighteenth century. Whereas their colleagues in the line regiments were invariably deployed shoulder-to-shoulder in relatively cohesive formations under the watchful eyes of their officers, such troops were more often than not scattered across (often broken) terrain in extended order and little clusters. Seeking to avail themselves of any available cover and advancing, standing or retiring according to the needs of the moment, theirs was a relatively mercurial fight which contrasted starkly with the ordered movements of the line troops. If the activities of these skirmishers were to be adequately coordinated and controlled, it was realised that not only would they need a more generous allocation of commissioned and non-commissioned officers to supervise their numerous, disjointed sub-units, but also a system for controlling them remotely which would have to be as mobile as it would have to be relatively sophisticated. Accordingly, just as the traditional, camouflaged dress of the *Jäger* was adapted for military purposes, so too were the other trappings of the hunt, including its music. As drums, particularly those with metal shells, were rather cumbersome, heavy instruments that were ill suited to the fluid operations of light infantry, bugles, horns, cornets and trumpets were relied upon instead, just as they were in the cavalry. Furthermore, whereas drums produced a rhythm of no definite pitch, these instruments permitted signals, in the form of tunes, to be played, which could be simple, brief and yet distinctive. For example, in Rottenburg's *Regulations for Riflemen*, which were followed by most British light infantry battalions during the Napoleonic Wars, we find an extensive collection of bugle-calls, including not just directives, such as 'advance', 'retire' and 'cease firing', but also some which permitted basic facts about an opponent to be relayed to friendly units further afield. Thus, there are flourishes that identify the enemy as being infantry or cavalry, or a mixture of the two.[25]

As the geographical scale of their operations grew, armies found that progressively more resources had to be committed to locating adversaries and establishing their strengths, weaknesses and intentions. The need to extend the radius of effective command increased commensurably, too. Chappe's semaphore 'signs' permitted the encoding of fairly complex ideas, but we have noted their limitations. Similarly, during the Napoleonic Wars, the eponymous emperor occasionally used great salvoes of artillery fire as a mechanism for signalling to distant corps. Clever though it was to use guns like drums, this medium only permitted the crudest of messages to be sent; indeed, they had to be pre-arranged signals to be intelligible to the recipient at all. Even after Samuel Morse was to substitute electrical impulses for drumbeats to produce, in 1838, a highly sophisticated, rhythmic code, the issuing of timely, detailed instructions to units remained problematic. As was suggested by early experience with light troops operating on the tactical plane, this remained especially true of forces which, whether functioning at the strategic or tactical level, were not merely scattered but also on the move; for, although basic information might be acquired by an army's headquarters through, say, semaphores or electric telegraphs, between the nodes of such static systems messages continued to be passed by couriers on foot or horseback or, later, in crude motorcars. Even the advent of field-telephone networks offered no solution to this conundrum; they were of little use in controlling manoeuvring units, their cables were very vulnerable (not least to clumsy feet) and the signals they carried attenuated over distance. Although by the time of the Boer War the British were experimenting with radio,[26] many decades were to pass before it could be fully exploited. Indeed, at the end of the nineteenth century, musical instruments were arguably of as much importance as a battlefield communication medium as they had been at its beginning.

Two types of musicians were typically encountered in European armies throughout our period. The first comprised those who were primarily responsible for the passing of basic tactical instructions to combat units. So far as the infantry were concerned, these men would normally be snare or tenor drummers in a line regiment, or buglers or hornists in a light unit. (The British 71st Light Infantry, as befits a Highland regiment, was accompanied by bagpipers.) Cavalry regiments normally favoured bugles, trumpets or cornets, all of which could be played on a moving horse without undue difficulty. Typically, an infantry company or cavalry squadron would have two or three such musicians, with the regiment's entire complement frequently acting together under the direction of a drum- or trumpet-major.

In addition, the regiment or battalion would also have a band – 'the music' – which, in the case of the infantry, consisted of woodwind, brass and percussion, while cavalry supplemented their usual instrumentalists with trombonists and, sometimes, kettledrummers, who had to be mounted on suitably sturdy horses. Unlike the 'field musicians', the band's role was primarily ceremonial and social. Although most colonels preferred them to play their regiment into action, if only from a position of relative safety to the rear of the fighting line, they did not always go on campaign and were frequently to be seen entertaining the general public in parks and at the seaside. Moreover, since music was used to establish the tempo of marches both on and off the battlefield, whenever and wherever troops were on the move, the local population would get a rare chance to hear and see it being performed. As, for instance, George Simmons of Britain's 95th (Rifle) Regiment, wrote to his parents in May 1809, explaining that his battalion had been ordered to Dover, where it was to embark for some 'profoundly secret' destination: 'Our men are in very high spirits, and we have a most excellent band of music and thirty bugle-horns, which through every country village strikes [sic.] up the old tune "Over the hills and far away." '[27]

If Simmons was familiar with this 'old tune', then there were doubtless those who were not, including most of the inhabitants of the Iberian Peninsula, his ultimate destination. War, whether it took place on the home territory of the European states or in their colonies, was an important vehicle for the export of musical ideas, among them the very concept of what constituted music. Then, as now, tastes in this regard all too often reflected not just cultural but also class divisions. In Europe, the mixture of marches, songs and popular tunes that military bands, together with street barrel-organs, performed constituted the great bulk of the secular music that the masses got to hear. At the very end of our period, recorded music was still an expensive novelty which few could afford, as was attending performances of works by the great masters. As Beethoven was to discover with his *Die Schlacht bei Vittoria*, which depicted Wellington's victory of that name in 1813, military music had a popular appeal which far surpassed that enjoyed by most mainstream classical pieces. Scored for a full orchestra backed by battlefield sound-effects, which were initially furnished by Johann Mälzel's 'panharmonicon' – a gigantic, bizarre, if ingenious, machine that, powered by compressed air, incorporated fifes, cymbals, triangles, drums and other instruments – the piece, with its gunfire and extracts from patriotic songs, such as 'Rule Britannia', proved immensely successful in its time.[28]

That Beethoven, a native of Bonn living in Vienna, the world's musical capital, evidently knew authentic British and French war-songs, trumpet-calls and drum-beats reveals how widespread armed conflict accelerated the proliferation of music that the peacetime migration of musicians gave rise to. Here and there in some of his compositions one hears traces of themes that appear in French Revolutionary songs. He almost certainly first heard these in his youth, when the Rhineland was penetrated by French armies, and subsequently adapted them, much as he created the modern scherzo by accelerating the tempo of the classical minuet. In the course of the Napoleonic Wars, Vienna was seized twice by French troops and, during both the 1805 and 1809 occupations, Beethoven would have had ample opportunity to familiarise himself with the martial music of Napoleon's forces, not to mention the homely, sentimental and patriotic songs which soldiers often entertained themselves with while on the march,[29] even if they did not always confine themselves to the original lyrics; 'Dans la Rue Chiffonniere', for instance, was frequently corrupted into 'On va lui percer le Flanc'.*

Leaving aside the common soldier's liking, if not need, for the bawdy and darkly comical, it was clearly easier to memorize and adapt tunes than words, particularly if the lyrics in question were in some alien tongue; and, even without them, a melody could convey emotions forcefully enough, as could certain noises. One sees this phenomenon very clearly in Franz Joseph Haydn's Symphony in G of 1794, 'The Military'. Twelve years before this work appeared, Wolfgang Mozart, in his *Die Entführung aus dem Serail* had employed so-called 'Turkish' instruments to emphasize the exotic, foreign setting of the opera. The type of music associated with the Janissaries had penetrated European culture via conflict in the Balkans, a process that had culminated in the Turks besieging Vienna itself in 1683. For Viennese audiences, in particular, it had long had threatening undertones. In fact, throughout Mozart's time it was still perceived to be a terrifying or exciting noise rather than music, for it had no definite pitch, being produced on percussion instruments that seemed appropriate enough in military bands, but were not regarded as having a legitimate place in a classical orchestra: the so-called 'Jingling Johnnie' or '*Chapeau Chinois*', an ornate staff surmounted with a decorative frame and adorned with numerous little bells; assorted cymbals; the Turkish drum, which is struck alternately with a heavy stick and a small whip or a bundle of birch twigs, evoking the impression that somebody is being flayed and beaten; and triangles hung with metallic rings.

Today, these instruments might be familiar enough to the concert-goer, but Haydn's use of them in a classical symphony was a truly revolutionary

---

* Best translated as, 'We're going to stab [the enemy] in the ass.'

step. In 'The Military', he employs them to enthrall the audience and, simultaneously, convey a sense of war's repulsiveness. Contrary to what one could be pardoned for expecting, there is no heroic march theme in the work at all. Instead, relaxing, tender melodies are abruptly interrupted by a grotesque, descending chord, which is as depressing as it is prolonged, by trumpet fanfares and, above all, by thunderous interventions from the Turkish instruments. Haydn went on to make similar use of percussion's ability to engender awe and a sense of irresistible power in his so-called 'Kettledrum Mass' of 1796. The popular title stems from the prominent use of timpani in the Agnus Dei, though the composer's own description of the work, as a *Missa in tempore belli*, is revealing.

Haydn died in Vienna on 31 May 1809, a little over two weeks after Napoleon's army occupied the city for the second time. Once again, its streets and squares reverberated to the sound of martial music. Beethoven, who, as fearful for his failing hearing as he was for his life, had taken refuge in a cellar during the bombardment, emerged to find 'nothing but drums, cannon and human misery of every kind.'[30] He, however, would have been the last to deny the attractiveness of marches in particular. Like dances, these carry the listener along with them and do not so much end as stop. Mozart had produced several, while the works of Schubert, another Viennese composer and no less prolific, included a celebrated 'Marche Militaire'. Although Beethoven barely concerned himself with the genre as such, so many of his compositions have a march-like quality about them. The boisterous finale and the second movement of, respectively, his seventh and ninth symphonies are good cases in point, while the vast *Sinfonica Eroica: per festeggiare il souvenire d'un gran' uomo*, which was originally to have been dedicated to First Consul Bonaparte, contains a lengthy 'Marcia funebre', the inclusion of which was, according to a friend of the composer, occasioned by the rumour that Admiral Nelson had been killed during the Battle of the Nile in 1798.[31] In the celebrated finale of the ninth symphony of 1824, too, we find a stirring 'Alla Marcia' tenor solo, complete with woodwind and percussion accompaniment.

Since armed forces tend to mirror the societies that spawn them, it is unsurprising that, during the early 1800s, when regiments were so often regarded not so much as the property of the state as of their colonels, who frequently contributed to their upkeep from their own pockets, bands became both a focus of unit pride and their commanders' whims. They were often dressed in expensive, flamboyant clothing with lashings of plumes, lace and braid. A widespread practice among regiments that had facings on their uniforms was the dressing of musicians in 'reversed colours'. This yielded bands clothed in tunics of, say, bright green, yellow, or sky-blue, which contrasted sharply with the relatively sombre facings on their cuffs and turnbacks. Mounted musicians were usually still more garish, riding upon immaculate white horses with elaborate tack and furniture.

Good musicians were always coveted. Their duties called for both musical talent and tremendous courage; not only did it take years of training and practice to produce, for instance, a drummer whose repertoire included all of the *batteries*, but also he had to be able to play them amidst the stress and strain of battle, regardless of what was occurring all around him. As one French colonel recalled of the Imperial Guard's advance at Waterloo:

> I ... saw the Emperor go past followed by his staff.... He moved off along the road which was swept by a hundred enemy guns. One hundred and fifty bandsmen now marched down at the head of the Guard, playing the triumphant marches of the Carousel as they went. Soon the road was covered by the Guard marching by platoons in the wake of the Emperor. Bullets and grapeshot left the road strewn with dead and wounded.[32]

In all of this, attempts to achieve an optimal blend of the inspirational and the fearsome made exotic musicians and outlandish instruments particularly sought after. Coloured percussionists, dressed as often as not in gaudy, oriental garb which gave them an intimidating yet dashing appearance, were a common feature of European military bands throughout our period. Indeed, fanciful though much of all of this might sound, behind the seemingly eccentric splendour was a good deal of pragmatic reasoning. Instrumentalists' distinctive uniforms and, where appropriate, horses made them easier to locate amidst the confusion of an engagement or in darkness. A commander who could not find his musicians, or whose musicians were incapacitated, faced ruin. At the Battle of Dirnstein in 1805, for instance, Marshal Mortier, discovering that his drum-corps had had their instruments smashed in the fighting, resorted to having them beat out their signals on camp kettles borrowed from the infantry.[33] Music was also used to regulate the tempo of marches between battlefields and tactical evolutions on them. Particularly where manoeuvre in close-order was called for, keeping the soldiers in step was of considerable importance. Jaunty tunes helped them do this as well as exhilarate them, but a rhythmic drumbeat could suffice just as well.

In the French Army of the Napoleonic era, for instance, the former might take the form of the 'Marseillaise', or 'Le Chant des Combats', or 'Le Chant des Vengeances', all of which were composed by the musician and soldier Claude Joseph Rouget de Lisle. The 'Chant du Départ' and 'Chant de Retour', both written by the opera composer Étienne Nicolas Méhul, were very widely used, as were 'Veillons au Salut de l'Empire', 'Malbrouck se va-t-en guerre' and other old favourites. So far as drumbeats are concerned, there were *batteries de manoeuvre* and, for attacks, the *pas de charge*. There were also various regimental refrains that served as aids to identification and as rallying-calls. The Imperial Guard's 'La Grenadière' and 'La Carabinière' best exemplify these.

However, important as a communication medium though it was, music's contribution to the psychological side of warfare was no less crucial. Fear can maim just as effectively as any sword or shell. Indeed, as a coercive act, war is essentially all about psychology. With its intriguing capacity to simultaneously excite *and* frighten, music was of great significance when it came to disheartening soldiers or raising their spirits. With regard to the latter process, the recollections of one captain in the French army at Austerlitz in 1805 are a telling illustration:

> Contrary to custom, the Emperor had ordered that the bands should remain in … the centre of each battalion. Our band was at full strength, with its chief … at its head. They played a song we all knew well.* … While this air was played, the drum[mer]s … beat a charge loud enough to beat their drumheads in. … It was enough to make a paralytic move forward![34]

This, of course, was precisely the impact it was intended to have. On an opponent, by contrast, the very same sounds could have quite different effects, as, for example, one British veteran of the Peninsular War was reminded as he prepared to confront his old adversaries at Waterloo:

> About half-past eleven the bands of several French regiments were distinctly heard, and soon after the French artillery opened fire. The rapid beating of the *pas de charge*, which I had often heard in Spain – and which few men, however brave they may be, can listen to without a somewhat unpleasant sensation – announced that the enemy's columns were fast approaching. On our side the most profound silence prevailed, whilst the French, on the contrary, raised loud

---

* 'On va lui percer le Flanc', referred to above.

shouts and we heard the cry of '*Vive l'Empereur!*' from one end of their line to the other.[35]

Similarly, nearly 85 years later, as the 1800s drew to their close, Winston Churchill, captured by Boers in an attack on the armoured train in which he was travelling through Natal, was to hear a sound which he found even more dispiriting than that of shells: his captors singing psalms. 'It struck the fear of God into me,' he confessed. 'What sort of men are we fighting?' he wondered. 'They have the better cause – and the cause is everything – at least, I mean to them it is the better cause.'[36]

Morale, Discipline and Leadership

Morale is of fundamental importance in war; neither technology, however sophisticated, nor numbers are of use without the courage to employ them. Yet people have to be highly motivated to risk being injured (and perhaps maimed), or killed, or captured in pursuit of political objectives. This quality is less likely to be found among conscripts than among volunteers. Leading soldiers onto a battlefield is one thing; it is quite another to get them to fight, and yet another to get them to fight not so much for survival as in accordance with some tactical or strategic plan. Whilst there are theorists who endeavour to explain away war in terms of 'aggressiveness', which they depict as instinctive, particularly among males, if humans have any instincts at all then that of self-preservation is surely paramount. The difficulties involved in persuading people with feet of flesh and blood, if not of clay, to risk life and limb for political aims, particularly those with which they can barely identify, if at all, should never be underestimated.

Until the eighteenth century's very end, military discipline was dominated by the notion that soldiers should be more afraid of their officers than of the enemy. Not only did armies reflect the feudal polities they served – their officer corps were composed largely, if not exclusively, of aristocrats and gentry, while the rank and file tended to come from the dregs of society – but also the nature of battlefield tactics called for the suppression of initiative and unquestioning obedience to orders. This, as we have seen, made the introduction of free-thinking, free-firing light infantry into the armies of the *ancien régime* as much a political and social issue as it was a military one. Indeed, officers like Britain's Sir John Moore and Prussia's Gerhard von Scharnhorst incurred considerable unpopularity and suspicion by insisting that these troops, at least, ought to be treated more like human beings and less like automatons. Whereas they sought to motivate soldiers, not with the lash and the cane, but with education and the fostering of an *esprit de corps*, the over-whelming majority of officers had very different opinions. Some believed that exemption from flogging was a privilege, not a right, and resented the implicit elevation of those whom Wellington, for instance, dismissed as 'the scum of the earth' to the status of decent, reasoning men. Others, probably the majority, justified their attitudes more in terms of prag-matism than ideology: given the unpromising material from which soldiers (and many sailors) were fashioned, war's brutalizing effects and the quotidian privations of military life, relaxing disciplinary codes was simply not feasible, however desirable. Nevertheless, although soldiers might be executed, flogged or made to run the gauntlet for desertion or even lesser crimes, generally speaking those who engaged in intermit-tent, or even habitual, acts of cowardice were less likely to incur some formal punishment than lose the respect of their peers for having dis-graced their unit and let their comrades down.[37]

Indeed, most armed forces had to motivate their personnel, whether volunteers, conscripts or a mixture of the two, more through the nur-turing of an *esprit de corps* and by appeals to their sense of honour than to notions of nationalism or patriotism. It is noteworthy that, even in the French Army under Napoleon, where discipline was comparatively relaxed[38] and soldiers were, at least in theory, to be treated as fellow cit-izens who had a concept of, and a sense of loyalty to, *La Patrie*, regi-mental colours were emblazoned with the motto *'Valeur et Discipline'*. Flags in all armies of the period not only identified a unit and served as a rallying point, but also, like music, had an important role in main-taining morale in that they symbolized what men believed they were fighting for. As one despairing Prussian officer shouted to his wavering troops at Jena in 1806, 'See! Here is your standard; it you *must* follow.'[39] Presented by the sovereign with due pomp and ceremony, and often blessed by the clergy, colours were the focus of regimental pride and, if shot to shreds in action or superseded, were affixed to nets and rever-ently hung in churches. It is little wonder that great painters of the age regularly chose them as centrepieces. Gérard's vast canvas depicting General Rapp presenting Napoleon with standards taken from the tsar's Guards at Austerlitz is a good case in point, as is Louis David's *Napoleon Distributing Eagles to the Army*.

Whereas the capture of a standard was a great personal triumph for any soldier, to lose one in combat was a disgrace that might continue to haunt a unit for decades. Consequently, they were frequently the focus for acts of great gallantry and despair. One British sergeant recalled how, at Waterloo, 'About 4 o'clock I was ordered to the colours. Now I was used to warfare as anyone, but this was one job I did not like at all. That day alone 14 sergeants, and officers in proportion, had been killed or wounded in the duty and the staff and colours were almost cut to pieces.'[40] To be appointed to a colour-party was a great honour, but an immensely dangerous one, too. Indeed, standard bearers were normally officers who, if they had nothing else to recommend them, were outstandingly courageous.

The flamboyant uniforms of the time also played their part in making men forget their own vulnerability and feel bigger, stronger and braver than they actually were. In this sense, they were more important than as a guide to identity on the battlefield; such was the proliferation of designs and colour schemes that it was often very difficult to distinguish the troops of one polity from those of another, and 'fratricide' was a common if unfortunate occurrence. Epaulettes made narrow shoulders look broader, while a shako, helmet or, above all, bearskin bonnet added stature. A glass of spirits before going into action also gave many men Dutch courage. So it was that, when wondering why soldiers fought at all, one veteran concluded that:

> Dress...almost always makes the soldier. Among...[those] who heard...balls whizzing past, there certainly were many on whom their shrill discordant sound made a disagreeable impression; but, in this case, each is afraid of betraying weakness to his neighbour; he dreads the jeers, the taunts, that would be the inevitable consequences. Duty, honour, pride, all concur to combat fear; and I have often seen the greatest cowards the first to cry: 'Forward!'... [Those who form] part of a regiment, ... [are] forced to be brave.[41]

But, during the Napoleonic Wars, neither all combatants wore uniforms, nor did they all behave honourably. Whereas Napoleon could risk unleashing his troops in prolonged pursuits like that after Jena because he could be confident that the majority were sufficiently committed to remain with their eagles, in the wake of every army were packs of deserters who did nothing but rape, rob and murder, singling out the weak or defenceless for attack while seeking to evade vengeful provost officers. In the Iberian Peninsula, the Tyrol, Southern Italy, and Russia especially, alongside those who resisted occupying French forces on ideological grounds were gangs of cut-throats who, amidst the anarchy of war, found fresh opportunities for banditry and smuggling, just as, at sea, privateers – licensed pirates – plundered hapless merchantmen, frequently regardless of their flags.

In seeking to stave off the revolution emanating from France, the *ancien régime* was fearful of provoking another nearer home. For polyglot empires like that of the Habsburgs, to encourage nationalism was to undermine legitimism. Indeed, though debated, the creation of a nation in arms was one measure that absolute monarchies could not embrace precisely because it threatened their strength's very roots. If the scope for mobilizing a feudal state's manpower through conscription was constrained by such considerations, then actively encouraging civilians to turn on an invader was almost unthinkable. Waging war was the ultimate prerogative of the Crown, and anarchy threatened to follow any erosion of the state's monopoly on violence. Once people began employing it, or the threat of it, to determine their own futures and political liberties, they might be tempted to go on doing so – a point illustrated by the fate of two of the most celebrated guerrilla leaders of the Spanish rising against Napoleon, Juan Porlier and Don Juan Martin Diez, both of whom, having participated in subsequent liberal revolts, were hanged by the very monarch they had fought to restore.

Although the 'Declaration of the Rights of Man', which embodied the French Revolution's philosophy, insisted that 'the principle of all sovereignty resides essentially in the nation', in France itself this ideal was soon distorted, while, elsewhere in Europe, political consciousness was slow to develop among the great majority of the population. The bulk of Napoleon's empire remained quite untroubled by insurrection while, elsewhere, undisciplined mobs of armed civilians seldom confronted his legions with any success. Undeterred, some liberals, who dismissed regular armed forces as part of the corrupt, old order, and a few men of letters, who had rather romantic notions about bloodshed, joined together in advocating what Clausewitz was to term 'People's War'. Yet this prompted questions concerning political responsibility as well as power. With the blurring of distinctions between combatants and non-combatants, established just-war concepts became far harder to apply. During the Anglo-American conflict of 1812–15, many of Britain's soldiers and sailors felt that, since her adversary was not a monarchy but a republic, led by elected politicians, it was as justifiable as it was necessary to hold every and any citizen at least partly responsible for the US government's actions. Consequently, they punitively burnt and bombarded American settlements.

Somewhat ironically, the policy of making a politically active population suffer as an integral part of hostilities was to be carried to new heights by General Sherman during the American Civil War. However indirect, popular participation in hostilities ineluctably had many consequences, not the least of which were the changes it spawned in the iconography of war. Up until the early 1800s, painters had concerned themselves more with depicting events than with chronicling them; they had tended to impose their own conceptions of warfare's realities, often representing it as a heroic, noble affair and generally sanitizing it for public consumption. This school was as strong as ever; Géricault's lavish, colourful *Officier de chasseurs de la Garde Impériale* embodies its approach. But, with his *Los Desastres de la Guerra*, Goya started a new trend. Delineating episodes of hand-to-hand fighting, rape, execution and torture in a harrowing, graphic fashion, he emphasized the barbarism of the 'People's War' against Napoleon in the Peninsula, his coarse, colourless sketches redolent of those grainy, if very much more anodyne, photographs that, nearly half a century later, Roger Fenton was to produce in the Crimea.

War is a revolutionary activity, generating changes to the *status quo* both between states and within them. The more 'total' it becomes, the greater the scope and intensity of those alterations. Invariably, it empowers the military, at the expense of other sectors of society, including its nominal rulers. It is fatuous to talk of apolitical armed forces, for they are inherently political entities and are the natural partners of politicians and bureaucrats in the formulation of military policy. However, their ability and willingness to show restraint in exercising the power at their disposal largely depends upon the stability of the political culture within which they exist, and of which they are the ultimate guardians. Should it crumble, they are likely to endeavour to fill the resulting power vacuum. Certainly, during the Napoleonic Wars, Sultan Selim III, Charles IV of Spain and Gustav IV of Sweden were all toppled by their rebellious guards; and Spanish generals turned against the elected *Cortes* in support of absolutism, just as, in 1812, Clausewitz and a score of other Prussian officers defied Frederick William III in the name of patriotism. Even Napoleon himself, who had risen to power as a warrior, completing the demise of the existing political order as he did so, was eventually pushed into abdication by some of his marshals.

Napoleon was the last truly great soldier-monarch. He led his army in the field, taking personal responsibility for the formulation of strategy and the direction of battles, while simultaneously presiding over the administration of his vast empire. Although he had talented commanders and governmental officials to assist him in these processes, they were expected to do little more than implement his will. He regularly gave advice, but, as the embodiment of supreme civil and military power, and conscious of his dynastic and political precariousness as a self-made man, he did not really seek to turn staff work into a didactic experience; whom would he have groomed as a successor and why? However, as war became an ever-more complex and grander affair, it all became too much for one man to control, even a Napoleon. Indeed, that he could not be everywhere at once was to be a major factor in his downfall; his enemies learnt to avoid confronting him while concentrating against his subordinates.

The absolute monarchs he fought against also found war to be too intractable to handle alone. State bureaucracies became increasingly professional during the Napoleonic Wars, and administrators joined kings and their admirals and generals in shaping military policy. Yet neither monarchs nor bureaucrats necessarily understood martial matters any more than soldiers and sailors were always politically astute, and such failings inevitably led to the sort of disputes that bedevilled the Allied headquarters during the *Befreiungskrieg* of 1813. As an exasperated Prince Schwarzenberg, who was nominally *generalissimo*, had to tell Francis, the Austrian *Kaiser*:

> His Majesty [Alexander] the Tsar of Russia ... leaves me alone neither in my headquarters nor even at the moment of battle. ... [H]e allows almost every general to give advice. ... [His senior commander] Barclay has neither sense of obedience nor understanding for operations, and is also jealous. ... I therefore find it absolutely necessary to request ... that either the Tsar ... be advised to leave the army alone, General Barclay be removed, and the corps of Kleist, Wittgenstein and Miloradovich be each advised that they are under my immediate orders, or someone else be entrusted with the command.[42]

Here we see a soldier appealing to one monarch to act as a counterpoise to another; and, once civilians, in the form of professional administrators, began interfering with the conduct of military operations, such relationships inevitably became more tangled still. Indeed, as, in the course of the 1800s, European states gradually became more liberal, popular participation in government increased and military advisers were formally or informally incorporated into cabinets, crowned heads became less significant when it came to reconciling competing views on policy. Nevertheless, they retained a symbolic importance that often proved an awesome burden. Certainly, as the sovereign and titular commander-in-chief, they felt obliged to behave like warriors, regardless of their aptitude for such things.

Napoleon was regarded by many, not least his nephew, Louis Napoleon, as the example to follow; yet neither he nor any other European monarch of the 1800s had comparable ability. As Sir Walter Scott concluded in his biography of the great emperor, if too much of a soldier among sovereigns, no one could claim better right to be a sovereign among soldiers than Napoleon I. Although, towards the end of his career, he forgot that war is, or at least should be, the continuation of policy by other means, and ultimately failed to fulfil his ambitions, he consoled himself with the enduring value of his domestic reforms, notably *Le Code*, and the fact that, whereas most great commanders' martial reputations rest on a single, spectacular success or a few victories, he had won nearly all of the 50 pitched battles he had fought. Certainly, none of the crowned heads who opposed him could begin to match his qualities as a strategist and leader of men. Napoleon gained such a moral ascendancy over most of his adversaries that, *as a matter of policy*,[43] they eventually declined to confront him at all except when they had overwhelmingly superior forces. Even Wellington, one of the very few who were not utterly terrified by the mere sight of that famous hat, readily acknowledged that just its presence on a battlefield was worth 40 000 men.[44] In his capacity for heroism alone, Napoleon was in a class of his own: though they were not devoid of courage, it is impossible to picture Tsar Alexander, Francis, or Frederick William III strolling, as Napoleon would, through a hail of shells, teasing soldiers for ducking, while nonchalantly examining splinters which fell nearby and musing on the effect they might have had, *had* the gunner's aim been somewhat better.[45] But even if he had died somewhat earlier, the overall impact he had on European history, not only during his lifetime but also throughout the nineteenth century and beyond, would have remained incalculable. Indeed, it lingers yet.

2

FROM WATERLOO TO THE CRIMEA AND SOLFERINO

It ultimately took the other European powers no fewer than seven coalitions and almost 25 years of virtually uninterrupted warfare to contain and defeat the threat posed by, first, Revolutionary and, then, Napoleonic France. Conflict on this scale had immense ramifications, only a few illustrations of which must suffice here. In France alone, it claimed the lives of around 38 per cent of the male generation born between 1790 and 1795; this is some 14 per cent higher than the mortality rate among the generation of 1891–95, the foremost victims of the carnage of the First World War. There were few families that had not had at least one male member killed or wounded, many of the latter being horribly maimed, if not by the weapon that had struck them, then by the crude, radical surgery – notably amputation – that was habitually resorted to as the only way of saving the lives of the badly injured. In looking for partners, many women were obliged to redefine their notions of male beauty.

Britain's maritime, commercial and industrial power had reached new heights, very largely because of the protection against invasion that her insular nature had afforded her. By contrast, many of Europe's largest towns and cities, including Saragossa, Hamburg and Moscow, had been ravaged, while innumerable smaller settlements had been expunged completely. Indeed, enormous tracts of countryside, such as the Elbe valley, the focus of the final struggle for Germany, had been devastated, either by actual fighting or by the mere presence of armies of unprecedented size. Creating these had required commensurable efforts on the part of the belligerents and had led to appreciable political upheaval. This included the demise of several polities and dynasties and the fatal weakening of others. Feudal and other reforms had, however, benefited the aristocracy more often than not, while Europe's growing *bourgeoisie* aspired to join the ruling classes rather than overthrow them. As always, war had brought out the best and worst in people. Scores of thousands of human beings had been transformed by their experiences on and around the battlefields, while millions more had been touched by the wider impact of a conflict that was more total than anything that had gone before: trade patterns, labour markets, investment, commerce, industry and agriculture had all been affected, though neither uniformly nor always adversely. Many people had lost everything – their homes, property, livelihoods, family. Yet, if law, order and normal life had collapsed in many areas, elsewhere it had survived almost unscathed; poverty and its symptoms, such as prostitution, were more evident in many places, whereas others enjoyed unparalleled prosperity; while the war-weariness, defeatism, bitterness, disillusionment and despair of some was juxtaposed with the triumphalism, optimism and addiction to '*la gloire*' evinced by others.

The more decisive a conflict is, the longer the ensuing peace is likely to prove. However, much also depends upon the quality of that peace. Endorsed in 1814, the First Treaty of Paris granted France far more lenient terms than she had any right to expect, but the immense problems created or exacerbated by the war swiftly overwhelmed the restored Bourbons who had inherited them. Scarcely liked to begin with, Louis XVIII could neither satisfy his subjects' aspirations at home nor reconcile their perception of France's position in the new European order with the realities of her situation. For too many people, it was just too tempting to conclude that she had been humiliated and subjected to an unjust peace, which had included the imposition of a maladroit, anachronistic regime.

Napoleon attempted to exploit this discontent by making one last bid for power. Having escaped from exile on Elba, in March 1815 he marched on Paris at the head of his bodyguard. It proved an essentially bloodless revolution. Troops sent against '*le petit caporal*' rallied to his cause, and the Bourbons fled. The Allied powers, however, convinced that they could never secure an enduring peace with the 'Corsican Ogre', promptly formed the Seventh Coalition and prepared to invade France. Napoleon, proclaimed emperor once more, responded with a pre-emptive blow against the Prussian and Anglo-Dutch armies in the Low Countries, but, after some initial success, was given a dose of his own strategic medicine and heavily defeated at Waterloo.

Abdicating a second time, he was exiled to the remote island of St Helena, where he was to die six years later. Although his last great adventure had lasted just 100 days, the Allies' victory could do no more than limit the extent of the upheaval provoked by his *coup d'état*. At the very least, Napoleon's gamble had compromised any hope of national reconciliation, and the French were soon in the grip of the 'White Terror'. This included attempts to purge the army. Marshals Brune and Ney met their ends at the hands of a royalist mob and a firing squad, respectively, while Grouchy, Soult, Davout and Suchet were all banished or otherwise disgraced. Leading generals who had rallied to the Bonapartist cause also suffered, notably Vandamme, who was exiled, and Drouet d'Erlon, who, proscribed and condemned to death in his absence, fled abroad. Traces of Revolutionary and Imperial influence were eradicated or reduced by other means, too. A Royal decree of August 1815 formally disbanded the army to facilitate its reconstruction. Conscription was suspended and was to remain so until 1818, when Gouvion Saint-Cyr – a Napoleonic marshal who had turned a blind eye to his former master's return in 1815 and was subsequently rewarded with the post of war minister by the Bourbons – introduced the '*Appel*', which required men to register for military service; 40 000 were then selected by ballot, with the customary exemptions being granted to the eligible. Between 1815 and the inauguration of this system, many personnel were demobilized and the remainder reshuffled, while the Napoleonic architecture of *corps* and divisions was demolished. Even the established regiments did not survive: whereas the *infanterie légère* all but disappeared, the *ligne* was reorganized into 'legions', each of which comprised several battalions supported by cavalry and artillery detachments. Besides being relieved of the eagles and tricolours that had been restored to them during the '100 Days', all units also lost their identifying numbers and were instead given departmental or regional titles. As a final political precaution, moreover, legions were raised in one district and garrisoned in another.

Needless to say, Napoleon's 1815 *coup* did nothing to diminish the Allies' fears and suspicions of France and, although the Second Treaty of Paris duplicated the first in so far that it paved the way for her to rejoin the concert of great powers as an equal partner, it was inevitably more punitive. If only in a bid to prevent any recidivism, the French were saddled with a war indemnity amounting to 700 million Francs as well as an army of occupation. Enormous though this force was, the need for the bulk of the Allies' military machine seemed to have passed. Much of it was promptly dismantled. Nevertheless, most states preserved some mechanism by means of which they could quickly supplement their martial strength, should that prove necessary. For instance, anxious to preserve

Britain's maritime security and power, and mindful that most of the lengthy period required to build a sailing vessel was needed for the construction of the hull and superstructure, the Royal Navy had warships built without masts and rigging. Their upper decks covered with a protective roof, these vessels were then laid up in river estuaries or harbours. In the event of an emergency, the roof could be removed and the ship completed in a matter of days or weeks.[1]

By contrast, the emphasis in most other European states was on land warfare. This was especially so of Prussia. Her geostrategic position was a vulnerable one and, in 1806, her partial, slow and ineffectual mobilization had contributed to a débâcle that had brought her to the very brink of annihilation. In precipitating reform, however, military defeats often prove to be better catalysts than victories. After the Napoleonic Wars, Prussia maintained and refined the conscription laws she had first devised for the *Befreiungskrieg*. These required all able-bodied men of 20 to serve for three years with the colours and two years with the reserves. For a further 14 years thereafter, they were liable for duty with the *Landwehr*, a discrete, territorial service. Besides yielding a sizeable standing army, this approach gave Prussia a large pool of trained manpower that she could tap to flesh out embryonic *Armeekorps*. Raised on a provincial basis, their composition was fixed at one cavalry and two infantry divisions, together with artillery, cavalry and engineering units.

The coming of new forms of transport that promised to speed up the tempo of military operations both facilitated the timely activation and concentration of armed forces and accentuated the importance of such capabilities. Indeed, over the next few decades, the utilization of the steam engine in this regard was a major factor in the erosion of the technological consistency that had prevailed in military affairs since Marlborough's time. Railways offered comparatively rapid, inexpensive transport and communication. One authority has estimated that they reduced haulage costs per kilometre by between 80 and 85 per cent.[2] They helped create integrated internal markets, accelerated the growth of towns and, like other machines, changed the relationship between humankind and its tools. Even people's concepts of time were transformed. Once related to the natural and essentially local world – the rising and setting of the sun, the turning of the seasons, the varying speed of travel achievable by horse or on foot – time now became an absolute. Trains could move with a regularity and predictability that the horse-drawn mail coaches could not match. The very notion of timetables demanded the synchronization of time.

Built between 1822 and 1825, the Stockton to Darlington line trig-gered a railway-construction boom that quickly radiated across the home of the industrial revolution to the European mainland and the eastern seaboard of the USA. Traversed by George Stephenson's *Rocket* at speeds of up to 56 kilometres per hour, the Liverpool to Manchester line opened in 1830, bringing these cities within two hours' travelling time of one another. The 'Railway King', George Hudson, was pre-eminent among the early railroad entrepreneurs. He made a fortune in northern England between 1836 and 1847, only to lose it over the next two years as the initial bonanza petered out in Britain. The same occurred in France, too, where the first major railway – a coal-freighting line between Andrézieux on the Loire and St Étienne – had opened in 1828. *Laissez faire* attitudes towards railway construction led to wasteful duplications of effort on some routes and the neglect of others, a plethora of gauges, a disjointed network and, particularly in the larger, nodal towns, a surfeit of separate termini – several of which were named after great battles – belonging to different companies. Such inefficiencies were largely responsible for the 1847 crash in Britain and, despite calls for more gov-ernmental regulation, persisted after the rationalization caused by the slump. In France, by contrast, the main problem was one of too much state interference, albeit of an indirect kind. Here, in the years 1835–44, railway investment averaged only 34 million Francs, climbing to 175 mil-lion between 1845 and 1854. During the next nine years, however, it soared to 487 million.[3]

This pattern of events is largely explained by the rather suffocating relationship between the French government and the Bank of France, which had been established by Napoleon in 1800 to regulate the state's finances. He certainly recognized the value of state-directed investment in transport, not least because of its military ramifications, and built or improved some 64 000 kilometres of roads and 200 of canals during his reign.[4] Yet, most of the bank's capital had to be devoted to the para-mount function of servicing the debts incurred during his wars. The 1815 indemnity only added to this burden. Later, under the Bourbons and Louis Philippe alike, different priorities and an ethos of *laissez faire* stifled investment by the *haute banque* in industrial development. Entrepreneurs had to find credit elsewhere, the *Commandité* banking sec-tor serving as the main source of capital between 1837 and 1848. Amidst the turmoil caused by the revolution of that year, however, the *haute banque* seized control of this, too, intensifying the dearth of investment funds – a situation that might have persisted had the Second Republic not soon succumbed to a *coup d'état* instigated by the president, Charles Louis Napoleon Bonaparte. His rise to power owed much to his exploitation of the legend surrounding his uncle and, presented as the saviour who would reunite the French nation through firm but efficient leadership, he was overwhelmingly confirmed by plebiscite as Napoleon III, hereditary emperor.

No nineteenth-century French administration did more to stimulate industrialization than *l'empire autoritaire*. Combining Bonapartist militarism with economic *dirigisme*, it promoted railroad expansion with capital that was raised from small investors and channelled through the *Crédit Mobilier* bank. Before 1851, the French railway system essentially comprised several spokes which, radiating from Paris, rather neglected the manufacturing centres. Thereafter, its growth, by network and region alike, boosted employment, agriculture and the iron, steel and coal industries especially, while improving access to emerging markets in North Africa and the Middle East through the gateway of Marseille.

However, Germany and the USA were the principal beneficiaries of rail construction in the period 1850–70. More will be said about the latter country elsewhere, but, between 1855 and 1859, rail construction absorbed all of 19.7 per cent of the former's total investment.[5] Although, again, *laissez faire* attitudes prevailed, there was appreciably more control of the development of the network in the German states, particularly in Hanover and Baden, than in France or Britain. From 1842 onwards, the Prussian authorities also sought to foster railroad construction by guaranteeing interest repayments for those entrepreneurs willing to invest in such ventures.

If, like Wellington, E. F. Kankrin – finance minister to Tsar Nicholas I – feared that railways, by allowing the lower classes to move around, threatened the established social order and could lead to concentrations of malcontents in inconvenient places,[6] there were others, particularly Germans, who were struck by the advantages that this new mode of transport offered for internal and external security alike. Within three years of the opening of the Manchester to Liverpool line in Britain, Friedrich Harkort, the politically active Westphalian entrepreneur and publicist, was calling for a rail network designed with military purposes in mind, while, in 1842, Karl Pönitz, a Saxon, published a book which underscored the importance of this concept. Perhaps of most significance of all, however, were some comments made at the same juncture by Helmut von Moltke, future chief of staff of the Prussian Army: 'Every new development of railways is a military advantage; and for the national defence a few million on the completion of our railways is far more profitably employed than on our new fortresses.'[7]

This was an interesting observation on opportunity costs. The relative utility of fortresses had been in decline for some time. Whereas, during the 1700s, they had frequently acted as the very foundations of the supply networks within which armies moved, making sieges a common occurrence, the manoeuvre warfare emphasized by Napoleon had relegated them to a secondary role. Apart from in the Iberian and Italian Peninsulas, where large areas of barren, difficult terrain constrained the movement and concentration of armies, not least by limiting their scope for living off the land, fortresses proved of limited value during the Napoleonic Wars except as hinges for mobile forces. In fact, leaving aside the campaigns in Spain, Portugal and Calabria, major sieges were almost unheard of. Danzig had the dubious distinction of enduring two, in 1807 and 1813, while Hamburg, Magdeburg, Torgau and several other strongholds in Germany were also besieged during the course of the *Befreiungskrieg*. Even many of these cases occurred as much by accident as design, however, and did not involve elaborate siege operations; as the French were rolled back towards the Rhine, the garrisons of these places found themselves cut off from Napoleon's main army and, encircled by enemy troops, were mostly beaten into submission, not by sapping, bombardment and assault, but by demoralization, starvation and disease.

If the value of fortresses was not what it once had been, the utility of railways was rapidly becoming apparent. Barely had Britain's Manchester to Liverpool line opened in 1830 than it was used to move a regiment of infantry; in two hours, they covered a distance that they could not have marched in under two days.[8] The Austrians, too, were quick to exploit the strategic flexibility bestowed by trains. In 1851, at a time of tension with Prussia, they employed them to reinforce their Bohemian garrisons at speed; they moved all of 14 500 personnel, 8000 horses, 48 guns and 464 wagons some 300 kilometres in just two days. Similarly, during the Franco-Austrian War eight years later, the French were to transport a total of 604 000 personnel and 129 000 horses within a period of 86 days.

Where available, trains greatly simplified the movement of armies. Providing they had sufficient coal and water, these machines, like ships, could keep going round the clock; they merely needed an occasional change of crew. Travelling by train at night or in poor weather posed far fewer problems than movement by road did at such times, and, spared gruelling, lengthy marches, units arrived at their destination, not only far faster, but fresher and with fewer losses, too. Railways were also capable of carrying a variety of loads, from troops to guns, foodstuffs and munitions. They enabled forces to be succoured from afar, though the difficulty of distributing supplies from the railhead to units in the field – units that might themselves be on the move – remained and was not always overcome with complete success, as French experience in their struggle with Austria in 1859 attests. Although, for the siege of Sevastopol during the Crimean War, the British and French reduced their need for pack animals and horse-drawn vehicles by constructing a railway between the port of Balaklava and their positions on the Saboun Hills, some ten kilometres away and 400 metres above sea-level, they could not eliminate it. Whilst this line enabled the allies to move *matériel* – notably ammunition for their heavy artillery, which, in all, devoured over 250 000 rounds – at a rate of up to 200 tonnes per day, then, as now, continuous supply required a continuous transport 'loop'.

At first glance, the introduction of railways meant that the size of armed forces was now constrained only by the dimensions of a state's manpower pool, the political and economic ramifications that would arise were it to be tapped, and the government's practical ability to do so in terms of financial, bureaucratic and material resources. Yet, experience in the Napoleonic Wars had already indicated that, as armies became larger, so too did the problems surrounding their command and control. At a time when so few people could read and write, simply finding sufficient soldiers who were capable of discharging even rudimentary administrative functions was hard enough; those with the skill and aptitude to fulfil the demanding duties inherent in the work of a general staff were in still shorter supply. Because of widespread illiteracy, training manuals, if they could be produced at all, were not always helpful. In any event, most of the theoretical works that were written during this period focused on tactical and strategic considerations; the majority of armies, with results that were frequently debilitating, neglected the essential but far less glamorous work performed by staffs. In the 1809 campaign, the lack of appropriately schooled personnel at his headquarters and dependable subordinate commanders prevented the Archduke Karl from securing much benefit from the structure, based on *Armeekorps*, that he himself had introduced into Austria's forces. Indeed, in the midst of the fighting, he was compelled to all but abandon it.[9] During the wars of 1807 and 1812–14, the Russians, too, struggled to furnish their massive armies with staff officers who had any inkling of doctrine and logistics, never mind standardized procedures and vocabulary. Thanks to the efforts of

Scharnhorst and her other military reformists during the aftermath of Jena, Prussia, by contrast, fared appreciably better; she had an educational process that yielded tolerably good staff officers, notably Neithardt von Gneisenau, who translated Marshal Blücher's strategic vision into detailed orders and disseminated them systematically and efficaciously.

Napoleon's own headquarters was a model of efficiency by the standards of the day. Known as 'the cabinet' and located in either the largest and most conveniently placed room in the building where he was living, or in a tent adjacent to his own, this was, as Baron Odeleben, an eyewitness, recalls,

> always arranged with the greatest particularity. In the middle...was placed a large table, on which was spread the best map that could be obtained of the seat of the war. ...This was placed conformably with the points of the compass...[and] pins with various coloured heads were thrust into it to point out the situation of the different *corps d'armée* of the French or those of the enemy. This was the business of the director of *bureau topographique*,...who possessed a perfect knowledge of the different positions.... Napoleon...attached more importance to this [map] than any want of his life. During the night [it]...was surrounded by thirty candles.... When the Emperor mounted his horse,...the grand equerry carried [a copy]...attached to his breast button...to have it in readiness whenever [Napoleon]...exclaimed 'la carte!'
>
> In the four corners of the [headquarters]...were...small tables, at which the secretaries of Napoleon were employed. He most commonly dictated to them...pacing up and down his apartment. Accustomed to have everything which he conceived executed with the greatest promptitude, no one could write fast enough for him, and what he dictated was to be written in cipher. It is incredible how fast he dictated, and what a facility his secretaries had...in following him....
>
> These secretaries were like so many strings attached to the administrative war departments,...as well as to the other authorities of France.... It is really astonishing how he made so small a number of persons suffice for such a load of business.... Neither keepers of records, nor registrars, nor scribes were seen in the cabinet;...there was one keeper of the portfolio...and all the...archives, in which was included the *bureau topographique*.[10]

Whilst Napoleon's seemingly boundless energy and the phenomenal capacity of his memory removed the need for masses of paperwork and

assistants, all of this also testifies to the fact that this particular headquarters was custom designed for him alone. Although it met most of his
needs and complemented his talents, lesser mortals would have found it
wholly inadequate. Without him, it could not have functioned at all.
Even with him it could not take full responsibility for everything that
affected the army's performance in the field. As Odeleben further
observes, the cabinet itself dealt with 'only those matters wherein
Napoleon was particularly engaged'. This comprised, above all, the formulation and implementation of strategy. Yet, although the emperor
knew 'with great precision the position of the armies, the composition
of the different masses, their combination and employment', the issuing
of detailed directives to his forces was the responsibility of Marshal
Berthier, the Chief of Staff, and his many *aides-de-camp*.[11]

It would be unkind but not inaccurate to describe Berthier as
Napoleon's head clerk. 'I am nothing in the army', he once conceded.
'I receive, in the name of the Emperor, the reports of the marshals, and
I sign his orders for him.'[12] Together with his assistants, he also compiled the *résumés and carnets* that his master regularly perused. However,
he was neither a tactician nor a strategist. Indeed, on the one occasion
when the emperor's absence obliged this normally calm and courageous
officer to take command, he was reduced to abject panic.[13]

Napoleon's immediate entourage also included several Imperial *aides* –
high-ranking officers who, if necessary, could act as his executors in
remote sectors of a battlefield while he tried to orchestrate proceedings
from a central position. Talented though many of them were, these men
could only represent him; they were not his equals in skill and, whilst
mandated by him, might be reluctant to try to impose any authority they
had on *corps* and wing commanders who were often distinguished marshals of France with correspondingly inflated egos. In fact, the very
devolution of power that the demise of monolithic armies entailed could
make it that much harder for a commander to maintain a firm grip on
events. It was not just that, with the concomitant expansion of troop and
unit numbers, military machines became more complex, increasing the
scope for minor and major breakdowns alike: human beings are that
much less predictable than machines, and it was quite an achievement
for one man to know even his immediate subordinates sufficiently well
to predict how they would react to a given set of circumstances. Those
further down the pyramid were commensurably unfamiliar, yet might
have pivotal positions thrust upon them in the course of an engagement
or campaign; during the Battle of Wagram alone, the French Army

saw 32 of its generals and 1121 other officers killed or wounded, while the Austrians' casualties included 793 officers, among whom were 17 generals.[14]

Just as Napoleon's inability to be everywhere and do everything obliged him to rely on lieutenants of varying quality to implement his strategic plans, so too was he compelled to leave other concerns to subordinates, not all of whom were as reliable or professional as his cartographers and secretaries. This was especially true of the department that was supposed to satisfy the troops' needs for foodstuffs and drinking water. Though competent, the military personnel attached to the *Intendant-Général* were far too few to regulate every arrangement for the supply of a force as enormous as the *Grande Armée* of 1812–13. The impact of Russian 'scorched earth' tactics during Napoleon's march on Moscow was not insignificant, but it was not so much a lack of supplies as an inability to get them to where they were required that had really hampered the French offensive; too often, the sheer immensity of Russia combined with her execrable roads to break what should have been a continuous transport loop. Even during the subsequent campaign in Germany, where supplies should have been relatively abundant, the logistical support for Napoleon's forces was again undermined. Odeleben blames the 'misconduct and cupidity' of private contractors for the resulting shortfalls. However, this can only be part of the explanation. Whilst it is astonishing that Napoleon's staff managed to control as many things as well as they did, the very innovations that the emperor and his contemporaries had embraced with such enthusiasm – conscription and semi-autonomous *corps* – had generated forces and operations of almost unmanageable dimensions.

All of this underscored the need for dedicated professional staffs to support a commander. With the advent of the use of railways for military purposes, established specialists, such as cartographers, had to be joined by officers with a detailed knowledge of networks, rolling-stock, timetables and so on. Clearly, potential candidates had to be identified and given appropriate training in peacetime. This led to the introduction of new curricula within military and other educational institutions as part of a wider partnership between the armed forces and private railroad companies. As the train became central to the state's security, these links ineluctably became more formal, culminating, in Germany's case, in the establishment of the Imperial Railroad Office which, from 1873, purchased one railway after another in a gradual process of nationalization that was primarily motivated by military considerations.

One innovation that, figuratively and literally, appeared alongside the railways was the telegraph patented by Morse in 1837. Whereas the Chappe system had relied upon visible signals, this used 'dot and dash' patterns of electrical impulses as a code. As such it owed much to the pioneering exploration of electromagnetism that had been undertaken in the late 1700s and early 1800s by Luigi Galvani, Alessandro Volta, André-Marie Ampère, Georg Ohm and Michael Faraday. Morse collaborated with Alfred Vail to construct the first system, between Baltimore and Washington, in 1844. As they attenuated over distance, signals were relayed from one transmitting station to another. However, the addition of rubber insulation to the wires not only reduced this problem, but also permitted cables to be laid underwater, creating the prospect of transoceanic links.

The electric telegraph revolutionized strategic communication and, like the train, was quickly exploited for military purposes. If of limited use for the issuing of tactical directives on the battlefield, it offered a means of rapid communication between sedentary headquarters and other nodes within a state's political and military hierarchy. Whilst this greatly facilitated processes like mobilization, it also made it possible for remote authorities to intervene more readily in military operations. So it was that, in 1855, General Pélissier – the latest in a succession of commanders nominally responsible for the French forces participating in the Crimean War – was reduced to impotent rage by Napoleon III, who, having been persuaded by both his own advisers and the British government not to lead his army in person, could not resist the temptation to meddle in Pélissier's plans by means of a newly-laid telegram cable. 'Your Majesty must free me from the narrow limits to which he has assigned me', fumed the wretched general, 'or else allow me to resign a command impossible to exercise in cooperation with our loyal allies at the somewhat paralysing end of an electric wire.'[15]

Exasperating though this must have been for Pélissier, whereas he eventually emerged triumphant, others were less lucky. On 25 February, 1896, General Oreste Baratieri, commander of the Italian army in Ethiopia, was to receive a telegram from his prime minister, Francesco Crispi, in Rome. This castigated him for pursuing a strategy that was as fruitless as it was chary, before concluding with the fateful words: 'We are ready for any sacrifice to save the honour of the army and the prestige of the monarchy.'[16] However justified his misgivings about confronting the Ethiopian army were, this missive spurred the hapless general into setting them aside. His troops promptly forsook the security of their entrenched position and were soon embroiled in the greatest colonial battle of the century, Adowa. Fighting against opponents who had been dismissed as racially and militarily inferior, in the space of a few hours Baratieri's forces lost half their strength, the rest being driven from the field in headlong rout. Swiftly relayed to Italy by telegraph, news of the catastrophe aroused a sense of humiliation and indignation among the populace that manifested itself in widespread riots and demonstrations. Crispi's administration fell and its successor was quick to acknowledge Ethiopia's independence formally by concluding the Treaty of Addis Ababa.

Although it spawned an Italian desire for revenge that was destined to help Benito Mussolini in his quest for power and lead to his invasion of Ethiopia in 1935, the débâcle of Adowa truncated Italy's participation in the 'scramble for Africa' that, as the nineteenth century wore on, had increasingly preoccupied the European powers. Only established as a unified kingdom in 1861, she was a relative newcomer to the international stage and her role in Africa had always been a comparatively minor one. This was not so of France. At the very end of the 1700s, her 'Army of the Orient', under Bonaparte, had sought to use Egypt as a steppingstone to conquests further east, only to be thwarted by the staunch defence of Acre and Nelson's triumph at the Battle of the Nile. British naval supremacy and General Abercromby's victory at Aboukir in 1801 spelt the end for the French presence in Egypt, which was formally restored to the Porte in 1802. However, Mehemet Ali, the Khedive from 1805 to 1848, made extensive use of French advisers to develop his province's army and economy, while one of his successors, Mehemet Said, also encouraged French influence, not least by permitting the construction of the Suez Canal. Although this was undertaken by an international company formed in 1858, it was one that was initially dominated by Frenchmen, notably the engineer Ferdinand de Lesseps, who was a cousin of the Empress Eugénie. Indeed, she was to open the canal formally when, after ten years' work, it was completed in 1869.

Mindful of Bonaparte's ambitions at the start of the century, and Paris's support of Mehemet Ali during his struggle with the sultan during the 1830s, the British government remained pardonably suspicious of any French involvement in the region and from the outset feared that the canal was another bid by Britain's greatest rival to gain a toehold in the Levant from where she might menace India. However, the thrust of France's African ambitions went in another direction. In June 1830, Charles X's regime embarked on an invasion of Algeria. This was largely intended to divert attention from the growing internal strife that manifested itself in anti-government factions securing a huge majority within the elected Chamber of Deputies. France's last Bourbon king and his prime minister, Prince Jules de Polignac, responded by issuing the Four Ordinances of St Cloud, which triggered the July Revolution. Charles's purges of the army, together with his other policies, had alienated it along with so many other sectors of French society. If there were any plans for the suppression of a rebellion, there was neither adequate resources nor sufficient will to implement them. With its best units in or *en route* for Algiers, the army had just 12 000 troops left in the vicinity of Paris, many of whom now deserted. Control of the capital was lost, Charles fled and the parliament proclaimed his cousin, the duke of Orléans, king.

With the Bourbons removed, the way was clear for the '*reliques de l'Empire*' who had been excluded from the army to return to its ranks. Among those who offered his services to the July Monarchy was Soult, the most distinguished of the surviving Napoleonic marshals. Appointed as minister of war in November 1830, on the death of Casimir Périer in 1832 he also became president of the king's council. In both these capacities, he laboured tirelessly to revitalize and enlarge France's neglected armed forces. Indeed, one of the first laws he introduced as Louis Philippe's prime minister sought to strengthen the army both qualitatively and quantitatively. As a result of the Bourbons' reforms, only about one third of its manpower comprised regular volunteers. The balance was made up of conscripts, the fruit of the *Appel* system, who were obliged to serve for six years. By cutting the number of exemptions to boost the size of the annual draft, Soult aimed to create a force of 500 000 regulars backed by 200 000 reservists. However, too many politicians saw the latter in particular as a potential source of instability and insisted that the annual draft be limited to 80 000. This yielded insufficient conscripts for the fulfilment of Soult's objectives, leaving France's disposable forces far weaker than he would have wished. Similarly, the implementation of his plans for the fortification of Paris were postponed on a mixture of aesthetic, financial and political grounds. On the other hand, Soult himself was sceptical about the political allegiances and military capabilities of the *Garde Nationale*. Intended purely for defence, this organization, revived at the behest of Louis Philippe, was dominated by the *bourgeoisie* with whom the king so closely identified, but contained more than a sprinkling of republicans who might be tempted to exploit domestic upheaval. Indeed, whilst those of Prussia and Russia especially were to emerge as the great swords of conservatism during this era, most European armies found themselves faced with either the prospect or reality of policing assignments. Just as, beyond the Channel, Wellington had to contemplate the possibility of a Chartist insurrection between 1838 and 1848, Soult, his old adversary in the Peninsular War, had to cope with serious disorder in Lyons during 1831 and 1834, when silk weavers, protesting over wage cuts, went on the rampage. Paris, too, was affected by this second wave of rioting which, like the first, was quashed with great savagery and loss of life.

The commitment in Algeria was another source of political strife and a drain on France's resources. Attempts to pacify the hostile natives soon sucked the French inland from their footholds along the littoral. The initial expeditionary force had amounted to 37 000 troops, but, by 1847, the operation was absorbing all of 108 000 men – one third of the entire army. Although, until the Second Boer War of 1899–1902, this was to constitute the single largest force of Europeans seen in Africa, combat in Algeria predominantly consisted of mercurial, small-scale actions. The concept of the massive, rapid mobilization that was being accorded ever more importance in European strategic planning was irrelevant here. Against a ruthless, elusive and often anonymous foe dispersed across a gigantic, inhospitable landscape, a combination of unorthodox military tactics and political stratagems was called for. Whilst there were some large engagements, notably that at Isly in 1844, on the whole there were neither worthwhile targets for heavy artillery nor many opportunities for the employment of horsemen *en masse*. Useful though it was for reconnaissance, sudden *coups* and sweeps, cavalry was, in any case, that much more vulnerable to the volume of firepower that, as we shall see, a new generation of small arms was making possible. This gave infantry correspondingly more protection from the once formidable threat posed by horsemen. Increasingly, foot troops deployed in just two ranks for most purposes and in three for repelling cavalry. The hollow square, with its impenetrable hedge of bayonets that had so often saved infantry from being hacked to pieces, not least at Waterloo, had yet to disappear from the drill books of many European armies, but it was becoming as much of an anachronism as the swords of the cavalry it was intended to ward off.

A brutal conflict, waged by adversaries who saw no prospect of a durable peace, the struggle for Algeria laid the country waste and too often threatened to become a war of annihilation. Its hallmark was the *razzia* – the raid – in which swiftly moving columns of, above all, infantry bore the brunt of the fighting. Backed by a few light guns and squadrons of cavalry, they used mule trains to supplement the supplies that they gleaned from the land. Besides the threat posed by hostile tribesmen, they faced formidable foes in the form of malaria, cholera and inadequate water supplies. These were as implacable as many of the tribesmen confronting them. Although the French and other Europeans frequently, and often sincerely, viewed their interference in the 'Dark Continent' as an obligation, the 'White Man's Burden', it ineluctably stimulated solidarity among its victims. The Amir of Algeria, Abd-el-Kader, who, like many African rulers, was the embodiment of both secular and religious authority, called for a *jihad* against the infidel invaders as early as 1832, but the French endeavoured to divide and rule, exploiting the nuances within Algeria's indigenous politics. Here as elsewhere, this led to the fusion of civil and military power, as the military not only took responsibility for the colony's administration, but also strove to shake off metropolitan control. Indeed, Soult consistently argued that the '*Mission Civilisatrice*' in Algeria was primarily a matter for the military and he bluntly refused to appoint a civilian governor. Predictably, Louis Thiers and François Guizot, his leading civilian colleagues, took a different view and, in July 1834, the dispute culminated in Soult tendering his resignation.

After representing France at Queen Victoria's coronation in 1838, this grand old man of the French Army was again appointed as president of the council to Louis Philippe. Although his growing infirmity gradually reduced him to a mere figurehead, he was to retain this position, with just one short break, until 1847, when Guizot formally superseded him. He also undertook a second stint as minister of war. Whilst in 1840 he incurred Lord Palmerston's wrath by throwing his weight behind Mehemet Ali – an error that led to the brief eclipse of the marshal's power and to the temporary isolation of France – on the whole he pursued a conciliatory foreign policy while trying to build up his country's martial strength. He reformed the *Corps d'État-Major*, creating reserve sections to support its regular personnel in times of emergency, detailed the organization of the army's foot regiments and oversaw the construction of concentric fortifications around Paris. However, he also found himself increasingly preoccupied with events in Algeria, where the commander of the occupying forces, Thomas-Robert Bugeaud de Piconnerie, was in danger of becoming a law unto himself.

'*Père*' Bugeaud was one of the many '*reliques de l'Empire*'. A country squire, he had spent the period 1815–30 tending his estate before being recalled to the colours. A courageous down-to-earth soldier who believed in born leaders, he disliked the army's '*Polytechniciens*' almost as much as he loathed politicians. A constant irritant to Guizot and other civilians in Louis Philippe's cabinet, he would accept orders from Soult alone and acquired a ring of admirers which extended beyond *l'Armée d'Afrique*. Among the younger officers he was to have an impact on were Louis Trochu, who was to write *L'Armée francaise en 1867*, and Charles Ardant du Picq.

Bugeaud's victory on the River Sikka in 1836 dispersed Abd-el-Kader's main army and ushered in a protracted period of desultory, scattered resistance. A veteran of the Peninsular War, Bugeaud had considerable experience in quelling opposition of this kind. Above all, he understood the distinction between controlling and holding territory, and the futility of the latter policy in counter-guerrilla operations. His toughness, political acumen and skilful use of the *razzia* yielded results, and he was rewarded with the governor generalship in 1840 and a marshal's baton three years later. Following his triumph there in 1844, he was also made duke of Isly.

Bugeaud's success opened up the prospect of large numbers of French civilians settling in Algeria. He dreamt of colonizing it exclusively with soldiers and their families. However, there were already areas, notably in the province of Constantine, where the military regime he favoured appeared incongruous. Elsewhere, tribal authority under the auspices of moderate Muslim leaders seemed to offer a viable solution to the conundrum of integrating immigrants and the indigenous population. In any case, French intervention in Algeria had always been motivated by more than the superficially noble notion of 'La Mission Civilisatrice'. There was the desire to expand trade, exploit the fabled wealth of what was actually a poor country and, at a time of growing economic hardship and political troubles at home, find new lands for potential emigrants, particularly the dangerously disaffected.

Of these, there were more than a few; and, all too often, they came to blows with the soldiers of their own country. If the rustic, old-fashioned Bugeaud had anything in common with General Louis-Eugène Cavaignac, a sophisticated *'Polytechnicien'*, it was a willingness to cow France's urban poor in particular. While Cavaignac was destined to mastermind the suppression of the 'June Days' revolt of unemployed artisans and unskilled labourers in 1848, it was the colonial commanders, *'Les Algériens'*, within the army who, above all, were to the fore in the actual coercion of French workers both then and in 1834. The estranged proletariat of France's growing cities never developed much enthusiasm for her colonial ambitions and harboured more than a few grudges against the distinctive units of the *Armée d'Afrique* in particular. Military tailors, however, greeted them with open pocketbooks. Alongside the 49 *ligne* and 13 regiments of *infanterie légère* that served in Algeria between 1830 and 1848, several famous units were created during this epoch. Among them were: the *Zouaves*, European soldiers clothed in the apparel of the Berber tribes, which comprised an ornate, vividly coloured waistcoat and a *chéchia* that was encased in a white turban with yellow tassels; the Foreign Legion, whose attire included the characteristic *casquette d'Afrique*, the *képi*; the *Spahis*, Arab horsemen who wore the burnous, the Moorish hooded cloak, and the *Infanterie Légère d'Afrique*, with their Algerian trappings. Once again, eye-catching uniforms were used to glamorize a way of life that, if not always fatal, was invariably hazardous, austere and poorly paid; to make soldiers feel bigger and more courageous and powerful than they really were; to foster an *esprit de corps*; and to make them look as fearsome as possible, whoever their opponents might be.

If Louis Philippe's policies progressively alienated some parts of French society, others were frustrated by his failure to act in certain areas at all. It was not just radicals who were disappointed by the cautious, conservative approach of the July Monarchy, which included *laissez faire* attitudes to electoral reform and to the management of the relations between employers and the employed. Too little of the prosperity that the commercial classes enjoyed until the depression of 1846/7 trickled down the social ladder to alleviate the plight of the urban workers. Although, in 1839, a small armed rising inspired by Louis Blanqui, who was to devote much of his life to the causes of revolution and communism, gained no popular support, the harsh economic conditions of the 1840s helped create a receptive environment for Louis Blanc's *L'Organisation du Travail* (1839), which put forward socialist solutions for the country's ills, and his *Histoire des Dix Ans* (1841), which was scathingly critical of the Orléanist regime. The 1833 Primary Education Law introduced by Guizot benefited the *petite bourgeoisie* more than any other social group, yet he refused them the vote. Foreign policy, too, seemed inordinately unadventurous in his hands. 'Let us not talk about our country having to conquer territory, to wage great wars, to undertake bold deeds of vengeance', he insisted. 'If France is prosperous, if she remains rich, free, peaceful and wise, we need not complain.'[17]

In 1840 Thiers briefly replaced Soult as president of the council. Whilst the latter owed his rise to power essentially to his Napoleonic connections, he had also been careful not to be associated too closely with the Bonapartist cause. However, Thiers – whose fascination for Napoleon was to manifest itself not least in the colossal *Histoire du Consulat et l'Empire* that he was to publish between 1845 and 1874 – successfully urged Louis Philippe to try to enhance the prestige of his own regime by exploiting the 'Legend of St Helena'. So it was that, at the end of 1840, in a ceremony of portentous splendour arranged by Soult, the remains of Napoleon, which were remarkably well preserved, were brought back to France and placed in a sarcophagus at the heart of the Invalides. Moreover, the plinth in the Place Vendôme was again adorned with a statue of the emperor, while the Arc de Triomphe, the greatest architectural monument to his victories, was finally completed. Last, but by no means least, Soult became only the fourth soldier in France's history to be awarded the title of marshal general.

That two bids by Louis Napoleon to seize power had come to naught suggests that there was little active support for Bonapartism up to this point. However, Louis Philippe's idolization of Napoleon ineluctably led to unfavourable comparisons being drawn between the lacklustre July Monarchy, with its *bourgeois* values, and '*La Gloire*' of the First Empire. Indubitably, efforts to depict military successes in Algeria as the equivalent of the emperor's victories aroused widespread contempt, as did other attempts to aggrandize the regime. Hector Berlioz, nineteenth-century France's most flamboyant composer and one of the most innovative, found himself embroiled in this process when the government commissioned him to produce celebratory pieces for some of its showpiece events. One of these, the *Symphonie funèbre et triomphale*, which was scored for military band, strings and chorus, was performed during the sepulture of Napoleon's remains. Four years later, to mark the Paris Industry Festival, Berlioz arranged the 'Marseillaise' in his own inimitable style, drawing on the services of an orchestra, a male chorus, soloists and a large choir of children. The instrumental and vocal forces he deployed for his *Messe des Morts*, however, were of Napoleonic proportions. Intended to create an effect of 'horrifying grandeur' and originally intended for use at a service to commemorate the dead of the 1830 Revolution, this work was actually first performed in December 1837 as part of a ceremony in Les Invalides to honour General Damrémont, who had been killed while storming the walled Algerian city of Constantine, which had defied subjugation for a whole year. As well as an enormous choir and orchestra, which included eight sets of timpani, Berlioz's scoring for the mass called for four brass bands, one in each of the corners of the church, to represent the heralds of the Last Judgement.

This event marked the climax of Berlioz's popularity in France. Thereafter, he found far more acclaim abroad than he did in his native country. Indeed, he was conducting in London when the 1848 Revolution broke out in Paris. Encouraged, no doubt, by the success of the tea-parties and public lectures held by the British Anti-Corn Law League in the early 1840s, those factions within the French opposition who favoured electoral reform staged a series of banquets, one of which, scheduled to occur in the capital on 22 February, was banned by a nervous government. Nevertheless, crowds began to gather. Guizot was dismissed and it seemed that Louis-Mathieu Molé, his successor, would make adequate concessions without further ado. However, what began as a peaceful campaign by the *bourgeoisie* for parliamentary reform suddenly degenerated into violent confrontation when, on 23 February, Bugeaud's soldiers fired on the protestors. Barricades promptly went up all over Paris as, egged on by socialist and republican agitators, masses of workers and students took to the streets. Rather belatedly, the *Garde Nationale*, normally Louis Philippe's instinctive supporters, was mobilized, but even they now gave the king a lukewarm reception. Although his regular troops would almost certainly have remained loyal, the mere thought of the bloodshed that would have attended any attempt to secure a city of over a million inhabitants, half of whom seemed to be in rebellion, proved repugnant to this elderly, well-intentioned man. He promptly abdicated in favour of his grandson, only to see this attempt at compromise swept away by the proclamation of the Second Republic.

The new regime quickly abolished slavery in the French colonies and introduced universal male suffrage at home. However, the great majority of the votes cast in the elections for the new National Assembly went, not to the radicals and socialists like Blanc who had formed a caretaker administration, but to Orléanists, legitimists and moderate republicans. They were, above all, votes for order. For, in Paris, demonstrations, including one by elements of the *Garde Nationale* that were threatened with dissolution, began within weeks of Louis Philippe's departure, while elsewhere, his overthrow ushered in violent attacks on property, clergymen, Jews, tax-collectors and major business proprietors. Moreover, events in France acted as a catalyst for revolutionary turmoil further afield that, here and there, also jeopardized the peace between the major European powers. Indeed, on 15 May, Blanqui and other extremists tried to overturn the French electorate's decision by occupying the Assembly and setting up a rival government that threatened Russia and Prussia with hostilities if they did not restore Polish independence. No sooner had the *Garde Nationale* smothered this threat by quashing the *putsch* than the Assembly's decision to abolish Blanc's national work-shops, which had been providing some relief for thousands of unem-ployed urban labourers, unleashed another: that of civil war, in Paris at least. Instructed either to enlist in the forces or depart for the provinces, the men of the workshops, supported by almost the entire population of the working-class quarter, took to the barricades. They were joined by some disaffected members of the *Garde*, which had recently opened its ranks to volunteers from outside the propertied classes. Cavaignac, who had returned from Algiers to become the new government's war minis-ter, declared the metropolis to be in a state of siege. For six days, regu-lar troops, backed by 100 000 loyal National Guardsmen rushed from the provinces by train, grappled with the 'Army of Despair' in a savage house-to-house fight. Some 1600 soldiers were killed. Estimates of the casualties among the insurgents vary, but they seem to have been well in excess of 10 000, while 14 000 more were arrested.[18] Blanc fled to England, but other perceived or actual ringleaders were transported to the French colonies, notably Algeria.

The heavy casualties inflicted on the Paris insurrectionists can be explained partly by the sheer ruthlessness of their opponents, who were out to teach them a gory lesson, but mostly by the growing sophistica-tion of the armaments at the government troops' disposal. As we have seen, rifled weapons had but a peripheral role on the battlefields of the Napoleonic Wars. This was very largely because of the tactical con-straints their nature made them subject to. The process of forcing bul-lets through the muzzle and down to the bottom of the barrel was made far harder and, consequently, more time-consuming by the resistance from the rifling. This meant that, whereas a smoothbore musket was not as accurate as a rifle, it was capable of being loaded and discharged more rapidly. Indeed, in any contest that pitted similar numbers of mus-keteers and riflemen against one another, once the range between them diminished sufficiently the superior precision of the latter's fire could be offset by the sheer volume of the former.

This state of affairs was transformed by, above all, a simple but inge-nious discovery made by a French Captain, Claude E. Minié. In place of the old musket ball, he substituted an oblong bullet that was made of soft metal and hollowed out at the rear. Of sufficiently small calibre to preserve the windage in the barrel, it could be rammed to the base quite easily yet, because of the heat generated when the propellant was ignited, would expand enough to grip the rifling as it shot out. The result was a weapon which, if a little more expensive, could be loaded and discharged as easily as a smoothbore while yielding a twofold increase in accuracy. Minié's invention thus offered tactical advantages that were too tempting to resist and made the mass-production and employment of rifled small arms both financially and operationally worthwhile.

The replacement, undertaken mostly by the early 1840s, of the old flintlock mechanism with a percussion cap also increased the reliability of the rifled musket and marginally enhanced its rate of fire, too. However, it was the innovations of Jahn Dreyse, a Saxon, that permitted dramatic improvements in these respects. In 1836, he produced a viable screw-breech, succeeding where Baker and other Napoleonic gunsmiths had failed. He had already devised a percussive needle some years before. This penetrated the base of the chamber to detonate the propellant and, integrated with the breech, led to a rifled weapon which could not only fire shots six times as fast as a smoothbore musket, but could also be comfortably loaded while the soldier was kneeling or lying down to reduce his vulnerability. Dreyse's breech was not perfect; the seals tended to leak, resulting in a loss of pressure and, thus, range. Indeed, just as the old flintlock had tended to shower its owner's face with sparks, making him wince when he pulled the trigger, so too did the disagreeable blast of gas from the 'needle gun' discourage careful aiming; troops frequently resorted to firing from the hip.

This only exacerbated the concerns about ammunition wastage that had dogged the old *Repetierwindbüchse* and persuaded many armies that adopting breech-loading weapons could prove a mixed blessing. The Prussians, undeterred, equipped their forces with Dreyse's gun as early as 1843, but the British, French and Austrian Armies preferred to depend upon muzzle-loading, rifled muskets for many years after. Most, but not quite all, of the British infantry units that fought in the Crimean War used the Enfield, which fired Minié bullets; first produced in 1853, it was still being distributed when hostilities broke out. In the main, the Russians, by contrast, continued to rely on old-fashioned, smoothbore muskets. Likewise, whereas the great majority of the French and Austrian troops employed muzzle-loading, rifled muskets during the war in Italy in 1859, a single squadron of the cavalry of the French Imperial Guard carried a breech-loading rifle designed by Antoine Chassepot which could achieve a rate of fire of five rounds per minute. Superintendent of the arsenal at Châtellerault, he had perfected a way of sealing a breech by means of a rubber ring that was compressed when the gun was discharged. This prevented any seepage of gas, maximizing pressure and, thus, reach. Together with its small-calibre ammunition, which – being lighter, could also be carried in greater quantities – this rendered Chassepot's rifle capable of propelling a bullet nearly three times as far as Dreyse's, the reach of which was, at 600 metres, already impressive.

Again, however, the limitations imposed by the human eye and by the realities of combat, which despite improved propellants that maximized energy and reduced clogging, still included clouds of gun-smoke, could often mean that the effective range of any firearm was appreciably less than its theoretical, maximum reach. It was one thing to test a gun under ideal, laboratory conditions against an inanimate target; using it amidst the physical and psychological strains of combat was another. In reporting on a celebrated episode during the Battle of Balaklava, William Russell, the London *Times* correspondent in the Crimea, revealingly noted that, when the 93rd Highlanders came under attack from Russian horsemen, their first volley, at around 600 metres, was ineffectual because the distance was 'too great', whereas a second, at under 150 metres, carried 'death and terror into the Russians.' In fact, so destructive was rifle fire at this distance that Sir Colin Campbell, the Highlanders' commander, not only had the confidence not to order his troops – 'a thin red streak tipped with a line of steel' – to redeploy into square but also ' "did not think it worth while to form them even four deep!" '[19] By the time of Inkerman, Russell was convinced that the Minié rifle was 'the king of weapons.' Here, he observed how:

> The regiments of the Fourth Division and the Marines, armed with the old and much-belauded Brown Bess, could do nothing with their thin line of fire against the massive multitudes of the Muscovite infantry, but the volleys of the Minié cleft them like the hand of the Destroying Angel, and they fell like leaves in autumn before them.[20]

Combatants are always afforded a degree of protection by the limitations of their opponents' weapons. The new generation of firearms, however, substantially increased the vulnerability of troops, particularly if they were deployed in open terrain and in close-order formations.

Yet new technology was replacing older forms faster than it was undermining accepted military wisdom. In 1848, seeking to exploit the Habsburgs' preoccupation with the rebellions then underway in much of their empire, and anxious to distract attention from the growing problems posed by the *Risorgimento* within his own kingdom, Charles Albert of Sardinia advanced against the Austrian forces in northern Italy. His opponent, Marshal Josef Radetzky, had served as Schwarzenberg's chief of staff during the *Befreiungskrieg*. Now 82, he was perhaps too old to be taught new tricks. The ones he had learnt from Napoleon, however, more than sufficed. That July, using interior lines to concentrate against the centre of his adversary's army while it was spread across a front of 72 kilometres, he routed Charles Albert's forces at Custozza. Barely had Johann Strauss the elder, father of the 'Waltz King', commemorated this victory with his celebrated *Radetzky March* than the grizzled marshal, imitating Napoleon's manoeuvres in the Marengo campaign, inflicted another heavy blow on his astonished enemy at Novara.

Fought in March 1849, this battle proved decisive. However, in the interim the example set by Sardinia in seeking to exploit revolutionary turmoil in order to rewrite the 1815 treaties by *force majeure* had tempted Prussia into backing a rebellion by the German population within Schleswig-Holstein. Sweden responded by sending troops to support the Danes, while Britain threatened the Prussians by sea. Russia sided with Denmark, too, if only diplomatically. Although Prussia's mobilization might have proceeded more smoothly than it did, her troops performed well enough and the Danes were pressed back. Nevertheless, their control of the region's waterways prevented the Prussian army from securing a conclusive victory. In July 1848, Frederick William IV, alarmed by his country's isolation and anxious to distance himself from the German liberal movement, concluded an armistice without even consulting the Frankfurt Parliament and its newly elected members from Schleswig-Holstein. His forces withdrew from the duchies, leaving the rebels to their fate.

Officially, the First Schleswig War only ended in July 1850. The violence spawned by the revolutionary and counter-revolutionary fervour in Hungary and parts of Italy and Germany also lingered on until the summer of 1849. Elsewhere, however, it proved strikingly ephemeral, not least because the unwavering loyalty of their military forces helped restore the confidence of the old ruling élites and enabled them to reassert their authority. In June 1848, Marshal Alfred zu Windischgrätz bombarded the Prague rebels into submission and then imposed martial law throughout Bohemia. By October, control of Vienna had been regained by similar means, while the Prussian army, withdrawn in the Revolution's early stages, again occupied Berlin. The following June, as Russian troops entered Hungary in strength to assist in curbing resistance there, Württemberg cavalry dispersed the hundred or so radicals who, as the last fugitives from the Frankfurt Parliament, were trying to reassemble in the Stuttgart Town Hall. Around the same time there were brief, if bloody, acts of repression in Berlin, Breslau and Dresden, while, in Baden, two Prussian *Armeekorps* overwhelmed the brave defiance of some civilian volunteers who were backed by the mutinous garrisons of Rastadt and Karlsruhe. The rising here ended with Rastadt's capitulation on 23 July and the summary execution of several of the revolutionary leaders.

France had sneezed and Europe had caught a cold. Among the ruling houses, the only one to fall as a result of the 1848 Revolutions was that of Louis Philippe. That development and the proclamation of the Second Republic revived international fears that France might again attempt to destroy the Vienna settlement by force of arms. Yet it soon became apparent that, whilst moderate republicans like Alphonse de Lamartine had to be seen to condemn the treaties that had ended the Napoleonic Wars in order to appease French popular opinion, Paris was actually eager to avoid hostilities with the other great powers. War would not only have strengthened the hand of the French left, but would in all probability also have culminated in the defeat of France and the imposition of a far more punitive settlement than that of 1815.

Certainly, by the fall of the July Monarchy, France was still relatively vulnerable from a martial perspective. Many of her troops were tied down in Algeria, while Soult's bid to expand her armed forces had, as we have seen, been truncated. The construction of fortifications around Paris devoured funds that, given evident strategic trends, might well have been more profitably devoted to the building of a steamboat fleet or to railways designed with mobilization plans in mind. Indeed, largely because of the gaps and weaknesses in her communications network, too much of France's economic and military potential remained unexploited, even though Louis Philippe's reign had witnessed some significant attempts to rectify this state of affairs. The act of 1836 that led to dramatic, if gradual, improvements in France's rural road grid; the opening, in 1837, of her first major railway line, that between Paris and St Germain; the launch of her first transatlantic paddle steamer in 1840: besides forging links with distant countries and bringing her various regions into a more intimate union, all of these bolstered her capacity to deploy armed forces at speed and *en masse*. Above all, French naval thinkers were struck by the possibilities that supplementing ships' canvas with steam engines created. Though often much uglier and seldom faster than traditional sailing vessels, the hybrids this innovation led to were far less dependent upon favourable winds and currents. This enabled them to operate in all but the worst weather and to take far more direct routes to many destinations, thereby reducing journey times. One strategic implication of this was highlighted in 1844 by a rather pugnacious article that appeared in the *Revue des Deux Mondes*. Written by a French admiral, the Prince de Joinville, this argued that, thanks to steam power, a French amphibious force could dart across the Channel under cover of night, catch the Royal Navy unawares and overcome any local opposition. Both Guizot, then the French foreign minister, and his British counterpart, the earl of Aberdeen, had only recently spoken of the existence of an *entente cordiale*. However, this enjoyed little firm support in either Britain or France, and the two countries all too frequently found themselves at loggerheads, notably over the latter's policy in the Pacific, in Morocco during 1844 and over the Spanish Marriages question which led, in 1846, to the demise of the *entente* and a search for new partners among the eastern powers. As was the case during periods of Anglo-French tension later in the century, during all of this Britain was intermittently gripped by invasion hysteria. It seemed that the Royal Navy, traditionally her first line of defence, was no longer a sufficient guarantee of her security.[21]

On the other hand, the threat posed by France was often exaggerated. She lagged behind 'the workshop of the world', not least in the building of ships at a time when not only was sail beginning to give way to steam propulsion, but also timber was being supplemented or replaced by iron, a much stronger material, in the construction of hulls and super-structures. Isambard Kingdom Brunel, the greatest of this era's many outstanding engineers, was pre-eminent in this process, which led to vessels of unprecedented dimensions. As early as 1843, he followed up his impressive *Great Western*, which had a displacement of 2300 tonnes, with the *Great Britain*, the world's first screw-driven, ocean-going vessel. Within ten years, he was working to produce the largest ship yet seen, the *Great Eastern*, which had a displacement of 32 000 tonnes and a length of some 210 metres. Vessels like this, the liners of their time, very much simplified the projection of power overseas. In the age of sail, finding sufficient tonnage for the movement of even a few thousand troops had often proved as difficult as it was costly. British expeditions during the Napoleonic Wars were regularly plagued by such problems, while, for the initial invasion of Algeria, the French had had to spend an entire year assembling an armada of 675 ships to move 30 000 soldiers, including just one cavalry regiment, and their equipment and supplies.[22]

The steam and metal revolution had its greatest impact, however, in terms of warship design.[23] During the 1840s, the Royal Navy conducted tests on armour plate made from cast-iron sheeting. This was found to be counterproductive; dangerously brittle when subjected to gunfire, it disintegrated into a hail of razor-sharp shards that would have wrought havoc within any ship. Improvements in metallurgy overcame this problem and, in March 1858, the French admiralty stole a march on the British by ordering the *Gloire*, the first of three wooden ships clad in iron plates, each of which was nearly 12 centimetres thick. Sinister though this seemed to the Royal Navy, *Gloire* was an unstable vessel with a metacentric height of just over two metres. Her sister ships were, moreover, built with rotten timber and had to be scrapped within a few years. By contrast, the British answer to the *Gloire*, ordered in June 1859, survives to this day,[24] and was by far the most sophisticated and powerful warship yet seen. Completed, astonishingly, as early as October 1860, HMS *Warrior* was 128 metres long, with a beam of almost 18 metres. Much of her iron hull was sheathed in tongue-and-groove plating, each piece of which, some 15 square metres in area and 12 centimetres thick, weighed almost four tonnes. Her draft was nearly eight metres and her hull not only had a double bottom for much of its length but, amidships, also subdivided into 35 watertight compartments. Her single, retractable propeller, seven metres across and weighing some ten tonnes, was turned by the energy provided by ten boilers. Together with her sails, this enabled the largest and longest warship yet built to cruise the high seas at speeds of between 14 and 17 knots. Such a platform was, furthermore, capable of supporting a crew of 700 as well as an immense weight of ordnance. Their wrought-iron barrels reinforced with external coils and their carriages mounted on rails to channel and absorb the energy unleashed whenever they were fired, cannon developed by Sir Joseph Whitworth took pride of place. *Warrior* bristled with six of his breech-loading 100-pounders, double that number of 68-pounder smoothbore guns and four of his 40-pounder breech-loaders. By 1867, this armament had given way to a total of 31 of the latest muzzle-loading rifled guns of seven- and eight-inch calibre.

Like the ship that bore them, these guns were the products of better precision-engineering techniques and metallurgical processes, notably steel production which had been simplified and refined by, above all, Sir Henry Bessemer. Industrial chemists played their part, too; Siemens devised a way of removing the phosphorous that contaminated so much of the iron ore found in the Ruhr, thereby rendering it suitable for use in the Bessemer 'process'. This gave the German cannon foundries, notably Alfred Krupp's in Essen, a fillip. Unlike those made of bronze, cannon barrels cast from steel tended to develop potentially fatal flaws unless they were cooled evenly. This was difficult to achieve where such large, heavy objects were concerned. Small arms, on the other hand, were easier to produce but, scarcely cost-effective, found few buyers. Krupp had tried, unsuccessfully, to interest potential customers in steel rifled muskets as early as 1844. His perfection of a method of casting steel artillery, however, quickly secured him much of the world market for heavy weapons. An all-steel 6-pounder he displayed at the Great Exhibition in London in 1851 caught many an eye, and he was soon selling artillery to all the major European powers except for France and Britain, who preferred to depend upon their own manufacturers.

Seven years later, the French seemed to set new standards of excellence when they introduced a muzzle-loading rifled cannon designed by Napoleon III himself. Theirs was the first army to be wholly equipped with rifled ordnance, and the new guns certainly performed satisfactorily in the 1859 war against Austria. Yet, as at all times of extremely rapid technological advance, what constituted state-of-the-art equipment one day could all too easily be obsolescent the next. At the Paris Exhibition of 1867, Krupp put a massive steel gun on show. This typified the sophistication in artillery design that had just persuaded the Prussian Army to equip all of its field batteries with his steel breechloaders. Ergonomically, these offered obvious advantages over guns that were loaded at the muzzle, while steel's superior robustness permitted proportionately larger charges to be used than in bronze guns.

These qualities brought about an increase in the rate of fire and in reach, respectively. The latter could be further added to if the gun was discharged, not horizontally, but at an angle of up to 45 degrees. In any event, since the tapered, cylindrical projectiles fired from rifled guns did not ricochet like the cannonballs they supplanted, best results were achieved when the barrel was elevated. All of this called for numeracy, notably a knowledge of triangulation, as bombadiers, assisted by manuals specially produced for the purpose, had to calculate the bearing and elevation of targets as well as the amount of propellant required for a given projectile. With field-gun ranges lengthening to as much as 3000 metres, the problems posed by indirect fire grew, too. Long familiar to howitzer crews, these increasingly beset the artillery as a whole. Better arrangements for the accurate engagement of targets beyond the sight of the gunners themselves had to be formulated. In time, this spurred the production of maps overlaid with grids, which yielded a geometric relationship between elevation, range and bearing. However, in the absence of instantaneous communication between observers and batteries, dependable techniques for directing fire against mobile targets was to remain elusive throughout the 1800s. Damage assessment from afar was equally unreliable. Consequently, large, static targets, notably fortifications and towns, were the principal victims of remote, indirect bombardment, if it was attempted at all.

The assimilation and full evaluation of any new weapon frequently can, and normally does, take several years. Impressive though many armies found Krupp's steel breechloaders to be, that of France maintained its faith in the guns designed by the emperor, adopted, at great financial cost, in 1858, and tried and tested at Magenta and Solferino the year after. By contrast, as late as Sadowa in 1866, the Prussian artillery – then a mixture of Krupp's pieces and the old smoothbores they were gradually replacing – failed to make much of a contribution to the outcome of the fighting, whereas the Austrians', despite comprising seemingly obsolescent technology, covered itself in laurels, particularly during the battle's opening and concluding phases. This suggested that Krupp's guns were not as dangerous as some observers believed them to be, if, indeed, they were threatening at all. After all, few people in the late 1860s could have predicted with certainty that France and Prussia would shortly embark on hostilities against one another for the first time since 1815. History is replete with examples of, on the one hand, wars that were never foreseen and, on the other, those that were anticipated but never actually broke out. Whereas political intentions can alter, quite literally, overnight, the acquisition of military capabilities can take years if not decades. Then, as now, policy-makers had to steer between the Scylla of complacency and the Charybdis of premature or inappropriate investment. Certainly, committed to spending 113 million francs on the Chassepot programme and having already lavished huge sums on its ordnance, the French Army at this juncture simply lacked the funds to either revamp or replace its artillery for the second time in a few years.

Moreover, in war, doctrine can be just as important as technology. As we have seen, during the early stages of the Napoleonic conflict especially, French forces frequently made up for their quantitative inferiority by making relatively better tactical use of the manpower and equipment at their disposal. With varying degrees of success, Napoleon's opponents gradually copied French methods to try to cancel out this qualitative superiority. By the 1850s, with a new generation of small arms and ordnance increasing the intensity and reach of firepower, armies were again faced with a need to adjust their *modus operandi*. Essentially, two solutions to the problem presented themselves: first, troops might seek to close with an enemy as quickly as possible so as to deny him time to exploit his weapons' full potential; second, if an attritional battle could not be avoided, the tactics of dispersal, concealment and individual fire that, in Napoleon's day, had been the preserve of light infantry should be adopted as the norm.

After its experiences in Algeria, the Crimea and Italy, the French Army was persuaded that its professionalism, tactical flexibility and Gallic *élan* were the keys to success. If, especially at Inkerman in November 1854 and on the River Tchernaya in the August of the following year, Russian musketeers advanced with the bayonet in a forlorn bid to overwhelm adversaries armed with Minié rifles, in Italy in 1859 the French infantry's assaults on Austrians equipped with similar weaponry proved a good deal more irresistible. The *furia francese* was no more of a myth than were the bayonet charges executed by British troops in the fighting for Port Stanley in the Falkland Islands over 120 years later. Morale is always the single most important determinant in war. But courage, however necessary, is not always enough by itself to guarantee success. When, at the climax of the Battle of Sadowa, the bruised Austrian I *Armeekorps* advanced to meet the Prussians head on, the intense fire from thousands of Dreyse breechloaders cut down half of its remaining men in just 20 minutes of appalling slaughter.

The rifled muskets used in the Crimea and Italy in the 1850s were largely responsible for the sanguinary nature of the fighting there, too. The ease with which the Russians' steamers, with their shell-firing guns, demolished the Turkish sailing ships at Sinope in 1853 also highlighted the advantages that the latest types of equipment offered over the old. The British admiralty was quite confident that HMS *Warrior* and her sistership, *Black Prince*, could take on the combined fleets of the world and emerge not only victorious, but also relatively unscathed. Indeed, some observers were tempted to believe that technology alone could decide wars.

However, then as now, technical solutions were neither available for, nor applicable to, every problem. Alongside the great inventors of this era of extraordinary inventiveness were numerous frauds and crackpots. One who emerged during the Crimean War, for instance, endeavoured to sell the British government his 'Portable Bouyant Wave-Repressor' to subdue the storms which were causing such problems for the shipping in Balaklava harbour.[25] This particular bargain was treated with the scepticism it deserved, but other devices seemed more promising, at least superficially. In 1834, N. J. Løbnitz, the Danish gunsmith and inventor, followed in Girandoni's footsteps by devising a machine gun that used air as a propellant and was capable of firing 80 shots per minute. Tested by a Danish military commission, it was found to have sufficient penetrating power to punch its way through sheets of timber over two centimetres thick from a range of 80 metres. Impressive though this sounds, the weapon was adjudged to be of little practical value, for Løbnitz, like Girandoni before him, was unable to devise a compressor of manageable proportions. His machine gun was powered by a vertical pump with two enormous flywheels, which would itself have had to be mounted on an artillery carriage. This made it wholly unsuitable for mobile warfare at least.[26]

Moreover, if the growing sophistication of armaments made them more deadly, it could also make them more prone to failure. The shells fired by the new generation of artillery had to be fitted with either a timed fuse or a percussion detonator. As the former could only be set to a limited number of ranges – either 1200 or 2800 metres in the case of the French guns – hostile forces could often find safe havens at other distances. Furthermore, under campaign conditions, air-burst fuses all too often proved to be temperamental and performed erratically; percussion detonation, being far simpler, was that much more reliable. In inaugurating changes in tactics, the new firearms also exacerbated the old problems of commanding, controlling and motivating soldiers in the heat of battle. As what, in Napoleonic engagements, had been nothing more than cordons of skirmishers became the main striking force, the rationale for, and precise role of, the close-order formations that followed them came under mounting scrutiny. It appeared that, inordinately vulnerable to the enemy's fire, the regimental and battalion columns that had once been the real muscle behind any assault should now be kept out of harm's way. But such a policy would relegate them to acting as a mere manpower reservoir for the skirmish chain. Furthermore, it was found that, once deployed *en tirailleur*, units tended to lose all forward impetus as the bulk of their members, released from the grip of senior, if not all, officers and encouraged to employ their own initiative, too often reacted by going to ground and staying there.

Pardonable though this tendency was, it threatened to undermine discipline and make efficacious attacks – the key to deciding any engagement – all but impossible. Both the spirit of the times and the need to close quickly with the enemy to try to offset his firepower demanded that infantry press home their assaults. All of this suggested that shoulder-to-shoulder formations could not be renounced entirely. Was it possible to reconcile such contradictions? Only, it seemed, by combining an offensive at the strategic level with a tactical defence. By means of bold manoeuvre, territory that was as crucial to an adversary as it was easily defensible might be seized and then held against his riposte. Conversely, if, using exterior lines, quantitatively superior forces could be brought to bear against an opponent, even one entrenched in a strong defensive position, he might be destroyed with converging fire. Should, at any point in all of this, troops prove unable to bypass a position and be obliged to attack it across open terrain, it was essential that they be underpinned with sufficient firepower to suppress that of the enemy. This, in turn, implied that, instead of being kept in reserve for the climactic effort, the bulk of an army's artillery needed to be well to the fore from the outset. It could then give the infantry close support. Indeed, if all else failed, they might then be able to occupy ground that the guns had conquered.

So it was that the use of close-order formations persisted throughout the nineteenth century and into the next. Cavalry, too, did not go out of fashion, despite widespread worries about, and mounting evidence of, its vulnerability. Although its very mobility assured it a continuing role in communication, reconnaissance and *petite guerre* operations across theatres of war that grew ever larger, these functions were, as we have seen, traditionally performed by hussars, lancers, *chasseurs* and other light units. But what missions, in the era of the rifle and quick-firing artillery, remained for *cuirassiers* and other heavy horsemen? As opportunities for the shock action they were designed for became rarer, such soldiers were increasingly anachronistic. Yet the elegance of cavalry in general and heavy regiments in particular was just too bewitching. Even today, they are accorded pride of place in the ceremonial of the British and French Armies. This testifies to the social and political prestige that such horsemen still enjoy – a prestige that was so much greater in the 1800s. The partnership between man and horse was an ancient one that evoked images of the knights of old, and commissions in cavalry regiments were particularly sought after by those eager to cut a dashing figure. Even if some of their mounts were old nags rather than splendid steeds, cavalrymen looked down, literally and figuratively, on the 'poor bloody infantry', not to mention the technical arms. They were widely regarded as being superior, too, not least because of the way they were depicted in the *belles-lettres* of the period. It is revealing that Lord Tennyson, for instance, was inspired far less by the daily deprivations endured by Britain's humble foot soldiers in the Crimea than he was by the dutiful gallantry exhibited by her horsemen in a few fateful moments. By transforming a calamitous blunder into a shining example of heroic self-sacrifice, his 'Charge of the Light Brigade' further intensified the aura that, in the public eye, surrounded the cavalry. It is also noteworthy that the heroes in so many novels of this period take the form of a *beau sabreur*; the works of Thomas Hardy alone contain several.

Although he was not born until 1840, Hardy's writings also betray other aspects of the lingering influence of the Napoleonic Wars on so much of European life. In looking back from the twenty-first century at the period 1830–60, we should not be too critical of our ancestors who, for the first time in living memory, experienced real changes in the technology with which conflicts were waged. For 45 years after Waterloo, only a handful of European states had to mount a major military operation at all. Many of those that did occur were colonial conflicts or internal policing missions. Although they furnished more insights into the realities of combat than any peacetime manoeuvre could, neither the Algerian *razzias* nor the quelling of poorly armed mobs on the streets of Warsaw or Paris were much use as guides to what a full-scale war with another major European power might actually be like. Whilst no two conflicts are identical, wars bear more resemblance to one another than they do to any other human activity. The past was the only signpost to the future. In a dynamic situation, many people understandably, if sometimes mistakenly, clung to tried and tested methods; and the more prominent members of the older generation who had participated in the 'Great War' were repeatedly looked to as a source of counsel, if only because they were too distinguished to ignore entirely. Soult, as we have seen, became war minister and a marshal general of France, while younger Napoleonic commanders, such as Bugeaud, rose to prominence as much because of their pasts as anything else. Radetzky was still fighting battles at the end of the 1840s essentially because he had been Schwarzenberg's chief of staff during the *Befreiungskrieg* over 30 years earlier.

Similarly, Nelson was the bane and lodestar of the Royal Navy; despite the steam and metal revolution, conservatism reigned supreme within the admiralty for some 50 years after his death, with little, if any, thought being accorded to the evolution of maritime strategy. Likewise,

Wellington's reputation became as much of a burden as an inspiration to the British Army. Lord Raglan, who had never actually commanded so much as a company but had been present at Waterloo, where he had lost an arm, was adjudged to be qualified to lead the Crimean expedition simply because he had served under the 'Iron Duke'. Indeed, he had acted as Wellington's military secretary from 1827 until the duke's death in 1852, after which he took up the post of master general of the ordnance. Though a fearless man, he was first and foremost not a leader but a bureaucrat, while, in contrast to their French colleagues, most of his subordinates were ageing, well-to-do gentlemen rather than professional soldiers. With the exception of the youthful duke of Cambridge, who was appointed purely because of his royal blood, all of Raglan's infantry commanders had also seen action during the Peninsular or Waterloo campaigns, while his chief engineer, Sir John Burgoyne, Inspector-General of Fortifications, had been in the British Army since 1789. Lord Lucan, the cavalry commander, was a mere 54, but had officially retired from active service in 1838, while Cardigan, who led the ill-fated light brigade, had never seen a shot fired in anger before.

The French commanders in the Crimea mostly came from Bugeaud's ring. He had fallen victim to cholera in 1849 and Cavaignac, having stood as a candidate for the presidency of the Second Republic in 1848, was not among the army officers that Napoleon III trusted. By contrast, Marshal Saint-Arnaud had played a prominent part in Napoleon's *coup d'état* of 1851 and was duly rewarded with command of the French expeditionary force. His principle subordinates – Canrobert, Bosquet and Forey – were all Bonapartists, too, as, needless to say, was Prince Napoleon Joseph, the emperor's nephew, who was also given a command. In view of his inexperience, this appointment was evidently made for dynastic, political reasons and caused Saint-Arnaud some concern. Whilst conceding that the prince might know the emperor's thoughts, the marshal was also emphatic that if he did 'anything other than his job as a general of division,' he would be made to re-embark. 'I am the commander-in-chief!' Saint-Arnaud insisted.[27] Already dying of intestinal cancer when the conflict with Russia began, he was not destined to remain so for long.

But neither he nor Napoleon III initially expected the war to last more than a couple of months. Land operations were to be brief, inexpensive and centred on the Danube valley; there was no thought at this juncture of a landing in the Crimea, still less of a prolonged siege at Sevastopol. In fact, the emperor envisaged the whole undertaking as a *coup de main* that would require no more than 12 000 troops. These, it was believed, could be found almost exclusively from among the Zouave regiments policing the precarious peace in Algeria. Led by officers with appreciable combat experience, these seasoned veterans would be more than adequate for the task in hand.

Certainly, the soldiers furnished by *l'Armée d'Afrique* fought with distinction in the ensuing campaign, but the performance of their commanders was more uneven. After Saint-Arnaud's death, General Canrobert took control. He and the rest of *'Les Algériens'* were essentially infantry tacticians. In the Crimea, they encountered opponents who were mostly equipped with muskets that were little if any better than those that had been purchased from European suppliers by Abd-el-Kader for use by his warriors. Whereas their adversaries, as we have noted, had to contend with the threat posed by the latest Minié rifles, the French and British were spared this ordeal. As a result, the allies' experience in the Battles of the Alma, Balaklava and Inkerman did little to weaken their faith in their existing tactical doctrines. Commenting on the British, one Russian captain was astonished by their adherence to the linear formations and unhurried manoeuvre that had served them so well in Wellington's day: 'Throughout the whole ... war they distinguished themselves by their extraordinary leisureliness, [which] ... was the cause of their high number of casualties in the Alma battle.' By contrast, the French infantry 'excelled in their speed of movement and in this respect were superior', he admitted, to friend and foe alike. They were also 'outstanding in the rapidity with which they deployed into attack columns – for we Russians sacrificed speed for good order ... .'[28]

The handful of set-piece engagements aside, however, the land war consisted of little more than the attempts to reduce Sevastopol. These dragged on for 12 months. Thanks to Bugeaud's influence, the French commanders might have been imbued with the Napoleonic martial spirit, but they were almost wholly devoid of expertise in conducting full-blown sieges and in coping with the problems encountered in trying to furnish adequate logistical support for protracted, large-scale operations. In both these respects, the Algerian *razzia* was a poor guide. It soon became clear that Napoleon III had underestimated the degree of commitment required to defeat Russia and avenge the catastrophe suffered by his uncle in 1812. Acknowledging that far more resources would be needed, where he had once spoken of 10 000 men, the emperor now talked of fielding four separate forces of 60 000 troops each.

This was utterly unrealistic. Its existing responsibilities in terms of colonial and home defence were already imposing a severe strain on the French Army. Many units comprised mere peacetime *cadres* – the Parisian garrisons, for instance, could actually muster only a third of their nominal strength – and finding just 50 000 soldiers to send to the Crimea proved hard enough.[29] The expedition stretched France's military strength to breaking point and left her own frontiers dangerously vulnerable.

Difficulties also arose in getting what troops, stores and equipment were available to such a distant theatre of war. For lack of steamboats, too much *matériel* had to be transported by sailing ships, which were often slower and carried less. As late as the middle of August 1854 – just four weeks before Sevastopol was first invested – the French siege train was still stranded in Toulon, while Saint-Arnaud was complaining that his divisions had only one-fifth of the two million rations he anticipated they would need for the coming month.[30] Although the British government was chronically embarrassed by the relatively small contingent of soldiers it could field and was obliged to recruit Polish, Swiss and German legions to make up the numbers, its maritime resources, both civil and military, far surpassed those of the French, who, at the start of the siege, had all of 10 000 troops sitting idle in Marseille for want of ferries.

These men were eventually transported in British steamers. Indeed, the decisive and highly characteristic contribution that the British made to the war was the naval campaign in the Baltic, a region that was of traditional strategic concern to the Royal Navy because it was a prime source of iron, hemp, timber and other essential supplies. While scores of thousands of her soldiers were pinned down around St Petersburg and other vulnerable points by actual or expected amphibious assaults,[31] the rigorous maritime blockade had a disastrous effect on Russia's trade; exports fell by 80 per cent. Whereas, on dry land, their numerical strength made the French the senior partner in the alliance, on both the Black and Baltic Seas they were relegated to a subordinate role by not just the quantitative, but also the qualitative superiority of the Royal Navy, the relative sophistication of which had been amply illustrated by the Spithead review of August 1853; such was the enthusiasm for the adoption of steam by an otherwise conservative admiralty that 37 of the 40 participating vessels were already fitted with engines, however small.

To begin with, the French forces in the Crimea coped far better with the demands of expeditionary warfare than their allies did. Years of campaigning in Algeria had taught them the art of sustaining forces in an inhospitable environment, and they had developed medical and transport services that had proved quite sufficient for the needs of *l'Armée d'Afrique*. The quality of the French staff and *Intendance* sowed envy among the British. One embittered diarist noted that 'The organization of the French is beautiful, ours a perfect disgrace; and I do therefore hope that, if we have another campaign, we may get rid of all Peninsular heroes.'[32] Another was struck by the irony as well as the consequences of the British shortcomings in this regard: 'Wellington prided himself on thoroughly understanding how to feed an army! I fear his mantle has not fallen on any shoulders here.'[33] Certainly, the British troops in the field suffered severely as a result of the penny-pinching, complacency and neglect that had gradually engulfed the army since the heady days of Waterloo.[34] From the outset of the Crimean campaign, basic necessities, such as clean water, suitable clothing, and regular and comprehensive supplies of food and ammunition as well as the conveyances to transport them were lacking, as was an expert general staff to administer to the expeditionary force's needs. The Royal Wagon Train had been disbanded in 1833, and there was a dearth of pack animals and vehicles.[35]

However, the remoteness of the seat of the war from their home bases and the sheer scale and intensity of the challenge the French encountered in the Crimea steadily overtaxed them, too. Arrangements that had more or less sufficed for the support of comparatively small units scattered amongst the settlements of nearby Algeria proved ever-more inadequate as the size of the French contingent expanded. By spring 1855, its infantry alone amounted to eight strong divisions and, within a year, the army as a whole was faltering under its own weight. In the first three months of 1856, 53 000 patients were admitted to its hospitals, of whom 10 000 died just from typhus or cholera. By this time, the situation of the British was much improved. Not least because of newspaper reports of maladministration and the unnecessary suffering among the soldiery, Lord Aberdeen's coalition government had toppled in January 1855. As prime minister, Palmerston strove to prosecute the war as resolutely as Britain's resources and her French, Sardinian and Turkish allies permitted. General Sir James Simpson superseded Raglan, who, like so many of his troops, had perished from cholera. A timid, colourless leader, he resigned in the November, stung by ongoing criticism. He had, however, started a programme of improvements that his successor, Sir William Codrington, continued to add to: navvies were shipped in to build both huts to shelter the troops and a railway to expedite the movement of supplies; a new Land Transport Corps was established, as was a Medical Staff Corps which, together with Florence Nightingale's volunteer nurses, endeavoured to improve basic hygiene and the care of the sick and wounded; Brunel designed a wooden, prefabricated hospital that, ingeniously ventilated and comprising modular wards, surgeries, kitchens, wash rooms and laundries, was erected at Renkioi in Turkey; and, while pack mules were procured from Spain, arrangements were made for regular supplies of fresh meat and fruit from Malta.

The introduction of these measures owed much to the overhaul of Britain's complex civil-military relationships that Palmerston not only recognized as essential, but also, in the aftermath of the death of Wellington, the arch-conservative, was at liberty to initiate. He separated the colonial and war departments and, by steadily enhancing the powers of the new secretary of state for war, sought to furnish the British Army with the sort of centralized and unified administration that Sir James Graham had created for the Royal Navy in 1834. But as better collaboration between the civil and military powers improved matters in the British camp, in that of the French relations became more strained as the war, despite its soaring costs in blood and gold, failed to deliver the results Napoleon III had anticipated. In January 1855, a scathing, embarrassing pamphlet entitled *La Conduit de la Guerre en Orient* appeared that, although anonymous, was widely attributed to Prince Napoleon, not least by the emperor himself. Aware that the conflict enjoyed little active support in France, where too many people dismissed it as a consequence of perfidious Albion's manipulation of his own personal and dynastic ambitions, he was eager to curtail it with a triumphal flourish. He now reasoned that, having saved Turkey, he need only teach the tsar a lesson in order to re-establish France's stature within European affairs, confound his domestic critics and consolidate the position of his regime.

As early as July 1854, he had begun talking about taking command of the Crimean operations in person. The recently laid submarine-telegraph link had already enabled him to meddle in his generals' plans during the preceding three months, but, for all the relative speed of this method of communication, there was a delay of 24–36 hours between the transmission of any information and its receipt. A further time lapse ineluctably separated the issue of any instructions by the theatre headquarters from their implementation. Exasperated by this and anxious to emulate his great uncle's martial achievements, by early 1855 Napoleon had resolved to leave Paris for the Black Sea and, on 24 April, sent Canrobert word that, at the head of reinforcements, he would arrive shortly.

This declaration of intent filled France's high command, court and allies with consternation. Canrobert and his colleagues had been obliged to tolerate Prince Napoleon's presence, but they knew that, for all his pretensions, the emperor did not possess his great ancestor's strategic flair. Fearing the likely consequences of his interference for both him and them, they began submitting tactful, if sometimes disingenuous, protests: his majesty would find the Crimean War intractable, yet would not be able to return from it without victory; his domestic political opponents, already restless, would seize on his departure as an opportunity to cause serious trouble; his death or injury might precipitate the collapse of his dynasty. The British government, as eager to keep their armed forces out of Napoleon's grasp as they were to stop him ruining his own, also joined in by inviting the emperor on a state visit to London. This proved to be one of the more successful episodes of Anglo-French cooperation during the war, as, under pressure from both his own and the British establishment, Napoleon reluctantly abandoned his notion of assuming command.[36]

He did not cease to intervene, however. In May 1855, in response to untimely, inept orders cabled from Paris, Canrobert recalled the French elements of a joint amphibious expedition that had been launched against the Kertch Peninsula. The acrimony and embarrassment this caused made him step down in favour of General Jacques Pélissier, another of 'Les Algériens', who, defying his emperor, proceeded with the blow against the Kertch. It proved highly successful. Pélissier also injected more offensive spirit into the flagging siege operations and, over the next four months, the Allies redoubled their efforts to seize Sevastopol's main strongholds, the Malakhoff and the Redan. On 16 August, the Russian field army made one last attempt to outflank the besiegers and forestall the impending storm. Two large columns gallantly attempted to force their way over the River Tchernaya at Traktir in the face of French and Sardinian resistance but, swept by artillery and rifle fire, sustained 10 000 casualties to no avail. On 5 September, the Allies commenced their sixth great bombardment which, after three days, culminated in the detonation of several huge mines beneath the Russian defences. The French infantry then dashed from their forward parallel to capture the battered Malakoff, only 25 metres away. Their British counterparts were now expected to take the Redan in similar style, but here matters went badly awry. Rather than advance through the rain of Russian bullets, too many of the foremost soldiers, who were largely inexperienced recruits, merely exchanged fire with their opponents from the safety of their own trenches. Some even began to drift, or run, back from the firefight, further hampering the reserves' endeavours to move forward. Consequently, the attack was repelled, though the Russians soon withdrew beyond the Chernaya into the northern half of Sevastopol. Ashamed by the assault's failure and burdened with guilt for having survived an operation that had cost so many of his comrades their lives, one British officer spoke for the whole army:

> I stood in the Redan more humble, more dejected and with a heavier heart than I have yet felt since I left home. ... [On] the Malakov, there was the French flag .... No flag floated on the parapet on which I stood and if it had, I could have ... dashed it into the ditch we could not pass, or hid it in the bosom of the young officer, dead at my feet ....[37]

For nearly 40 years, British politicians had neglected the army. Much of the motivation for this stemmed from the primacy accorded the Royal Navy and the desire to minimize military expenditure as a whole. However, whereas defeat at Jena had compelled the Prussians to rethink their methods and rebuild their military machine from scratch, the British had managed to avoid any such exigency. This had occurred as much by luck as design. Neither the shock administered by the reverses of the First Afghan War of 1838–42, nor the panic that, caused by the French invasion scares, intermittently gripped Britain in the 1840s and early 1850s proved sufficient to end governmental complacency for any length of time. However, the failings in the Crimea were too glaring and too well publicized to be ignored. Writing in February 1855, Lord Panmure, Secretary of State for War, was damning, perhaps a little excessively so, in his criticism of the shortcomings revealed by the Crimean campaign. He argued that the British Army had to be 'something more than a mere colonial guard or home police; ... it must be the means of maintaining our name abroad, and causing it to be respected in peace as well as admired and dreaded in war.' For too long, salvation had depended upon the purely fortuitous emergence of outstanding soldiers like Marlborough and Wellington. The system, Panmure continued,

> by which an army should be provisioned, moved, brought to act in the field and in the trenches, taught to attack or defend, is non-existent. ... We have no means of making General Officers or of forming

an efficient Staff, as it has been the practice ... to keep the same officers ... till they have either become worn out, or so wedded to old
ways as to be useless ... .

[O]ur force in time of peace should never be under 100 000 bayonets .... Of these, three divisions of 10 000 each should be formed to
be placed in permanent cantonments and occasionally encamped in
such locations ... as afford sufficient space for training and exercise,
and easy access by railway ... .[38]

Sound though his suggestions were, once peace returned, Britain's
enthusiasm for military expenditure waned again. French and British
soldiers returned to capital cities and garrison towns that, over the next
few years, acquired scores of new boulevards, bridges and public houses
bearing the names of Crimean battles and heroes. The Russians, meanwhile, who had been widely regarded as Europe's greatest military power,
digested the awesome implications of having been beaten on their own
soil through offensives launched from the sea by opponents who were as
technologically advanced as they were comparatively democratic. The war
had highlighted just how economically backward Russia was. Europe's
leading producer of pig iron in the 1780s, she was now outclassed in this
respect by Belgium, while the amount of coal extracted from her immense
but scattered reserves was less than 12 per cent of the quantity mined in
Britain.[39] Her defeat might have been staved off had she possessed a railway system capable of bringing timely succour to the Crimean garrison
and circumventing the maritime blockade by increasing overland trade
with Central Europe. But, as late as 1855, her whole network amounted
to just 1056 kilometres of track. As well as hampering economic growth
by tying both labour and capital to the land, slavery's close relation, serfdom, also impeded military efficiency and social control; the army, judi-
cial system and local government were all products of feudalism.

Even if the economic rationale for reform was not overwhelming, the
military case was: a massive but feudalistic army was clearly no longer an
adequate defence against either external threats or the radical Populists,
the *Narodniks*, who were spawned by Russia's humiliating defeat. Though
their political doctrine was rather nebulous, they advocated the creation
of an egalitarian society rooted in peasant communes. When the people
failed to respond to the entreaties of these high-minded socialists, who
mostly came from middle-class backgrounds, some of the exasperated
Narodniks resorted to revolutionary terrorism. Indeed, one fanatical
faction succeeded in assassinating the tsar in 1881.

By this time, however, Alexander II had made appreciable headway in implementing the sort of far-reaching reform programme that major military defeats often precipitate. Serfdom had been abolished and the railway web expanded to 22 400 kilometres by a modernizing Russia that, as a result, now posed so much more of a threat than before to putative foes. Her inability to strike directly at the British Isles during the Crimean War had stimulated a quest for leverage elsewhere. India was the obvious weak spot, and expansion into Central Asia was duly hastened. Russian forces were soon in a position to menace the whole length of Britain's eastern strategic flank, which now stretched from the Baltic to Afghanistan. Austrian policy during the war had also alienated Russia, particularly after the help she had given Vienna in 1848. Conserving the political *status quo* in Central and Eastern Europe was now accorded less importance than regaining what had been lost, in prestige and other respects, further south. The pre-eminent consequence of this policy was that it facilitated Prussia's unification of Germany, which, in turn, had dire consequences for the recent efforts by France and Britain to contain Russia. No sooner had Prussia crushed France in 1871 than the Black Sea was remilitarized. This led, as early as 1877, to fresh fighting between Turkey and a revitalized Russia, in which the latter gained the upper hand.

Besides these, the Crimean and other conflicts of the 1850s had other, wider ramifications. The Russians employed undersea mines to help guard some of their Baltic strongholds. Moored below the surface, these weapons were detonated by either an electrical impulse or a chemical fuse, comprising sugar and potassium chlorate. Noting this and the Royal Navy's use, close inshore, of small, armoured steamers in its enforcement of the Baltic blockade, some naval theorists thought that they might be witnessing the beginning of a new trend in maritime strategy. In any case, just as it had during the Napoleonic Wars and the Anglo-American conflict of 1812–15, naval embargo as an instrument of economic warfare raised fundamental questions about the rights of belligerents and neutrals alike. The Paris Congress of 1856 yielded a declaration on disputed aspects of relevant international law which, as we shall see, was to be sorely tested by the American Civil War.

The fate of sick and wounded soldiers also aroused international concern. Some 675 000 men perished in the Crimean War, 80 per cent of them from disease and injuries, notably wounds that became infected. Florence Nightingale's endeavours were swamped by the sheer scale of the problem, but they set an influential precedent. At St Thomas's

Hospital, London, the Nightingale School for Nursing, the first of its kind anywhere, was established by public subscription, while, across the Eurocentric world, women joined volunteer nursing corps which were often organized along paramilitary lines. The conflict in Italy in 1859 had similar by-products, too. So shocking was the bloodshed at Solferino that it accentuated calls for some form of cosmopolitan medical service. These led, in 1864, to the establishment of the International Red Cross, which has been alleviating the suffering of those caught up in war ever since.

Many of the French Army's deficiencies that had been revealed in the Crimea were again highlighted during the fighting in Italy. Logistical shortcomings, inadequate transport, poor strategic planning and the inept leadership of Napoleon III and some of his generals plagued the operations of a field army that swelled to five *corps* and the Imperial Guard as the campaign unfolded. Their opponents mobilized their forces on a similar scale: 200 000 men clashed at Magenta, while Solferino involved a further 50 000 combatants, even though tens of thousands of soldiers were by now laid up with malaria and other diseases. Through sheer professionalism and their celebrated *élan*, the French troops, together with their Sardinian allies and in spite of their commanders, eventually clawed their way to victory. Nevertheless, withdrawing to the almost impregnable Quadrilateral, the Austrian forces, directed by the Emperor Franz Josef in person, were shaken rather than routed; any further fighting promised to be gorier still. It was mounting international pressure on the belligerents that really determined the next step, however. Alarmed by Prussian sabre-rattling, Napoleon quickly settled for spoils far short of those he had anticipated. These constituted, for all that, France's first territorial gains in Europe since 1815, while further weakening the Vienna settlement of that year. When they marched into Paris in August 1859, the emperor and his soldiers were acclaimed as heroes. It was to be the last occasion for almost 60 years on which the city would welcome a French army back from a victorious European war.

Solferino was the penultimate milestone on the road to doctrinal and tactical change. Although the then new French rifled artillery did not have so much of an effect as to precipitate the total abnegation of Napoleonic formations and techniques, the use, by both sides, of Minié-style muskets appreciably reduced the degree of protection that soldiers had hitherto derived from the limitations of their adversaries' weaponry. At Sadowa, just a few years later, the employment of the Dreyse rifle by the Prussians was to carry this evolutionary process still further; thereafter, breech-loading designs became the standard issue of all European armies. In reach and volume of fire, they were markedly superior to the rifled musket. Bayonets, which had always been of more psychological than practical value, were, together with the swords and lances wielded by horsemen, now definitely weapons of last resort, as opportunities for their use became ever rarer. Indeed, as the reach and lethality of firearms increased, so too did the size of battlefields and the intervals between the opposing sides. Combat took place at a distance, with firepower alone offering sufficient protection against even the most rapid of cavalry charges. This, together with the dispersal of forces in order to deny an opponent prime targets, exacerbated the problems of command and control. It facilitated the disengagement of armies and individual soldiers alike, making retreat an easier, and thus more tempting, stratagem, particularly for conscripts who were lacking in commitment and a sense of *esprit de corps*. On the other hand, with the decline of close-quarter fighting, it was now feasible for even mediocre irregulars to keep hardened veterans at bay through sheer firepower, providing their morale could be maintained.

This challenge was, as always, the paramount one in war, as was recognized by, among others, the French soldier-theorist Ardant du Picq, who had seen action in the Crimea and, subsequently, in Syria and Algeria. War is a human concept, and military institutions reflect the societies that give rise to them, including racial, technical and other characteristics. However much the technology employed in military operations might change, the nature of *Homo sapiens* remains constant. Performance in combat is thus shaped by the individual and the collective psychology of humankind. By means of various devices, including music, uniforms, alcohol, discipline and tactics, human beings had been enabled to overcome the instinct of self-preservation so as to risk life and limb in pursuit of political objectives. This process continues to this day in armed forces throughout the world. Yet Du Picq, in common with many other writers on war and peace in the mid-1800s, sensed that growing affluence and the influence of democratic thought and practice, however partial, was eroding *l'esprit militaire* in his and some other countries, while the ruling warrior castes within Prussia, Russia and Austria were managing to preserve it. He was particularly concerned with the implications that this might have for the morale and thus tactics of the French Army. Whereas long-serving professional soldiers developed a spirit of comradeship that underpinned unit cohesion, conscripts and reservist forces, particularly if they simply coalesced around kernels of unfamiliar regulars when mobilized, lacked these qualities. What was the point in having large armies if so many of the men comprising them were reluctant, if not wholly unprepared, to fight? Would a smaller, more professional force not prove more reliable?

By means of detailed questionnaires he circulated within the French officer corps in the late 1860s, Du Picq sought to gather data on the precise conduct of units and their constituents in recent engagements. Through this positivist, behavioural research, he hoped to produce, not some loose theory as many had done in the 1700s, but truly scientific insights into human nature and what motivated people to fight regardless of it. He concluded that, in the age of the rifle, shock-action's utility had faded to the point where *l'ordre profond* was not merely obsolete but suicidal. Killed in action in the Franco-Prussian War, he never completed his study, but it was published posthumously in 1880 under the title *Études sur le Combat*. Although its impact on military doctrine was far stronger in the early 1900s than when it first appeared,[40] it remains a fascinating, novel examination of some of the ramifications for warfare that flowed from the scientific revolution of the mid-1800s.

Certainly, the tactical changes ushered in by the widespread adoption of the rifle were unsettling to the likes of Jomini and Colonel William Napier, who believed that warfare would essentially conform for ever more to the Napoleonic paradigm they had experienced and so admired. The author of the epic, huge and controversial *History of the War in The Penisula*, which he had dedicated to Wellington, Napier dismissed the significance of Minié's innovation,[41] while Jomini, despite the impact of the rifled musket on the battlefields of the Crimea, still insisted in the 1855 edition of his very influential *Précis de l'Art de la Guerre* that tactics would never fundamentally alter. Even in the sphere of colonial warfare, however, there were already indications enough that Jomini and his disciples were wrong in making this cardinal assumption. After all, the very emergence of the Algerian *razzia* had persuaded Bugeaud, among others, that orthodox Napoleonic tactics and strategy were not universally applicable. During the mid-1800s, many African rulers especially embraced European armaments and methods to give them an advantage in conflicts with their neighbours and to enable them to resist European penetration of their lands. Although the use of manual weapons by some tribes survived far into the century, others acquired firearms one way or another at the earliest opportunity. Smoothbore muskets, either purchased from international traders or looted from dead or captured French soldiers, quickly became a part of the arsenals of the Algerian chieftains, while Paris provided Mehemet Ali's army in Egypt with both guns and advice on how best to use them. If, today, mechanisms intended to restrain the proliferation of advanced armaments too often prove ineffectual, they were virtually non-existent in the free-wheeling economies of the 1800s. As the leading European armies switched from smoothbore muskets to, first, Minié-pattern rifles and, thereafter, to breechloaders, a weapon cascade was created, whereby surpluses of older armaments trickled down to lesser powers, many of them overseas.

They included the Zulu and Ashanti Kingdoms. It has been estimated that between 30 000 and 60 000 shoulder arms found their way into the former region during the years 1875–77 alone.[42] Nevertheless, even at this late stage, the Zulus preferred to rely upon their traditional *assegais*. The Ashantis, on the other hand, who had prospered from their trade in gold and slaves, elected to equip much of their large army with smoothbore firearms at least. If, in the conflict with Britain during 1873/4, they failed to make optimal use of these guns, it was essentially because many of them were poorly maintained and no tactical doctrine had been elaborated for their employment.[43]

By contrast, the Samorian Empire emulated European methods to such a degree that its founder, Samori Touré, came to be known as the 'Bonaparte of the Sudan'. He began his military career during the 1850s as a young mercenary in his native Guinea Highlands and, a born leader, went on to carve out a realm centred on them. Originating from among the *dyulas* – a class of affluent, educated, long-distance traders – he promoted their values to the detriment of the old warrior chieftains and, as *almamy*, embodied both secular and spiritual authority. His policies brought peace, greater prosperity and a sense of unity to his diverse lands, the security of which was entrusted to a formidable army, backed by an efficient bureaucracy. Predominantly infantry, his troops were equipped with muskets or rifles that were purchased from European traders and often paid for with the revenue from the sale of slaves, among whom were prisoners captured in Samori's wars. Small arms of the very latest design were procured wherever possible, and there even seem to have been attempts to buy British artillery pieces. Certainly, over time most of his soldiers were issued with breechloaders, while his élite units were to acquire repeating rifles by the 1880s.[44]

Samori's forces favoured guerrilla warfare rather than set-piece battles. Through their tactical sophistication, they were destined to cause the

French serious difficulties in the Sudan. However, as early as 1857 the proliferation of rifled weapons almost brought about the collapse of British rule in India. When the East India Company punished 85 of its sepoys at Meerut after they had refused to handle cartridges issued for use with the new Lee Enfield rifle, all of its native troops in Bengal rebelled. The disaffected soldiers believed the ammunition to be greased with beef and pork fat – substances that were regarded as defiling by Hindus and Muslims, respectively. The company's armies in Madras and Bombay, which predominantly comprised Sikhs and Gurkhas, remained loyal, however. Together with reinforcements rushed out from Britain, they suppressed the rising.

Predictably, the British Army's ultimate success in quelling the mutiny strengthened the hand of those who opposed the sort of reforms called for by Panmure and others. Yet many people found this sinister and savage episode in colonial history hard to forget, not least because of the stimulus it gave to the depiction of warfare in the arts. The absence of an armed conflict among the major European powers in the period between the '100 Days' and the Crimea led to most painters, engravers and illustrators concentrating on historical subjects, notably episodes of the Napoleonic and still earlier struggles. Indeed, until the 1850s, historical motifs, particularly those with a military flavour, were as highly thought of in artistic circles as religious ones were. They had a wider appeal, too. Just as romanticized, and often very misleading, images of the *Befreiungskrieg* fed the growth of the militant nationalism that erupted in Germany in 1848, in France depictions by the likes of David of Napoleon's victories and other facets of the days of '*La Gloire*' all added to the 'Legend of St Helena' and the lure of Bonapartism. For British artists, Sir John Moore's death, the Peninsular campaigns, Trafalgar, Nelson, Wellington and Waterloo all had an enduring appeal as subjects. Indeed, such was the fascination George Jones evinced for the last of these that he acquired the sobriquet 'Waterloo Jones'. Sir David Wilkie, meanwhile, both immortalized and glamorized Augustina, the 'Maid of Saragossa', heroine of the sieges of 1808/9.

The production of such paintings coincided with and was influenced by works of literature at a time when numerous novelists and historians – including Marie-Henri Beyle (Stendhal), William Thackeray, Walter Scott, Victor Hugo, Thiers and Napier – were similarly intrigued by the Napoleonic era. For some of the canvases he produced during the early 1840s, Sir William Allan evidently derived inspiration from Captain William Siborne's *History of the War in France and Belgium in*

1815, published in 1844. Using eyewitness accounts that he had solicited from veterans of the battle, Siborne, at this juncture, was also busy constructing two dioramas of Waterloo,[45] which furnished Thomas Sydney Cooper, the celebrated painter of animals, with background details for a picture of one of the battle's cavalry actions. Cooper submitted this work to the competition that, held in 1847, selected pieces for the decoration of the new Houses of Parliament. Allan, too, was a competitor, though neither his nor Cooper's entry won a prize, unlike Daniel Maclise's *The Meeting of Wellington and Blücher after Waterloo*, which was a companion piece to his *The Death of Nelson*.

Compared with such great historical subjects, the various small wars of the 1830s and 1840s commanded little attention among artists. Numerous Dutch, German and French painters were as captivated by Waterloo as their British counterparts, with the French tending to emphasize the heroic sacrifice made by their countrymen in pursuit of a lost but glorious cause. By contrast, Sir Edwin Landseer's *Peace* and *War* juxtaposed the cruelty and waste of the latter with the former's blessings. Best known for his pictures of animals, the centrepiece of his *War* comprises two dying horses and their riders amidst the ruins of a house and garden.

This attempt to convey a given theme's essence reflected a wider trend in the portrayal of warfare by British artists as panoramic depictions of events gave way to a focus on particular details. As a subject, the Crimean War lent itself to this approach. Whereas French painters lauded the triumphs of the Second Empire just as they had those of the First with pictures of great victories and heroic commanders, British artists more often than not focused on the conflict's undercurrents. Chronicled by war correspondents whose reports, virtually uncensored and forwarded by telegraph or steamer, quickly appeared in newspapers that an ever-more literate population could understand, the deprivations suffered by the ordinary soldiers and their generals' maladministration and tactical blunders were as familiar to artists as they were to the rest of the public. Pictorial journalism, facilitated by lithography, also brought the realities of a distant war into people's parlours. Moreover, as the early cameras required subjects to remain stationary for several seconds while the photograph was taken, dynamic scenes were impossible to record, whereas static ones, such as small groups of soldiers relaxing in their encampments, could be captured.

By providing raw material for grander works created with paints and brushes, these snapshots of real life helped divert the attention of artists towards subjects that emphasized the quotidian, human aspects of service in the military. John Millais's *News From Home*, painted in 1857, is a classic example of this genre. That year also witnessed the outbreak of the Indian Mutiny, which quickly supplanted the Crimean conflict in the collective imagination of the British public especially. That soldiers could turn against the very authorities they were intended to support and that vassals could revolt against their colonial rulers was quite disturbing enough to European minds. Events in India, however, went beyond the violation of military oaths or even simple treachery. At Cawnpore, Delhi, Allahabad, Jhansi and elsewhere, British civilians – men, women and children – together with native servants and sepoys who remained loyal to them, fell victim to shocking atrocities that inevitably stoked the fires of racial and religious animosity. Mutiny, as the ultimate failure of discipline, had always had to carry the death penalty. But, as both retribution against those who had perpetrated the vile deed and as a deterrent to others, the punishment that was meted out to those involved in the Indian rebellion had to be seen to be a fate worse than physical death. Accordingly, where possible, methods of execution that exacerbated the spiritual fears of the condemned were utilized, notably dismemberment. This was achieved instantaneously by splaying the victim across a cannon muzzle and firing a round through his abdomen.

There were few major engagements in this ghastly conflict, which mostly comprised sieges and guerrilla warfare. Informed by newspaper reports and official dispatches, much of the British public monitored its progress with detailed maps that were rushed out to satisfy demand. By the end of 1857, as the tide began turning against the mutineers, their actions had already stimulated a huge amount of creative activity that had yielded exhibitions, books, songs, poems, porcelain and pictures. The plight of beleaguered garrisons was of prime concern to many people, and several painters and illustrators tried to catch the blend of fear, fortitude and hope that characterized the various isolated outposts as they awaited rescue. Edward Hopley's *An Alarm in India* and Frederick Goodall's *The Campbell's Are Coming*, which depicted the final relief of Lucknow, are two particularly celebrated products of these endeavours. Not everyone could be saved from the mutineers, however, as explicitly acknowledged by Joseph Paton in a painting of 1858 that was redolent of some of Goya's *Desastres*. It hinted at the fate in store for a group of women and babes-in-arms, who, having sought refuge in a Cawnpore cellar, had been discovered by blood-spattered sepoys.

This was too close to reality for much of the viewing public, and Paton was persuaded to withdraw the picture from exhibition and alter some of its details: the setting duly became Lucknow, the murderous sepoys were transfigured into the Highlanders who relieved the city and the work was dubbed *In Memoriam: Henry Havelock*. Sir Henry, who had been one of the stalwarts of the efforts to rescue the garrison, had perished in the fighting, thereby ensuring his place in the British pantheon. In any case, as an icon of Christian stoicism, *In Memoriam* played an eminent role in the rise of the cult of the Christian military hero that began with the Indian Mutiny and was to peak with General Charles Gordon's death at Khartoum in 1885.[46]

War, Philosophy and Natural Science

By the middle of the 1800s, academics and artists of every description were contributing to public debates about war on an unprecedented scale. Thanks to educational and school-building programmes, rudimentary literacy began to spread among the European population during the 1850s especially and, by the 1870s, over 80 per cent of bridegrooms and military recruits in Britain, Prussia and France were judged to be capable of reading and writing.[47] Moreover, literature was that much more available and diverse. Inexpensive transport, based on railways and steamboats, facilitated the harvesting and export of timber from the USA especially. Much of this cheap lumber was pulped and, when wedded to mass-printing techniques, yielded huge quantities of newsprint, books and pamphlets, the contents of which, however esoteric, were devoured by growing numbers of eager readers. A pamphlet by Gladstone on the Papal Decrees sold 100 000 copies in a month.[48] As armies and the societies that supported them became increasingly literate, battle was waged as much with the pen as with the sword. Not just officers, but also the rank and file now recounted their experiences in letters and diaries, while journalists, novelists and dons all participated in a war of propaganda.

Understanding the *mentalité* of the period that he or she is studying can prove a formidable hurdle for even the best of historians. Too often, contemporary values are applied in the analysis of events that occurred in a very different moral, technological and intellectual climate. As the ultimate challenge that any state and its constituent human beings can face, war *per se* is an issue that ineluctably arouses strong feelings. Each conflict has to be viewed in its unique context, however. Indeed, it is impossible to fully comprehend some characteristics of warfare in the 1800s without at least some reference to the major intellectual trends that shaped humankind's reasoning about not just war, but so much else besides.

The upheaval caused by the French Revolution was followed by a wave of counter-revolution and conservatism that permeated much of European politics and society, not least the military. As Christian values were turned to as a potential source of not just consolation, but also peace and order, in several states the established Churches found their relationships with the temporal authorities being formalized. The Holy See, for example, which had seen its secular power eroded over recent decades, was able to reassert itself in the Europe of the Holy Alliance, where rulers undertook to deal with one another and their subjects in keeping with Christian principles. The commitment of many princes to this ethical approach was, of course, superficial and opportunistic. Indeed, the re-establishment of order often involved the curtailing of political liberty, which, many democrats believed, was more than a little at odds with the importance accorded by Jesus of Nazareth to the individual. On the other hand, the collectivism and philanthropy espoused by Christ had an appeal that cut across political and even religious divisions. It was in Christian-inspired altruism that the Italian Carbonari, for instance, was rooted. Giuseppe Mazzini himself rejected the institutionalized Churches as the allies of despots, yet he saw the rise of nation states as part of a divine plan that would ultimately unite not just Europeans, but the whole of humankind. Consequently, the 'Young Europe' movement he inaugurated advocated a republican brotherhood of nations founded upon non-sectarian principles of Christian charity.

Yet, by the mid-1800s, Christianity, both as an institution and as a provider of moral concepts, found itself at the heart of the growing contest between the two great schools that have shaped Western intellectual thought. On the one side was that which, reaching back to Plato and Aristotle, depicted virtue as knowledge: it maintained that there was an answer to every genuine question and that all such questions could be answered; that all answers are knowable, learnable and teachable and, moreover, are compatible with one another. All of this implied that humankind's capacity to improve its quality of life would expand as its knowledge grew. However, as a result of German intellectual thinking especially, by the beginning of the 1800s an alternative opinion had arisen. This was that some things at least were not endowed with a discoverable structure. The world, indeed the universe, was in a constant state of flux. This implied that, although what one individual, class, group or nation wanted would not necessarily be compatible with what others desired, anybody with sufficient power and will could impose change, if only temporarily.

The classic, contemporary illustration of this phenomenon was Napoleon's attempt to create an empire governed in the light of his *Code* and other creeds that were regarded by him and other disciples of the Enlightenment as having universal applicability and value. Romanticism, by contrast, stressed the plurality of ideas at the expense of notions of absolute truth, thereby dismissing all generalizations as distortions of reality rather than revelations of it. This had awesome repercussions for notions of what constituted morality. The dawn of Romanticism undermined the conviction that those who failed to conform to certain patterns of behaviour were acting in a literally unreasonable fashion and were in need of correction. That acts committed with sincerity could, whatever their consequences, be laudable now became a widespread belief.

Once the morality of motive became as significant as the morality of consequence, values were transformed. This, in turn, stimulated changes in human opinion and conduct, not least with regard to war. However, as we have noted, there were those who were reluctant to accept that the essential nature of warfare might alter, despite the impact that new technology alone was having on tactics and strategy. The contrasting views held by Clausewitz and Jomini on this subject epitomized the differing approaches of, on the one hand, Romanticism and the German Movement and, on the other, the reasoning of the Enlightenment. Clausewitz's *magnum opus*, *Vom Kriege*, remains the most persuasive exposition of what war is – or should be, at any rate – because it transcended earlier military thinkers' achievements by identifying war's few enduring and universal characteristics. Whereas Jomini argued that Napoleonic warfare could furnish a paradigm against which the past could be measured and which could provide standards for the future, Clausewitz insisted that, for all his genius, Napoleon was not to be compared with the likes of Alexander, Caesar or Frederick the Great because of every historical event's uniqueness; each of these individuals waged war within the social, political and technological framework of his own time, just as great commanders, as yet unknown, would in the future. Much might change so far as warfare's details were concerned. Indeed, all that remained constant was the employment of violence for political ends.

This is an activity that is engaged in exclusively by *Homo sapiens*. Humankind possesses a unique capacity for conceptual thought and not only evolves theories about its own behaviour, but also allows its conduct to be influenced by them. Among our concepts are those of history and religion, our sense of the latter depending largely on our perceptions of the former, as does so much else. During the 1800s, historical scholarship revolutionized theology, dominated philosophical inquiry and became the basis of literary criticism, while scientists drew on the historian's methods in seeking to fathom the mysteries of geological and biological developments. As it was concerned with the exploration of what could and could not be known, natural philosophy also played an important part in the rise of natural science. The knowledge acquired from the latter was perceived to have a unique reliability and verifiability which had implications for everything, including the conduct of war; the strategic writings of Jomini and Adam Bülow, for instance, were heavily influenced by Newtonian physics and mathematical and geometrical theories. In so far that it could be discerned at all, reality, some people were now persuaded, was that which was revealed, not by Revelation, but by the likes of John Dalton, Americo Avogadro, Joseph Gay-Lussac, Ohm, Pierre-Simon Laplace, Volta, Ampère, Faraday, Geoffroy Saint-Hilaire and Friedrich Wöhler.

By the start of the 1800s, philosophers had already begun to ponder religion in new ways. In his *Dialogues Concerning Natural Religion* (1779), David Hume had explored theogony and theodicy as well as the atheistic notion that matter could exist and be ordered without the need for either some grand design or a divine creator. Treating the Bible as literature that could be subjected to analysis also became more acceptable at this juncture, while the ancient conundrum of theodicy and the institutional failings of the established Churches attracted new attention in a Europe where the ravages of protracted war had been followed by harsh political repression and the social and economic upheaval caused by growing industrialization. Certainly, the established Churches, accustomed to ministering to the needs of small, essentially agrarian communities, were ill-prepared for the explosive growth of towns and the rise of the urban labouring classes, who were not only tempted by all manner of new vices, but whose working conditions also left even the faithful with little time for religious observance. The Church's belated response to their plight only strengthened its detractors, though most of Christianity's leading critics at this time were as troubled by theodicy as by the social and economic evils stemming from *laissez faire* politics.

They included Arthur Schopenhauer, the British utilitarian James Mill and his humanist son, John Stuart. He was deeply influenced by French thinkers, notably Auguste Comte, the most prominent exponent of positivism, the dominant intellectual school of the Second Empire.[49] An outstanding mathematician, Comte sought to establish a humanist 'church', complete with apostles in the form of Adam Smith and enlightened despots like Frederick the Great. He styled himself as '*Le Fondateur de la religion universelle*' and the '*Grand Prêtre de l'Humanité*'. Comte's views on the enfranchisement of women eventually alienated John Stuart Mill, just as his growing admiration for Napoleon III disappointed some of his other followers. On the other hand, his thinking, and that of the positivist school as a whole, did much to deepen the secularist, anti-clerical tendencies traditionally evinced by the French republican movement.

Meanwhile, through the efforts of such literati as Samuel Taylor Coleridge, Thomas Carlyle and George Eliot, the British public was being introduced to new philosophical ideas and biblical criticism from, above all, that 'nation of poets and thinkers', the Germans. The great metaphysician Georg Hegel was to the fore in rejecting empiricism. His *Naturrecht und Staatswissenschaft im Grundrisse; Grundlinien der Philosophie des Rechts* (1821) expounded the theory of Idealism, according to which historical experience was shaped by an abstract '*Weltgeist*' that transcended the material world and was indifferent to the lot of individuals. History, therefore, comprised the only possible outcome to events in Hegel's view; success was an indication of righteousness, while power was to be used ruthlessly to determine one's fate. This, Hegel perceived, Napoleon – whom he described as the 'World Spirit on horseback' – had accomplished in the early stages of his career at least.

Hegel's admiration for power and authority, his disdain for party politics – which he regarded as divisive and so inimical to the state's interests – and his suspicions concerning unfettered market economies and individual liberty appealed to social engineers of every hue. Among the contrasting thinkers he influenced were Karl Marx, who, with Friedrich Engels, produced the *Communist Manifesto* in 1848, and the British philosopher Thomas Hill Green, whose socialism was coloured by Christian ideals.[50] In Hegel's opinion, religion, as a human, collective way of looking at creation, was an entirely subjective phenomenon, with one conception being superseded over time by another. Just as Christianity had supplanted older faiths, it in turn would come under threat from the ideas put forward by the Enlightenment and the

German Movement. Hegel turned to dialectical theories in exploring the implications of this process. In his *Phänomenologie des Geistes* (1807), he reasoned that if God was no more, then everything seemingly eternal and real could not be, including death. Was this, then, the end of God or a beginning?

Hegel's own death occurred in 1831, just three years before Heinrich Heine produced his *Zur Geschichte der Religion und Philosophe in Deutschland*, an immensely influential work. It was followed, in 1835, by David Friedrich Strauss's *Das Leben Jesu, kritisch bearbeitet*, which, like Heine's *Geschichte*, soon appeared in English, too. By setting their stories within the context of contemporary mythology, Strauss's textual analysis of the Gospels caused controversy, as did Ernest Renan when he depicted Christ as, not a deity, but a moral exhorter in his *Vie de Jesus* and his *Histoire des Origines du Christianisme*. Whereas Hegel had argued that human experience only made sense if seen as part of a divine order, in *Das Wesen des Christenthums*, which was first translated into English in 1854, Ludwig Feurbach opined that the concept of a divinity was a product of human history. In its preface, he asserted that his book would demonstrate that Christianity was 'a fixed idea, in flagrant contradiction with our fire and life assurance companies, our railroads and steam-carriages, our picture and sculpture galleries, our military and industrial schools, our theatres and scientific museums'.

Ironically, Christianity had played a huge role in bringing about the Eurocentric world's scientific and industrial revolutions, in so far that, more than any other faith, it encouraged people to manipulate and alter their natural environment for their own benefit and God's glorification. Feurbach neglected to add, moreover, that it was an idea that had moulded many Europeans' attitudes to, and thus conduct of, war. A decline in belief in the concept of ultimate truth, coupled with the appearance of the very modernism he highlighted, might be construed as progress, but did not necessarily augur well for humankind.

Certainly, by the middle of the 1800s, adherents to traditional Christianity were struggling to defend their beliefs in general and those in particular that were founded on literal interpretations of the claims made in the Book of Genesis. These clashed with emerging scientific explanations for the nature of the world that, many argued, conflicted with not only Judeo-Christianity, but with other religions, too. As early as 1785, James Hutton, in his *Theory of the Earth*, had suggested that the planet's surface had been – and still was being – moulded by aqueous and igneous processes that were so slow as to be almost imperceptible. If this cast the biblical assertion that God had created the world in six days into doubt, the works of Sir Charles Lyell disproved it completely. The most eminent geologist in a Britain where the study of fossils and unusual rock formations was a popular pastime, his *Principles of Geology* (1830), *Elements of Geology: Or the Ancient Changes of the Earth and its Inhabitants as Illustrated by Geological Monuments* (1838) and *The Geological Evidences of the Antiquity of Man, With Remarks on Theories of the Origin of Species by Variation* (1863) were read widely and avidly. Above all, however, it was Charles Darwin's *On the Origin of Species by Means of Natural Selection* (1859) that seemed to undermine literalism conclusively by showing that creatures were not the products of some discrete act of creation, but had evolved as they adapted to their environment. It provoked the fiercest of reactions. Each of its successive editions was more defensive than its predecessor as the book was condemned from the pulpit, not least for suggesting that humankind might share a common ancestor with the apes.

The ongoing arguments between materialists and spiritualists, scientific realists and theologues had immense ramifications, not least for people's attitude to war. Then, as now, the very existence of such suffering was never easy to reconcile with the notion of a merciful, just deity who cherished the individual. That God and Nature were evidently 'at strife', as he phrased it in his moving poem *In Memorium A. H. H.*, perplexed Tennyson for one. Yet, long before the scientific discoveries of the 1800s, theodicy had troubled many, while accepting Christianity's central message, that of the Resurrection, had always required a supreme act of faith. Indeed, amidst the realities of the fallen world depicted in the Bible, fulfilling the ideals of a religion that, among other demands it imposed upon its adherents, urged them to love their enemies, had always proved problematic. For hundreds of years, leading Christian clerics and other theologians had sought to give guidance on how and under what circumstances the faithful might legitimately engage in violence. As a propensity for conflict was a part of the imperfect world they inhabited, eliminating it permanently and completely seemed an unattainable goal. Just-war theory acknowledged this unpalatable fact while seeking to minimize the damaging effects that armed conflict inevitably entailed for people and their environment.

Darwinism or anything else that appeared to subvert Christianity, the very rationale behind such good intentions, threatened to undermine them, too. Whilst it is palpably unnecessary to believe in Revelation in order to have a sense of ethics or morality, codes that are supposedly based upon ultimate truth and have divine authority behind them are likely to be accorded that much more respect than those which are purely the invention of human subjectivity. As we shall see, Friedrich Nietzsche especially was to turn Christian values on their head and, by so doing, opened a Pandora's Box. But as Fiodor Dostoyevsky, among others, suggested, if God did not exist, then anything could be permitted; humankind and uncaring Nature were left as the supreme arbiters. Predictably, the message perceived to be in Darwin's theories was seized upon by some to justify the preservation of the political and social *status quo*. Natural selection, it was reasoned, underpinned the class structure, just as it vindicated the unbridled competition of capitalism. Wealth was proof of success, while indigence was an indication of unfitness to survive. Indeed, whereas Christ had urged people to care for the poor, social welfare programmes could now be dismissed as contrary to Nature's grand plan.

Racial concepts, too, were embedded in Darwin's discoveries. Even before *On the Origin of Species* was published, a debate was underway amongst European anthropologists about perceived racial inequalities and the impact that miscegenation might have on social cohesion and military effectiveness. For instance, the *Essai sur l'Inégalité des Races humaines* by Arthur de Gobineau first appeared in the early 1850s, though its full impact was not to be felt for another 20 years. In any case, it had long been believed that their racial characteristics gave certain men a natural aptitude for service as, for example, light infantry,[51] and we have already noted the respect that the *furia francese* commanded among France's adversaries. At the height of the Crimean War, several writers, notably Patrice Larroque, in *De la Guerre et des Armées permanentes* (1856) and Charles-Jean Letourneau, in *La Guerre dans les diverses races humaines* (1856), expressed concern that modern impressment techniques could have detrimental consequences for a nation's gene-pool. Even if they did not actually perish in the course of service with the colours (and many did), conscription removed large numbers of healthy young men from circulation in society for prolonged periods, whereas those who were physically unfit were left behind, fathering children.

Such notions were the products of a particular age rather than of a specific place. Indeed, Darwinistic theories were inevitably applied to the realm of international rivalry, turning that, too, into a contest in which, it was believed, only the fittest states would survive. This would foster the growth of *Weltpolitik* and rampant imperialism in the later 1800s. In the interim, however, the scientific and industrial revolutions continued to prove mixed blessings, not least for Richard Cobden, the doughtiest advocate of Free Trade. He was slow to appreciate this, however. Attributing the incidence of war to the malign influence of military and political patricians, he had been tempted to believe that this would gradually be smothered by the pacific mercantilism of the great mass of Europeans; the affluence and international partnerships generated by open markets would surely be sufficient to usher in the era of perpetual peace predicted by some of the Enlightenment's philosophers. Indeed, Cobden was persuaded that rationalist thought, railways, steamships, factories and the abolition of tariffs would all contribute to the world's civilized and peaceful development. Like too many people both before and after him, he reduced war to an accountant's balance-sheet, assuming that economic self-interest is somehow more compelling and fundamental than prejudices, ideas, emotions, political allegiances, moral commitments, religious convictions and social frustrations. That, today, so many Europeans have difficulty comprehending the importance that our ancestors accorded to the concept of honour perhaps reveals more about us than it does about them. Cobden, however, knew full well that many of his contemporaries were as likely to seek recompense for a perceived slight through a duel as through the courts, while a sense of failure pushed many others into doing what was euphemistically referred to as 'the honourable thing'. The embodiment of *laissez-faire* liberalism, he certainly had a faith in human avarice that, ironically, blinded him to the possibility that peace and plenty could make people that much more selfish.

This drawback was highlighted by Thomas de Quincey in his essay 'On War' of 1854. For all its awfulness, conflict was depicted here as not just a part of the natural order, but also a process that had positive, creative dimensions; it stimulated collectivism and inventiveness, enhanced people's appreciation of peace and one another and, by so doing, countered materialism. Similarly, whereas Karl Marx and Friedrich Engels were struck by the dehumanizing effects that industry and urbanization were having on society, Cobden could only lament the tendency to refine military technology and doctrine and thereby make 'the arts of peace and the discoveries of science contribute to the barbarism of the age.'[52] In contrast to the French anarchist Pierre-Joseph Proudhon, who, in *La Guerre et la Paix* (1861), pointed out that the very existence and legitimacy of states was founded on their capacity to wage war, he was reluctant to acknowledge that Britain's prosperity depended upon her security, which was derived at least partly from her possession of military power. He deplored the accumulation of weapons and the other peacetime preparations for conflict that he saw all over Europe. The Crimean

War disappointed him enormously, and his vociferous opposition to it ultimately cost him the parliamentary seat he had held since 1841.

The people of Europe, including his constituents, were evidently rather more bellicose than Cobden liked to think. But if the war with Russia constituted a setback for those who, in common with him, anticipated that Free Trade, industrialization, democracy and the decline of putative warrior castes would bring about perpetual peace, the harrowing conflict that was to engulf the USA before his death in 1865 should have shattered any such illusions for good.

3

THE AMERICAN CIVIL WAR

The waves of change unleashed by the scientific, industrial and political revolutions within Europe during the 1830s and 1840s quickly crossed the continent's geopolitical frontiers, most notably the Atlantic. Alongside the proliferation of such inventions as the railway and the rifled musket, mass migration took place. Whatever their precise motives, which ranged from a desire to escape poverty or political repression to a taste for adventure, millions of immigrants poured into the USA during this period in search of a new life. Certainly, with her system of republican government, based on a constitution and universal male suffrage, and her expansive and ever-increasing territory, she seemed to offer boundless opportunities for personal fulfilment and material enrichment. However, many immigrants were to discover that the reality of life in America often fell far short of their dreams. Like all political, economic and social systems, that of the USA had its winners and losers. Indeed, for much of the indigenous population, the arrival of the machine age, together with masses of outsiders with disparate ideas about the shape the future should take, threatened the very virtues that they had inherited from the Founding Fathers and from George Washington, Thomas Jefferson and Benjamin Franklin.

In many respects, the USA's weaknesses were her strengths carried to excess. There was perhaps more scope for individualism and freedom than was reconcilable with the maintenance of unity. Whilst most indigenous Americans possessed a developed sense of common heritage, experience and ideas, this relatively new polity had neither a religious authority, nor a stable class hierarchy, nor an educational élite, nor a political establishment. Jeffersonian principles of agrarian simplicity and decentralized government reigned supreme. The USA's federal structure deliberately dissipated power and, in the absence of a strong core, was a formula for division and disintegration, particularly as there was no discernible external threat that might have bolstered internal cohesion. Above all, the presidency had yet to acquire much of a pro-active role in the country's management. The tradition of keeping that office weak and reactive was wedded to the Congress's reliance on shift-ing political coalitions and to the use of procedural and structural checks and balances to avoid divisive confrontations. In fact, many of the constitution's provisions had never really been tested, and every major legal issue was exhaustively debated in the light of interpretations of that sacred document.

The mid-1800s witnessed an ultimately futile bid to reconcile social, political and economic change with the Founding Fathers' simple pre-scriptions. During this period, not only did millions of people arrive in America from overseas, but also the internal dynamics of the country were transformed. The population soared from 17 million in 1840 to 31 million by 1860. Much of this stemmed from immigration into the towns of the Northeast, which rapidly turned into urban and industrial centres of hitherto unseen dimensions. At the time of her rebellion against Britain, America's largest town was Philadelphia, with just 42 000 inhab-itants. By 1850, New York had well over 500 000, who all competed for jobs and accommodation. Besides the move from the farm to the factory that this trend entailed, a thread of new transport systems, primarily comprised of railways, an instrument and symbol of unity, steadily wove discrete, local economies into a national market on which thrived, above all, the Northeast's middle classes. Better communications also facili-tated the mass migration of people westwards across the grain of the continent from the Eastern seaboard, the cradle of the USA, until, by 1860, no less than half of the population was located beyond the Allegheny–Appalachian mountain chain, mostly in the central basin of the Great Lakes and the Mississippi.

By 1861, the original 13 states had been joined by 20 new ones, mostly in the West; and, as ever more Americans moved into this region, the informal alliance between the South and the Northwest that had operated during the first 50 years of US history began to break down. It was not just that the balance of the relationship between the states and the Federal government was affected, but also that the West became the focus of rivalry between the North and South, which had contrasting social and economic systems. The institution of slavery set the South apart more than any other single characteristic. This had been abolished in the northern states just after the revolution and an ordinance of 1787 had excluded it from many others. It was not until 1819, when the question of Missouri's status arose, that attempts to preserve the symmetry between free and slaveholding states encountered any serious problems; and they were overcome.

Indeed, the Missouri Compromise worked well enough for some decades precisely because it was the product of the bargaining that was the hallmark of American politics during this era. In the USA as a whole, there were comparatively few people who, as late as 1860 if not still later, favoured the outright abolition of servitude. Even the notion of confining it to a distinct geographical region did not command overwhelming support, as illustrated by the repeated rejection of the 1846 Wilmot Amendment by the US Senate. In fact, despite the influence of Harriet Beecher Stowe's *Uncle Tom's Cabin* (1852), over 1 500 000 copies of which were sold within a year, further trade-offs and compromises were achieved during the 1850s which consolidated slavery's position; and, on coming to power in 1861, Abraham Lincoln and the Republican Party were committed to going no further than the containment of bondage within the slave states and its elimination from the territories.

Certainly, it should not be thought that the 22 million Americans in the country's northern half were generally less prone to Negrophobia than the 9 million in the southern states; any dislike for the concept of human bondage was not necessarily founded on a belief in racial equality. The very existence of slaves gave even the poorest of whites some social standing at least. Moreover, contemporary scientific opinion, notably extrapolations of Darwin's theories, maintained that Negroes were inferior to white people, while slavery was criticized as often on economic and constitutional grounds as on moral ones. Even Lincoln, who was to emancipate the slaves in the course of the Civil War and has since been figuratively if not literally beatified for his liberality, was praised by many contemporaries for his conservatism with regard to racial issues. He took the view that

> There is no reason ... why the negro is not entitled to all the rights enumerated in the Declaration of Independence – the right of life, liberty and the pursuit of happiness. ... He is as much entitled to these as the white man ... [though] he is not my equal in many respects, certainly not in color – perhaps not in intellectual and moral endowments; but in the right to eat the bread without leave of

anybody else which his own hand earns, he is my equal and the equal ... of every other man.[1]

However, the scope for further compromise began to run out as the disagreements over slavery and everything that it represented gradually intensified.[2] The 1852 presidential election proved a disaster for the Whigs, who split into Southern and Northern factions – the latter sub-dividing again to form the Republican Party after the passing of the Kansas–Nebraska Bill in 1854. The public mood steadily became more confrontational as slavery's moral, racial, social, political, constitutional and economic ramifications slowly unravelled the established pattern of politics which, for decades, had offset the South's weakness in its deal-ings with the more populous North. Indeed, in the 1856 presidential contest, of the 1 300 000 votes secured by the defeated Republicans' can-didate, John Frémont, only 1200 came from non-slaveholding states. Then, on 6 March 1857, just two days after the inauguration of the vic-torious Democrat, James Buchanan, the Missouri Compromise of 1820 was finally undermined by the resolution of the Dred Scott Case, whereby the Supreme Court ruled that slaves were property, not citizens, and, as such, could lawfully be taken anywhere.

This jeopardized even the relatively modest goal of containing slavery; it either had to be everywhere or nowhere. The abortive attack by John Brown on the Federal arsenal at Harper's Ferry in 1859, which was intended to spark off a slave rebellion across the South, culminated in him being arrested by Colonel – later General – Robert E. Lee, tried for treason against Virginia and, with 6 others, hanged. Months later, the cli-mactic, tangible manifestations of the collapse of national cohesion were provided by the splitting of the Democratic Party at its convention in Charleston in the spring of 1860 and Lincoln's victory in the presiden-tial election later that year. His name did not even appear on the ballot-slips in some parts of the South and he won no support at all in ten states. Although he secured an overwhelming majority in the Electoral College, he received somewhat less than 40 per cent of the popular vote.

Even now there was an evident reluctance on the part of the southern states to break away from the Union, and not even all of the 15 slave-holding states decided to do so. South Carolina's departure was quickly followed by that of Florida, Mississippi, Alabama, Georgia, Louisiana and Texas, but the delegates called to the Virginian convention to vote on the matter rejected secession by a majority of two to one as late as 4 April. Lincoln, whilst refusing to recognize the legality of these states' actions, hoped to avoid violence. However, he resolved to reprovision the Federal garrison of Fort Sumter, an outpost in Charleston harbour, and advised South Carolina's governor of this intention, stressing that force would only be resorted to if the stronghold or the supply flotilla came under attack. Responsibility for the initiation of any hostilities was thus passed to the secessionists. Sure enough, after the garrison rejected an ultimatum to surrender, the surrounding Confederate batteries opened fire on 12 April 1861. Three days later, deeming the South to be in a rebellion, Lincoln called for 75 000 volunteers to suppress the rising.

That its bid to ward off the changes that were occurring within the American federation had led to violence only served to strengthen the South's conviction that it was the victim of Northern aggression. Indeed, the war was to prove the ultimate test of what the concept of union actually amounted to. The Crittenden Resolution of July 1861, that was passed almost unanimously by the US Congress, stipulated that the objective of hostilities was the salvation of the Union and the protection of the constitution, not slavery. However, as the conflict progressed, becoming more protracted, costly, bitter and intense than all but a handful of people had ever anticipated, the North's aims inevitably become more complex. This, in turn, divided policy-makers within the Federal camp: on the one side were those who favoured the pursuit of a conciliatory agenda; on the other were those who wanted to impose a radical, punitive settlement on the rebellious South.

Certainly, the war was to complete the amalgamation of the North's sense of identity with its own peculiar concept of American nationalism; and the US Army, which ultimately swelled to some 1 500 000 personnel, was to become both the single most tangible demonstration and the greatest symbol of this unity. At the outset, however, very few Americans envisaged either a conflict or forces of such magnitude. Something more along the lines of a glorified duel, which might be decided by a solitary battle, was expected. Many people found it hard to believe that a prosperous, democratic society that had been presented to the world as a model of civilization would really tear itself apart. Only when the fighting had dragged on into 1862 did hopes of a compromise peace give way to a quest for total victory. Indeed, the war seemed somewhat phoney to begin with: both sides hastily mobilized their manpower, but three whole months passed before the first major engagement took place, and another six were to elapse before the next big clash occurred.

By civil war standards, the geographic separation of the two sides seemed exceptionally clear, but, in practice, clarifying the demarcation line between them was not so straightforward. If Delaware, where there were very few slaves, never seriously contemplated secession, allegiances in the putative battlespace of the other borderlands – notably Maryland, Missouri and Kentucky – were mixed. The social structure here was akin to the South's, but the area depended on the North as far as trade and commerce were concerned. Lincoln's wife, Mary, came from Kentucky, as did John Crittenden, whose sons Thomas and George became Union and Confederate generals, respectively. Similarly, the 4th Kentucky Regiment of the rebel army and that of the US Army were destined to come to grips with one another in the fighting on Missionary Ridge during the Battle of Chattanooga in 1863.[3] Their mother state, if not its inhabitants, had tried to remain neutral until September 1861, when, its territory violated by forces from both sides, it had finally sided with the North. Much of the population of western Virginia were also Union sympathizers and went so far as to establish their own state in April 1862, which, ironically, was unconstitutional. The situation in Missouri was also bewilderingly complex, but the Union eventually secured the upper hand here, too.[4]

That four borderline states did eventually secede was a severe blow to the Unionists' cause. However, the essential ones were retained. Had West Virginia, Kentucky and Missouri joined the South, both the geostrategic situation and the balance of resources between the antagonists would have been transformed. As it was, the loss of the borderlands left the Confederacy woefully inferior to the North in terms of the quantities of manpower and other means at its disposal. Moreover, the fact that Washington and the rebel capital at Richmond were just 190 kilometres apart dictated much of the strategic planning of both sides. Too much of what little industry the South did possess was dangerously close to the epicentre of the fighting, as were its armies' sources of horses and food. The North, for its part, was acutely aware of the vulnerability of Washington to a sudden Confederate thrust. Indeed, as late as July 1864 General Jubal Early carved a path up the Shenandoah Valley, routed the Union forces guarding the Monocacy and penetrated to the very gates of the metropolis. Lincoln himself came under fire while visiting the city's outer defences, which, hastily reinforced, deterred Early's 12 000 troops from mounting an attack in earnest. They withdrew, leaving Washington in turmoil.

By that stage of the conflict, the South was being worn down by an essentially attritional strategy. She had always lacked the means for this type of warfare, and it is truly astonishing that, despite all the shortcomings in their mobilization and application, her comparatively meagre resources were made to last for as long as they did. What they lacked in numbers and *matériel*, the Confederates strove to make up for with improvisation, skill and determination. They enjoyed a good deal of success, which is all the more remarkable when one considers the sheer disparity in the resources that, on paper at least, were at their and their adversaries' respective disposal.

Indeed, one could be pardoned for being tempted to believe that, from the outset, the war's outcome was a foregone conclusion. Leaving aside divided Kentucky and Missouri, the 11 states that comprised the Confederacy had just 9 000 000 inhabitants, including 3 500 000 slaves, whereas the North's population amounted to all of 20 000 000. So far as white males who were considered at all suitable for active military operations are concerned, that is to say those between 17 and 40 years old, the South could muster perhaps 1 000 000, compared with the 4 000 000 to be found within the North. Once disillusionment with the war began to set in and the initial rush of volunteers petered out, the Confederacy had to introduce conscription ahead of the Union in April 1862, although the regulations permitted exemptions and substitutes, as was customary in Europe. The North followed suit in March 1863, when the methodical tapping of its male population further enlarged its vast and numerous armies. In a bid to redress the balance, the Confederacy strove to release manpower for its armed forces by employing large numbers of women and Negroes for other tasks. Thousands of slaves were requisitioned or hired from their owners for hard, dangerous labouring work near the front lines; and, after 1864, as the South began to run out of white manpower, their use as troops had to be considered at least.

This prompted obvious questions about the purpose of the war. It was being fought at least partly to protect the institution of bondage, which was now threatened as much from within as from outside. By this time, many slaves had either fled into the enemy's lines or been released by advancing Union troops, while the possibility that those who remained might turn on their masters *en masse* constantly haunted the South's white population. In fact, whether viewed morally, financially or militarily, slavery was becoming increasingly burdensome. That numerous owners were already being deprived of the services of their slaves through impressment and abscondence was quite bad enough; it was unthinkable that the Negroes should be expected to defend their own servitude. It was argued that they would, at best, make unreliable soldiers who would be regarded with resentment and suspicion by their white colleagues. On the other hand, if the war were to be lost, it was apparent that the slaves would be freed anyway. If they were to be offered their liberty in return for their services, they might indeed fight for the Confederacy, which would then have a better prospect of securing international recognition. Such arguments eventually proved overwhelming and, in March 1865, the Congress authorized President Davis to call on each state of the Confederacy for a quota of 300 000 men, regardless of colour. Some black units were actually formed, but too late to see action.[5]

The North was comparatively unconstrained in its use of blacks as soldiers, though Negrophobia made it a very sensitive issue here, too. In August 1862, Lincoln stated that

My paramount object in this struggle *is* to save the Union, and is *not* either to save or to destroy slavery. If I could save the Union without freeing *any* slave I would do it, and if I could save it by freeing all the slaves I would do it; and if I could save it by freeing some and leaving others alone I would also do that.[6]

But the Union had foundered because, above all, of a failure to accommodate the institution of servitude within its changing shape. The war could not leave slavery untouched if only because an attack on it would also be a blow against the South. If, on the other hand, as Lincoln maintained, secession was unlawful and the war was one against rebels, it was difficult to use the conflict as a pretext on which to alter slavery's constitutional position. Any move of this kind risked the alienation of not only the border states and the Democrats in the North, but the great mass of Unionists as well, however popular a moral crusade against slavery might have proved with the outside world. Arming blacks and using them as troops had obvious advantages, not least that of saving white lives, but what incentives would the Negroes be offered to get them to risk injury or death for the Union? More generally, if the policy of containment were to become one of abolition, what would the fate of former slaves be?

While talk of repatriating them or establishing colonies for them dragged on, the need for some official policy declaration became pressing, for Federal soldiers on the front line were encountering ever more runaway or abandoned slaves. Initially, they were treated as contraband of war. However, General John Frémont's declaration of martial law in Missouri in August 1861 also proclaimed the emancipation of all slaves whose owners were actively aiding the rebellion against the Union. Lincoln, fearing that this was premature and that it was his responsibility, not the military's, to take political decisions of this magnitude, reprimanded Frémont, despite the widespread support for the general's actions in the North. Any other considerations aside, Lincoln recognized that significant progress towards the Confederacy's military defeat was a prerequisite if any declaration freeing some or all of the slaves was not to prove counterproductive.

Indeed, it was not until 22 September 1862, just after the Battle of Antietam, that he issued his preliminary emancipation proclamation. Although Lee had given the Union forces a magisterial and gory lesson in tactics, it was apparent that the latest rebel offensive had lost its momentum and that the Confederacy was not going to reap the rewards, notably international recognition, it had been hoping for. Lincoln's proclamation cunningly left servitude in the border states untouched, while heralding the liberation of all slaves in rebel territory as of 1 January 1863. This was enough to head off any prospect of outside interference – which, irrespective of its precise nature, could only have benefited the South – while simultaneously stoking the Confederacy's fears of a slave insurrection.

On the day that his preliminary emancipation proclamation came into effect, Lincoln issued a second. This granted liberated, suitable Negroes admission to the US armed forces. A handful of units, comprising fugitives from Missouri and Arkansas, had already been formed, but this measure opened the floodgates. Charged with coordinating recruitment, the Bureau of Colored Troops was established within the War Department during May 1863 and, within 18 months, had formed all of 50 regiments. Altogether, some 179 000 blacks, mostly former slaves, passed through the US Army, while a similar number found employment as teamsters, labourers, cooks and other auxiliaries. Even limited liberty came at a price, of course. If taken prisoner, Negro soldiers invariably faced maltreatment and, sometimes, as seems to have happened at Fort Pillow in Tennessee during April 1864, systematic murder at the hands of their captors.[7] Even many of their white comrades harboured, at best, ambivalent feelings for them. One song that was popular with the Irish Brigade extolled 'Sambo's Right to be Kilt.'[8] It was a privilege that many black soldiers were to exercise, not least the men of the 54th Massachusetts Infantry, who, with their heroic if futile assault on Fort Wagner in July 1863, dispelled any doubts about the courage and commitment of the Union's coloured troops.

Certainly, the ultimate test of loyalty to the Stars and Stripes had to be seen to be applied as rigorously to blacks as it had been to whites; and, whenever volunteers were not sufficiently forthcoming, impressment was resorted to. This was particularly so after March 1863, when disillusionment with the war was mounting and Washington was obliged to introduce the draft to compensate for the diminishing number of white volunteers. The demand for officers to train and lead the numerous black regiments that were formed over the next few months offered many a white subaltern a good chance to secure promotion by leaps and bounds, while the addition of hordes of Negro troops to the Union's disposable forces further increased their numerical advantage over the Confederates in the field.

The South's inferiority in manpower was, however, just one of her problems. Her relative weakness was no less marked as far as her means of transport and industrial production were concerned. That of even small Northern states like Massachusetts exceeded her total manufacturing capacity. Of the 1 016 260 tonnes of pig iron produced by the USA in 1860, just 37 390 originated in the South. Had the key border states and their output been secured, the quantities of this basic commodity in Confederate hands would have increased threefold. As things turned out, however, the South had to rely very heavily on the production of the Tredegar foundry at Richmond, which was one of the few pieces of heavy industrial plant in the entire region.[9]

The South was similarly deficient in transport infrastructure and sizeable towns – she had just six with more than 20 000 inhabitants. This hampered the forging of an integrated economy. Whereas the North had 35 400 kilometres of railway track, the Confederacy's network amounted to just 14 500 and was more disjointed, too; several different gauges were in use and very few termini could act as interchanges. Improving the system was almost impracticable in wartime. The South had traditionally depended upon the North for investment credit and skilled labour. With both of them, and raw materials, in short supply, simply preserving what railroads she had proved difficult enough. She had built just 19 out of the 470 locomotives produced in the USA in 1860, and she failed to forge a single length of rail throughout the conflict; little-used spurs were cannibalized to keep the main routes open. Rolling stock was rare, too, and, more often than not, the private companies that owned the railways tended to allocate it to those best able to pay, regardless of the war effort's needs. As engines broke down for lack of proper maintenance and spares, tracks and wheels became dangerously worn with incessant use, bridges fell into disrepair, and the incidence of accidents and damage inflicted by Unionist raiders increased, average journey times doubled and timetables became meaningless. Indubitably, the movement of people, goods and words was that much slower and more problematic than in the North. A few stretches of track were, at either the behest of the Richmond administration or that of the relevant state, added to the network to assist essential military operations, but a general reluctance to interfere with free enterprise, coupled with shortages of funding, expertise and time, inhibited the Confederacy's attempts to exploit her railways as an instrument of war. Even after May 1863, when Congress reluctantly granted the War Department the right to commandeer trains in an emergency, such powers were used sparingly. Not until the conflict's closing weeks was the power to assume total control of the railway network vested in the government, by which time it was too late to do so, even if the political will had been present.

Railways made an immense contribution to the Union war-effort. They made the conquest of the South feasible by enabling military force to be projected quickly over tremendous distances and the replenishment of armies from afar. Just as, during the Peninsular War, seapower had sustained Wellington's troops behind the Lines of Torres Vedras for weeks on end, so too did railways permit armies to remain stationary for prolonged periods, oblivious to the exhaustion of local resources. Although an act of 1862 authorized the president to take control of the North's railways, Lincoln invoked this prerogative abstemiously. The system as a whole was much more integrated and functioned far better than the Confederacy's, enabling the competing demands of civil and military traffic to be accommodated comparatively easily. Normally, only those lines in the immediate vicinity of battle zones were placed under governmental superintendance, which was usually provided by the US Military Railroads, a branch of the War Department. Headed by Daniel McCallum, formerly of the Erie Railroad, this possessed some 400 locomotives, 6000 vehicles, 17 000 workers and an unrivalled reputation for civil-engineering prowess. One of its most celebrated feats was the spanning of the Potomac Creek with an enormous bridge that carried a line directly to General George Meade's army at Gettysburg. Completed in less than 40 hours, this work was supervised by Brigadier General Herman Haupt, McCallum's deputy in the eastern theatre of war. Similarly, by laying new, repairing old and exploiting captured tracks, often with extraordinary speed, MacCallum was to furnish General

Sherman with crucial logistical support during his Atlanta campaign of 1864.

Whilst few wars are inexpensive, the struggle between the Confederacy and the Union was as financially costly as it was intense and protracted. Indeed, the respective abilities of the two sides to finance their war-efforts were an important factor in determining its outcome. Inspired by Jeffersonian reasoning, President Jackson's attacks had precipitated the demise of the Bank of the USA during the 1830s; and, with the passing of the Independent Treasury Act in 1846, the disentangling of the banking sector from the American state was complete. Although this arrangement satisfied the peacetime needs of a central government that was as inert as it was diminutive, it was wholly inadequate when confronted with the challenges posed by the Civil War. By barring Federal funds from being lodged in any bank and stipulating that all government transactions were to be conducted in gold, within a few months of the start of hostilities this law brought the Union's financial system to the brink of collapse. Nobody had foreseen the scale of the conflict and its concomitant costs, and the loans and handful of special taxes that the government initially expected to survive on proved woefully insufficient. An acute specie shortage began to develop which, had it not been alleviated by the Californian Gold Rush and payments from European countries for grain purchases that were fortuitously large, would have culminated in an economic slump. Before the end of 1861, the government had been compelled to suspend specie payments and was being accused of, not merely financial mismanagement, but also betraying traditional American values. In February 1862, the Legal Tender Act introduced the greenback, which, like Pitt's income tax in Britain, had to be presented as a wartime expedient, misleading though this proved. Similarly, Lincoln exploited the unprecedented circumstances created by the war to establish a National Bank, which issued new notes and coins through 1500 participating banks.

Over the medium term, the greenbacks steadily lost their value against the gold dollar, which was coveted in both the North and South. However, they never amounted to more than one-sixth of the total war debts incurred by the former, whereas the Confederacy, which started the conflict with no more than $30 million in bullion reserves, was essentially dependent on paper money by 1863. Even after the US Congress passed the Revenue Act of 1862, which introduced an income tax that was ratcheted up over the next couple of years, taxation only yielded $675 million towards the cost of the war. The gap was bridged with loans, some $2000 million being raised through bond sales and credit of one kind or another.

Together with the general buoyancy of the Northern economy,[10] all of this helped to contain inflation, which, in the South, was to prove almost as destructive as the invading Union forces. Tied up in land and slaves, much of the Confederacy's capital could not be released, and there was neither the political will nor the bureaucratic machinery to impose taxes; attempts to do so proved ineffectual and divisive. Having traditionally looked to the North for investment and financial expertise, once the war began the South was left with inadequate knowledge and institutions to manage her finances competently.[11] Instead of using 'King Cotton' – the one asset that might have secured her credit abroad – to fund the purchase of arms and other necessities from Europe, she squandered the chance, imposing an embargo on cotton exports in a vain attempt to extract diplomatic recognition from Britain and France especially. This conduct not only damaged the European textile industries, which accounted for 80 per cent of the South's raw cotton market, but also won her few friends. In fact, and much to the North's relief, no foreign state was ever to formally recognize the Confederacy.[12]

Meanwhile, her armed services' appetite for weapons, munitions, wagons, clothing and equipment could never be satiated by her own stunted and essentially agrarian economy, which was geared to meeting purely local needs. Indeed, whereas the North developed its own peculiar brand of American nationalism and rallied round the Union as the fountainhead of executive power, the South comprised a region of regions, which were as parochial as they were varied. Neither her structure nor her methods could easily be adapted to satisfying wartime demands, and her constituent parts too often resisted Richmond almost as much as Washington. So lacking in political roots was Jefferson Davis's regime that even Alexander Stephens, the Vice-President, spent most of his time in Georgia, his home state, championing its rights against those of his own administration.

The Montgomery Constitution was virtually identical to that of the USA. However, unlike the North, the Confederacy began the conflict without even the makings of a governmental machine. Constructing one proved, as did so much else, a matter of trial and error; there were five secretaries of war within four years, for instance. Richmond did establish armouries, nitre beds, chemical plants and mines, but most production remained in private hands and the allocation of what resources were available was too haphazard. Although there was appreciable overland trade via Mexico and with venal Northerners, the US Navy's blockade of Southern ports compounded the shortage of manufactured goods especially, while the requisitioning of wagons, horses, labour, forage and foodstuffs that alone made it possible for the Confederate Army to keep functioning had detrimental repercussions for the rest of society. Not only was the 1863 Impressment Act that authorized this practice resented as an attack on private property, but it also turned too many producers into consumers. This compounded the growing shortages of every conceivable commodity, from salt to metal implements, leather and paper.

There were bread riots, too, such as the one in Richmond on 2 April 1863 that Davis himself, through a conspicuous display of sheer willpower and personal courage, brought to an end. So that more edible crops might be grown, the production of cotton was cut back from 4 500 000 bales in 1860 to just 1 000 000 in 1862, and substitutes were found for sugar, dyes, conventional medicines, tea and coffee. Nevertheless, coupled with the reckless printing of money, the insatiable demand all of this created within the economy caused rampant inflation: prices rose twenty-eightfold between September 1861 and September 1864, after which they spiralled to almost incalculable levels. In order to eke out an existence, despairing civilians were reduced to hoarding, speculation, forgery, prostitution and crime, while rampaging deserters and draft-dodgers added to their misery. Law and order all but collapsed in many areas, necessitating the declaration of martial law and the suspension of habeus corpus. However, already divided over requisitions and conscription, Congress members were so angered and alarmed by these fresh assaults on the rights of states and individuals that they rescinded the necessary powers, leaving the executive hamstrung and much of the South with neither military nor civil law.

Meanwhile, Confederate fortunes on the battlefield had taken a turn for the worse, too, with dire consequences for the home front. The great defeats of 1863 – Vicksburg, Gettysburg and Chattanooga – not only sapped the strength of the Confederate armies but also led to the loss of crucial stretches of territory. This fractured both the political and military cohesion of the South. Indeed, in the Congressional elections of that year, whereas the electorate in the regions contiguous to the fighting recognized Davis's administration as their sole hope of salvation, in more remote regions many of his supporters were swept away by voters who simultaneously disapproved of his policies for winning the war and his failure to do so. Yet his opponents could no more solve the

conundrum than Davis could. Whilst the measures he took were criticized for being too extreme, they were not in fact radical enough to save
the Confederacy; for all their diversity, he and the other Southern politicians were essentially conservatives who found themselves trying to
manage a revolution.

The ruling party in the North had difficult periods, too. In the 1862
Congressional elections the Republicans sustained a setback, while
Lincoln was frequently gloomy about his prospects during the 1864 presidential contest,[13] which became something of a referendum on the continuation of the conflict. During that year, as in the next, there was
widespread frustration and war-weariness, as the North, in spite of all its
power and advantages, struggled to deal the tottering South the lethal
blow. Lincoln's emancipation proclamations and his reference, in his
Gettysburg Address, to 'a new birth of freedom' had, it seemed to the
annoyance of many whites, transformed the contest from one for the
Union into one for the blacks. An anti-war movement arose – notably
among Democrats in Iowa, Michigan, Ohio, Indiana and Illinois – including secretive societies of so-called 'Copperheads', such as the 'Sons of
Liberty' and the 'Knights of the Golden Circle'. Although disaffection
struck some units of the Army as well – the 138th Illinois was reduced to
just 35 men by mass desertions – not only did the Union triumphs of
September 1864 at Atlanta and in the Shenandoah Valley help swing popular opinion in Lincoln's favour, but also soldiers' votes made a major
contribution to his victory in the election that followed; Illinois, New
Jersey and Indiana, the legislatures of which were dominated by
Democrats, were the only Northern states that did not permit serving
troops to cast their ballots in the field. Men who had evidently been willing to sacrifice all for the Union were, at this stage, unlikely to settle for
anything less than the overthrow of the Confederacy.[14] Certainly, three
out of every four soldiers backed 'Old Abe', their Commander-in-Chief,
who also secured 54 per cent of the popular vote and a majority of 191 in
the Electoral College. His own military connections notwithstanding, his
opponent, General George McClellan, only managed to take Kentucky,
Delaware and New Jersey.

For all the political problems that beset Lincoln in the North, he
knew that they were as nothing when set against the rifts within the
Confederacy. Secession had left comparatively few Democrats in the US
Congress and, by the end of 1864, the Republicans had big majorities
in both chambers. Faced with a choice between being seen as patriots
or traitors, nearly all Democrats chose the former, becoming either

unstinting supporters of the president or his loyal opposition. Indeed, whilst some of the more moderate ones among them were often critical of the administration's methods, they all backed the war in principle. The electorate remained generally supportive, too.[15] Although conscription was never popular – the implementation of the draft sparked off numerous demonstrations, notably the riots in New York in July 1863, which claimed over a hundred (mostly black) lives[16] – and the conflict's cost in blood and gold was immense, the majority of the Northern population was spared the worst tribulations of war: relatively little territory was devastated, any occupation proved short-lived and, for the most part, production kept abreast of the demands made upon it by civilians and the military alike.[17] If there was little attempt to interfere with private enterprise's handling of the economy, Lincoln did make extensive and imaginative use of his prerogatives as commander-in-chief, testing the constitution to an unprecedented extent. Ever the consummate politician, his leadership was as inspiring as it was skilful, and he was fortunate to have the services of not just talented field commanders like Grant[18] and Sherman,[19] but of administrators of the calibre of Edwin Stanton and Montgomery Meigs. Above all, the Union possessed an ideological strength that greatly surpassed that of the Confederacy and sustained it in its darkest hours.

By contrast, the demoralization that acute shortages, rampant inflation and political wrangling inflicted on Southern society could not be offset by even the most dazzling of Lee's successes on the battlefield. Even they were too often won at the cost of disproportionately heavy casualties. The draft might have enabled Richmond to truncate some of the states' powers, but, lacking the support of a bureaucracy capable of administering and enforcing it, it proved inefficient, not least because of the complex exemption and substitution mechanisms, which also created enormous scope for anomalies and unfairness. Whereas the sheer size of the North's resources rendered any deficiencies and wastefulness in its system inconsequential, the South had to cast its net ever wider; by February 1864, all white males between the ages of 17 and 50 were theoretically obliged to serve.

Reluctant draftees rarely made good warriors, however. The least suitable might be allotted auxiliary roles, but, in a war waged by two democratic societies, bitterness inevitably arose between those who had volunteered to fight and those who had not. In both camps, life was made uncomfortable for the latter group, while the Union went so far as to offer bounties of $300 to the former.[20] If such largesse attracted bounty jumpers – men who enlisted and deserted repeatedly, pocketing payments time and again – in both the South and North the right to purchase substitutes was one that only those with sufficient wealth could actually exercise. This inevitably gave rise to the conviction in some quarters that this was a conflict fought for the rich by the poor, with the bitterness among many indigent, white Unionists being compounded by Lincoln's perceived attempts to turn it into a war to end slavery.

For all the South's relative weakness in means, the inherent contradictions within its war aims merit greater emphasis in any explanation of the conflict's outcome. When the Confederacy needed more power to save itself and them, far too many Southerners clung stubbornly to the very principles that had brought them into conflict with the Union; they undermined their own unity and cause through atomistic individualism and parochialism. Lee himself, whilst regarding secession as a calamity, was a Virginian first and last. Rather than betray his home state, at the conflict's very start he not only resigned his commission in the US Army, but also turned down an invitation to command the Federal field forces. Although he emerged as one of the most outstanding military leaders of the 1800s, he consistently viewed the war essentially from a Virginian perspective. Again, this was part of a wider malaise that, among other things, led to governors squabbling with Richmond over the control of the forces their respective states had furnished and to a failure to appoint a general-in-chief to orchestrate the Confederacy's various military operations. Glaring though it was, this particular shortcoming was not rectified until as late as February 1865, by which time the war was irremediably lost; and even then the calls for action were motivated more by petty political intrigues than by a desire to create an efficacious fighting-machine.

Nevertheless, it took the Union four years of tremendous effort to bring the Confederacy to heel, not least because the political and strategic conundrum it faced was that much more complex than that confronting the South. The latter, after all, had comparatively modest aims: it needed to conquer neither the North nor its territory, but simply demonstrate that its own claims of independence were not mere words. If this demanded the breaking of Washington's resolve through military success, that goal did not appear beyond reach. Indeed, for the first 30 months of the war, the outcome was to hang in the balance and, even after the triad of Union triumphs in 1863, there were periods when the North's morale oscillated wildly. Although the fate of recent European revolutionary movements was not encouraging, the Confederacy, it was argued, was surely strong enough to accomplish as much as the 13 American colonies had in 1783. The need to defend every square kilometre of their own soil would be a political imperative that would ineluctably limit the rebels' strategic choices, yet the Union, by contrast, would face the seemingly impossible tasks of transforming any tentative penetration of Southern territory into a comprehensive occupation and any temporary conquests into permanent acquisitions. Coercing the Confederates would ineluctably involve threatening their homes and their whole way of life. For them, the war would become a fight to the finish, whereas the threat to the North would be that much more circumscribed. The likelihood of foreign intervention would, moreover, also grow with time and could only help the South.

To many, it seemed very probable that, under these circumstances, Union morale would crumble as soldiers and voters came to the conclusion that the game was not worth the candle. Yet, however much it wobbled, the North's fighting spirit did not implode. The Union was saved, though its nature was changed substantially. This was true not least of the USA's armed forces and their attitude to war *per se*. All of the conflicts waged prior to 1861 had been undertaken with means that were often more limited than aims: the rebelling colonists had relied extensively on the support of allies during the revolution against the British; the Anglo-American conflict of 1812–15 was a peripheral, small-scale affair, as was the Mexican War of 1846–48; and the rolling back of the continent's native Indians by white settlers was assisted by detachments of the US Army that rarely reached even regimental size.[21] In fact, General Winfield Scott's campaign in Mexico saw the largest all-American force – some 15 000 men, including volunteers – that had ever been assembled; while, on the eve of the Civil War, the entire US Army amounted to just 16 367 personnel. The War Department, with only 90 employees at the start of 1861, was commensurably small, too, both armed forces and bureaucracy reflecting the traditional American conviction that the role of government, particularly that of the Federal authorities, should be highly circumscribed and inexpensive.

In military matters as in so much else, the emphasis was on the role of the Union's constituent states. At the very start of the secession crisis, Lincoln followed the time-honoured practice of looking to their militias as the cardinal source of military strength; he mobilized 75 000 men who, called up for just three months, were on the verge of returning home when Bull Run, the Civil War's first major battle, took place. These amateurs were pardonably more interested in survival than in being dead heroes, and many did not perform too well. In any case, the militia was an attempt to reconcile the need for some form of military power with American suspicions of standing armies; its very cheapness and lack of professionalism were its redeeming features. Although John Brown's ill-fated bid to provoke a slave rebellion in 1859 had kindled interest in parts of the South in the development of more effective reservist units and had thereby helped to lay the foundations of the Confederate armies that were to be formed in 1861, generally speaking, the militia was a palpably unsuitable model for the sort of forces that might withstand and win a protracted, bitter, large-scale war.

However, nobody expected the conflict to turn out like that. In any event, there was just too little time, too little kit and too few professionals to do much with the immense masses of raw volunteers who came forward during the heady days that followed the outbreak of hostilities. The scale and speed of recruitment was quite overwhelming. The Confederacy quickly found itself with 600 000 volunteers on its hands, few of whom it could actually equip. So many would-be soldiers had to be turned away that, by the start of 1862, it had no more than 300 000 under arms. Many of them had, moreover, enlisted for a term of 12 months, which expired just as their enthusiasm for the war first began to wane. The ensuing manpower shortfalls made conscription unavoidable; and, as we have noted, the system proved as inefficient in its results as it was unfair in its execution. Nevertheless, the South managed to mobilize all of 900 000 men in the course of the war.

In the North, meanwhile, forces of even greater proportions were being amassed. In May 1861, Lincoln called for 42 000 volunteers to serve as part of the regular army for up to three years. Yet, whereas he had asked for just 40 new regiments, enough recruits for 208 were immediately forthcoming. In fact, the US Army was destined to have an average strength of around a million men during the war. At the beginning, there was no central authority to set and uphold standards and to channel resources to where they were needed. Yet, if financing, organizing, equipping and maintaining such a colossal force without any precedents or mechanisms for doing so seemed a daunting task, it was a challenge that the North, greatly facilitated by existing trends, rose to. Most immigrants, for instance, instinctively supported the Union because it constituted the America they had been attracted to and had benefited from. Indeed, immigration surged to new heights during the conflict's second half as the North's search for labour intensified. With hundreds of thousands of men being lured or pressed into the army, women,

Negroes, children and mechanization had to fill their places in the wider economy. Between 1860 and 1865, the number of farm machines in the USA increased fivefold,[22] while the expansion of the Federal civil service from 41 000 employees in 1861 to 195 000 in 1865 is similarly indicative of the scale of the demands imposed by the war-effort.

The contribution made by women to it is deserving of further comment, not least because it raised their prominence in American society and was to help stimulate the emancipation movement of later years. Most worked in factories, offices or schools or took over the running of the family farm, but many, especially those from the prosperous, urban middle classes, were active in the US Sanitary Commission and other private agencies that strove to relieve the deprivations faced by soldiers at the front. Most members of these organizations collected donations of fresh food, clothing and other creature comforts which were distributed by rail to the grateful Union troops, while others, most notably 'Mother' Mary Bickerdyke, a Quaker widow, worked alongside the military in the field. Similarly, Dorothea Lynde Dix, Clara Barton and Sally Tompkins emerged as the Florence Nightingales of the American Civil War, Barton going on to serve as a volunteer nurse in the Franco-Prussian War before returning home to establish the American Red Cross. As had happened in the Napoleonic Wars, a few women even sneaked into military combat units, if only in a bid to be with their husbands or sweethearts. One such woman was wounded and captured at Chickamauga. Her captors, promptly released her with a note that read: 'As the Confederates do not use women in war, this woman, wounded in battle, is returned to you.'[23]

To the Southern gentry in particular, the mere thought that women might engage in such 'unladylike' behaviour was repellent and yet more proof of Yankee barbarism. There can be no doubt, however, that the Northern troops benefited greatly from the selfless efforts of so many of their womenfolk, while some of the most vocal and ardent supporters of Dixie's cause were females.[24] Although there was a handful of Confederate relief organizations, their very nature encapsulated the South's fundamental disunity. State bodies exclusively dedicated to aiding soldiers from within their own borders, their ethos contrasted with that of the US Sanitary Commission, while the balance of resources lay, as always, in the North's favour: 'We were too poor', recalled one Confederate soldier; 'we had no line of rich and populous cities closely connected by rail, all combined in the good work of collecting and forwarding supplies and maintaining costly ... charities. With us, every house was a hospital.'[25]

Gory and destructive though it was, like most wars this one had its creative effects, too, a few illustrations of which must suffice here. Books, periodicals and newspapers played an important role in a country where there was a large and growing degree of elementary literacy. Although in the South shortages of cheap paper, printing machines and ink damaged the publishing trade somewhat, in the North they were comparatively abundant. Newspapers flourished and employed numerous war and other correspondents.[26] Among these was Walt Whitman, a journalist with the *Brooklyn Standard*, who was to compose some of the most famous war poetry of the 1800s. Though not always as eloquent as him, a sizeable proportion of the rank and file, as well as officers, also recorded their and others' experiences in letters and diaries.[27]

The many photographs taken by Matthew Brady, Timothy O'Sullivan and Alexander Gardner, especially, have proved another valuable and vivid source of insights into the fighting and its context. Indeed, photographers followed the armies around, producing not only portraits of individual soldiers – who delighted in enclosing snapshots of themselves in their finest uniforms with their letters to the folks back home – but also shockingly graphic pictures of war's harsh realities: of dead and dismembered men and horses, emaciated prisoners and devastated buildings and landscapes. Sketches, often to embellish newspaper reports, and paintings were also produced, notably by Winslow Homer, Theodore Davis, Henry Walke, Edwin Forbes and the Waud brothers, William and Alfred.

Last, but by no means least, was the role of music in the maintenance of morale. Some songs produced during the war remain among its most familiar and enduring legacies. Among those pieces favoured by Federal troops were: 'Tramp, Tramp, Tramp, The Boys Are Marching'; 'Rally Round the Flag, Boys'; and 'The Battle Hymn of the Republic'. The Confederates liked 'Dixie's Land' above all, but Lee himself was in no doubt as to the importance of music in general. 'I don't believe', he once observed after attending a band recital, 'we can have an army without music.'[28]

Armies required organization, too. The North's initial appeal for men yielded thousands of volunteers and, rather than dilute existing units with hordes of green recruits, the US Army created dozens of new regiments, each comprising, on paper at least, 1000 men divided into ten companies. Regiments were usually brigaded together in fives, with three brigades forming a division and three divisions a corps. As, however, there were no depot units to replenish them, most regiments shrank considerably once on campaign. Furnishing sufficient commanders proved similarly problematic. As experienced officers came at a premium, captains and lieutenants were normally elected by the rank and file and were lacking in vocational schooling. The more senior commanders were either established professionals or men who, because of political influence or social standing, held their commissions from state governors. In so far that it encouraged states to regard the troops they provided as their own property rather than that of the central government, in the South at least this practice led to divided loyalties within the officer corps and further complicated the task of resource allocation. Again, however, the Union's superior bureaucratic and political apparatus enabled it to overcome any such difficulties that much better than the Confederacy, while the latter's quantitative weakness in manpower and *matériel* rendered any degree of inefficiency in their exploitation commensurably more damaging to its cause.

Whereas the North put its trust in numbers, the South pinned its hopes on its limited aims, its perceived moral superiority and the prospect of foreign intervention. However, neither side found a promising strategy easy to formulate or execute. Land operations were on a grand scale and, at times, extended over 3000 kilometres from the Chesapeake Bay area as far as New Mexico. The war, moreover, was split into eastern and western theatres by the Appalachians: the former, a narrow, constricted area between the Atlantic and the mountains, lent itself to defence, while the latter, through which meandered the Mississippi, favoured the attacker. Whereas operations beyond that mighty river were virtually self-contained and frequently neglected by both Washington and Richmond,[29] between it and the Appalachians was a swathe of open terrain. Some 500 kilometres across and dissected by the Mississippi's tributaries, which penetrated deep into the South's heartland, this was an obvious Achilles' heel.

Indeed, simply defending this and the rest of its landlocked frontier against superior numbers would have been a difficult enough undertaking for the Confederacy, but it also had to contend with the threat posed by the Union's maritime power to its immense seaboard, the coastline of which amounted to some 3500 kilometres. Although, with just 42 vessels, the US Navy was rather weak at the start of the war and the coastal blockade it imposed was patchy, the Confederate littoral remained extremely vulnerable to amphibious attacks. As the British had demonstrated in the Anglo-American War of 1812, if exploited with skill and boldness, sea power's sheer flexibility could enable even small forces to wreak havoc. Indeed, as late as January 1863, all of a third of the rebels' land forces had to be committed to littoral defence assignments, while, with almost no merchant shipping of its own to protect, most of the tiny Confederate Navy was rapidly absorbed in these and counter-blockade missions.

The South's *guerre de course* enjoyed considerable if insufficient success. Still mostly wooden sailing vessels dependent upon favourable winds and currents, US merchantmen plotted courses that were highly predictable. Armed with shell-firing cannon, the Confederates' steam-powered raiders found them as easy to intercept as they were to destroy or capture, and some 200 ships were lost in the course of the war. Consequently, insurance became prohibitively costly and around half of the US merchant fleet was sold off to neutral countries. Whilst this obliged the Southern warships to venture ever further in search of their quarry, the US Navy had problems of its own, not least because of its rapid enlargement following the outbreak of hostilities. By the end of 1861, it had grown to 22 000 men with 264 vessels and ultimately swelled to almost three times this size. This astonishing rate of expansion was largely achieved through the expedient of converting merchant shipping. However, few of the vessels thereby produced were ideal for interdiction and pursuit missions, being either too slow or too big or having insufficient endurance. Still, they did provide the Union with a significant capacity for maritime operations which was put to good use in a series of amphibious assaults. As early as November 1861, Port Royal in South Carolina fell to a Northern coup and, within a few months, New Orleans, the South's greatest city and harbour and the key to the Mississippi, had been lost, too.

Gunboats, notably the 'Pook Turtles' devised by Samuel Pook, made a major contribution to the second of these victories and to the early establishment of Union control over the great rivers.[30] Among other things, this was to help bring about the fall of Vicksburg in 1863, cleaving the Confederacy down the line of the Mississippi. Similarly, in the spring of 1862, with a fleet of 400 vessels at his disposal, General George McClellan was able to land all of 100 000 troops on the peninsula between the James and York Rivers, threaten Richmond and capture the naval yard at Norfolk, obliging the Confederates to scuttle that celebrated ironclad the *Virginian* (formerly the *Merrimack*). The Peninsular Campaign was ultimately unsuccessful, as was a bid to seize

Charleston in April 1863. Nevertheless, the mere possibility of attack from the sea tied down thousands of rebel soldiers when they were desperately needed elsewhere. Moreover, the Confederates' best endeavours notwithstanding, by 1864 the only major ports left open to blockade-running vessels were Mobile and Wilmington. A Northern amphibious force effectively closed the former that August, while the latter's fall, in February 1865, helped seal the fate of both Lee's army and Richmond.

On the other hand, the Union blockade exacerbated one of Washington's dilemmas in so far that it threatened to provide the pretext for outside interference in what Lincoln was anxious to keep a purely civil war. Whereas the Anglo-American conflict of 1812–15 had stemmed primarily from Britain's enforcement of her economic sanctions against Napoleonic France, the *Trent* incident of winter 1861 highlighted the danger that the USA's endeavours to blockade Southern ports might be construed as violating the rights of neutral powers, the most significant of which was Britain. After all, the North insisted that the Confederates were merely rebels, yet, for a blockade to be lawful under the Paris Declaration, both sides had to be accorded belligerent status. Furthermore, international law stipulated that any blockade had to be genuinely efficacious, not merely proclaimed. Certainly, by testing the meaning of neutrality in an era when the limitations on war were being eroded, the conflict in America had tremendous ramifications for the interpretation of international law.

Moreover, its numerous and often overlapping political facets sowed dissension across the Eurocentric world, just as it had within America: although Lincoln denied that it was an anti-slavery crusade, those who wished to could easily reduce it to one; others perceived it to be a war for self-determination or minority rights at a time when many Europeans could empathize with either nationalist or liberal movements or both; alternatively, there were those who saw it as a struggle between, on the one hand, the supporters of legitimate authority and democracy and, on the other, rebels and the defenders of privilege.

Yet, however divided their citizens and rulers were by the war, all the European states evidently concluded that military intervention was neither in their best interests nor really practicable. Although France took the opportunity presented by the USA's preoccupation with the conflict to establish a Mexican Empire under the Austrian Archduke Maximilian and Spain entertained hopes of regaining her lost influence in Latin America, no foreign power embroiled itself in the fighting or recognized the Confederacy. Nor, contrary to widespread expectations, did the USA disintegrate. As she ruled the waves, Britain's essentially benign neutrality was largely responsible for this outcome. In May 1861, London issued a proclamation that granted the Confederacy belligerent rights and accepted that, irrespective of its physical frailty, the Union blockade was lawful. Britain thereby extracted a valuable legal exemplum. Indeed, scrutinizing the USA's every action during the war, she was able to accumulate a number of precedents that she was to cite to justify her own conduct in future conflicts.

Ironically, the Confederacy's attempt to wring recognition from the European 'states through its embargo on cotton exports was not only politically counterproductive, but also effectively performed the Union's blockade work for it at the time when the US Navy was too feeble to do so. This maritime weakness also helped undermine the so-called 'Anaconda Plan', the Union's initial strategy for winning the war that was devised by the ageing and sick Winfield Scott. He envisaged the gradual strangulation of the South through the coupling of the naval blockade with an advance down the Mississippi. Lincoln feared that an attritional struggle of this kind could prove too strenuous for Northern morale and wanted something that promised to deliver cheering results speedily. He was slow to recognize the possibilities that a penetration of the Confederacy's western flank would offer, but, by January 1862, had, like McClellan, who had superseded Scott as the Union's general-in-chief in November, come to the conclusion that pressure along the whole rebel perimeter was the best course of action:

> [W]e have the *greater* numbers, and the enemy has the *greater* facility of concentrating forces upon points of collision.... [We must] find some way of making our advantage an over-match for *his*; and this can only be done by menacing him with superior forces at *different* points, at the *same* time.... [W]e can [then] safely attack one, or both, if he makes no change; and if he *weakens* one to *strengthen* the other, ... [we can] seize and hold the weakened one, gaining so much [my emphasis].[31]

This was essentially the Trachenberg stratagem that had offset Napoleon's use of interior lines in Germany in 1813. However, during the Peninsular Campaign, McClellan – who was to stand as the Democrats' presidential candidate in 1864, disliked Lincoln and was loathe to discuss military matters with him – failed to make much headway. Although he had been relieved of the additional burden of being general-in-chief as early as March 1862, his leadership of the mighty 'Army of the Potomac' seemed so dilatory and lacking in determination that some suspected him of being motivated by cowardice, treachery, or both. That July, after being utterly overawed by Lee in the sequence of engagements known as 'The Seven Days', the man once hailed by the Northern press as 'Young Napoleon' was succeeded by General John Pope, while Henry Halleck took over as general-in-chief. The latter was adamant that Lincoln's proposals would not work: 'To operate on exterior lines against an enemy occupying a central position will fail, as it has always failed, in ninety-nine cases out of a hundred', he insisted. 'It is condemned by every military authority I have ever read.'[32]

Halleck was to serve as Union general-in-chief until February 1864, when, replaced by Ulysses Grant, the first American soldier to be given the rank of substantive lieutenant-general since Washington, he took up the post of chief of staff. The authority that he, like so many of his colleagues, revered above all others was Jomini, whose works were as avidly read in the USA as anywhere in Europe. While studying at West Point, Halleck, together with McClellan, was a member of a Napoleonic Club that had been established in 1848 by Professor Dennis Hart Mahan, the father of the great naval theorist, Arthur Thayer Mahan. The intellectual analysis of Jomini's works, notably the *Précis de l'Art de Guerre*, which was the West Point cynosure, was this society's principal pastime. Indeed, the translation of Jomini's writings into English was undertaken in, above all, America, Halleck himself producing an English version of his huge *Vie Politique et Militaire de Napoléon*. Seeking to schematize Napoleonic strategy, the *Précis* emphasized the exploitation of interior lines and rapid movement to achieve a local supremacy over adversaries who might then be defeated piecemeal. Although the destruction of the opposing army was presented as the cardinal objective, Jomini also advocated the seizure of an enemy's territory and capital for political effect. In contrast to Clausewitz, however, he generally accorded politics, ideology and public opinion little if any significance, while insisting that tactics remained essentially constant. Fascinated by the Napoleonic paradigm of manoeuvre warfare, he underestimated the changes being wrought by new technology, notably steam's impact on strategic movement and the need, on the battlefield, to offset improved firepower with better protection in the form of earthworks and fortifications.

However, as, in 1862, West Point prepared a translation of the (expanded) 1855 edition of Jomini's *Précis* for publication, too many of his assumptions had either already been discredited or were being so by the realities of the Civil War. Although some of the officers who directed it were a West Point brotherhood who knew one another and were trained on the same precepts, they reacted to the challenges it posed in contrasting ways. Grant, for one, paid Jomini little attention: 'The art of war', he observed, 'is simple enough; find out where your enemy is, get at him as soon as you can, strike at him as hard as you can, and keep moving on.'[33] Similarly, Lincoln's ideas about strategy barely concurred with those of Jomini,[34] while, as had happened in the Crimea, it was apparent that new technology was altering at least some aspects of warfare beyond recognition. Railways, for instance, played an important role from the outset, transforming the relationship between time and space. At the start of the very first Union offensive in 1861, General Joseph E. Johnston used the Southern railway network to rush his forces eastwards from the Shenandoah Valley to support his colleague Pierre G. T. Beauregard at Bull Run. This was followed, in 1863, by the most dramatic demonstration of power projection on land yet seen, when 20 000 fully-equipped Federal troops were loaded onto trains and, in just 12 days, travelled 1900 kilometres to help relieve General William Rosecrans's beleaguered forces at Chattanooga.

At the tactical level, too, the adoption of new technology steadily transformed the face of battle. On the eve of hostilities, there were perhaps 600 000 firearms in the USA, but all except 35 000 were smoothbores. Among the more sophisticated weapons that were available or soon became so were: the 1855 and 1861 patterns of the US rifled musket, the latter version of which, known as the Springfield, was capable of firing six rounds per minute and was accurate against individual targets at up to 300 metres; the Henry repeating rifle, which, if it did not jam, could discharge up to 15 light-weight bullets in just 11 seconds; the single-shot, breech-loading Sharps carbine, which could fire ten rounds per minute and had an effective maximum range of 400 metres; and the Spencer repeating carbine, which was fitted with a magazine holding eight rounds. Impressive though they sound, weapons like the Henry were untested novelties in armies that were barely accustomed to rifled muskets and only some 10 000 were utilized during the war. Springfields, Sharps and Spencers predominated, but more than a few Confederate troops had to be armed with 1842-pattern percussion muskets because of a lack of anything better. Indeed, during the first 18 months of the war especially, rifled shoulder arms, notably Lee Enfields, were imported by both sides, as were Whitworth, Blakely and Armstrong breech-loading field artillery which supplemented the Parrott, Rodman and Napoleon guns manufactured by the Americans themselves. William Hale produced a primitive rocket that was used by the Union forces, while the South deployed a few Congreve rockets purchased from Britain. Lacking proper guidance mechanisms, these projectiles were scarcely more efficacious than they had proved at Waterloo.

Among the most exotic armaments that featured in the Civil War were machine guns. Northern inventors and precision engineers especially were fascinated by the notion of such weapons and churned out design blueprints in overwhelming numbers. The Union Ager Gun was produced in small quantities during the conflict's early stages. However, not only was it prohibitively expensive and prone to mechanical failure, but also there was a lack of doctrinal thinking to underpin its use in battle. Consequently, on the few occasions it was employed at all, its impact was negligible. This did little to arouse official interest in other models, including that produced by Richard Gatling in 1862, though his was one of only seven out of the dozens of machine guns patented in the USA during that and the following year which were actually tested by the army or navy. Despite Gatling's lobbying efforts, the Ordinance Department declined to purchase his costly, hand-cranked weapon during the war, but was sufficiently impressed by a more refined version that he developed in 1865 to add it to the services' inventory the year after.[35]

If reluctance to embrace such innovative technology seems, with hindsight, like blind conservatism, it must be remembered that, whereas resources remained finite, in the midst of the scientific revolution, ideas for new weapons abounded; there were 240 patents for such devices in 1862 alone. Few even got beyond the drawing-board and, of those that did, too many did not live up to the promises made on their behalf, particularly when they were subjected to the rigours of an actual campaign. Certainly, British military observers at a test of Gatling's gun in 1862 were unimpressed by its mechanical fragility and operational inflexibility.[36] Furthermore, as was the case with those shoulder arms that were capable of extremely rapid fire, a machine gun that could discharge up to 200 rounds per minute devoured immense quantities of ammunition, much of which was essentially wasted. How would this demand be satisfied in the field, particularly if the slugs were of a distinctive design? It was only by a happy coincidence that Springfield and Enfield bullets, for instance, were interchangeable. In any case, as volumes of fire continued to increase, so too did the overall demand for ammunition.

This, together with the growing sophistication of equipment in general and the sheer size of the forces mobilized for the war, exacerbated the need for 'tail' as opposed to 'teeth' units. Napoleon I had had roughly 12 vehicles to support 1000 men. Under McClellan, the ratio within the US Army was 26 to 1000. By the time Grant assumed overall command, it had reached 33 to 1000. Even this proved inadequate. Although Federal troops were generally better clad, shod and fed than the rebels, foraging was unavoidable and inevitably generated animosity among the civilian inhabitants of the war zones. Neither, when it came to the provision of medical care for sick and injured soldiers, had much changed since Napoleon's day. There could never be enough surgeons and orderlies to give timely attention to the thousands of wounded that, often in the space of a few minutes, modern battles could generate. Disease, too, remained a major killer; twice as many Union troops were killed by it as by enemy action, and roughly one in every 13 of the war's 620 000 victims perished from such infections as typhoid and diphtheria.

The appearance of novel technologies also prompted debates on where exactly in the armed forces' structure they should be placed, what their precise role should be, who should have control over them and how many of them there should be. For instance, both the North and South made some use of air power in the form of balloons. The US Army's Balloon Corps was a brand new unit headed by 'Professor' Thadeus Lowe. Equipped with just seven balloons, it was tiny when compared with the overall size of the Federal forces, yet needed a lot of logistical support, including horse-drawn hydrogen generators to inflate the envelopes. Both these factors constrained its disposal and utility. During the Peninsular Campaign, it was attached to McClellan's headquarters as a reconnaissance unit, but was also called on to aid in the direction of artillery fire. For this purpose, Lowe tried installing a telegraph system in the gondola. This, however, posed as many problems as it solved. Balloons, as we have noted elsewhere, made errant observation platforms at the best of times, and it was not until the advent of dependable field telephones that the notion of forward observers became more viable. Certainly, the army was disappointed by the impact of Lowe's unit and disbanded it after the Battle of Chancellorsville.

The refinement of naval warfare was generally easier and more successful. The celebrated clash, in March 1862, between the *Virginia* and a Federal flotilla that was reinforced in the nick of time by John Ericsson's *Monitor* confirmed the supremacy of armoured over wooden ships. On the first day of the Battle of Hampton Roads, *Virginia*, shrugging off the fire of Union shore batteries, swiftly rammed and sank the sailing ship

Cumberland, ravaged the *Congress* with her heavy ordnance and so panicked the steamers *Roanoke* and *Minnesota* that they ran aground. The arrival of the *Monitor* the following morning redressed the balance, however. Her design included no fewer than 47 patented inventions. A much smaller vessel than *Virginia*, with what was ultimately to prove a fatally low metacentric height, most of her hull was submerged. Indeed, little could be seen of her except her pilot-house and her two cannon, the latter being mounted in a novel, revolving turret, which enabled her to keep her armament trained on a target without her having to change course.

The two ironclads bombarded each other for hours on end to little effect; the projectiles simply bounced off their plates, even when fired from point-blank range. Both ships managed to evade being rammed, too. Eventually, the *Virginia* sullenly retired into Norfolk where she was later scuttled. *Monitor* capsized not long after.

Unlike the Confederacy, however, the Union had the industrial capacity to produce dozens of ironclads and other vessels. Dixie was obliged to purchase many of her warships abroad, notably in Britain – a practice that was to intensify the legal disputes surrounding the rights and obligations of neutral powers, as epitomized by the *Alabama* case. That said, Southern naval architects did have their moments, producing, among other things, the *Hunley* submarine. Armed with a solitary spar-torpedo – a contact mine fitted to a lengthy probe – mounted on her bow, this submersible had a crew of eight and was powered by a hand-cranked propeller. She sank the USS *Housatonic* off Charleston in February 1864. However, this incident, like the Battle of Hampton Roads, highlighted both the problems and possibilities inherent in modern maritime warfare. Spar-torpedoes had to be driven into their quarry to detonate and, as the hapless *Hunley* discovered, the resulting explosion could prove fatal to both vessels.

Indeed, the very complexity of industrialized warfare created more scope for shortcomings, miscalculations, and mechanical and other failures. All fleets needed replenishment arrangements, including the availability of ports and drydocks, but, unlike sailing ships, steamers needed adequate supplies of coal or wood, as did railway engines. Whereas movement and communication by road and across open countryside were difficult to impede, telegraph and railway systems needed active defences. Railroads were immensely valuable in transporting and supplying armies, but only if they formed part of a continuous loop. This called for the competing demands imposed by civil and military traffic to be reconciled and for an adequate provision of trained personnel, marshalling yards, sidings, unloading bays and platforms, storage facilities, rolling stock and locomotives. In general, it was increasingly as important to be a better organizer and producer than an opponent as it was to outmanoeuvre and outfight him.

Massive and rapid mobilization also left people with that much less time and opportunity to adjust themselves to the transition from peace to hostilities. Hardly any of the volunteers who flocked to the colours in the early months of the American Civil War had had any military experience and, as such, had little real idea of what they were in for. Any training they had received was rudimentary and, if they survived to tell the tale, they could be pardoned for being disconcerted on discovering the effects that shellfire and Minié bullets, not to mention the hardships of camp life, could have on the human body and mind. The early engagements especially, notably Bull Run and Shiloh, were mostly fought by enthusiastic amateurs employing a blend of modern and old technology. Too many of them found that the battlefield is an unforgiving environment – more Americans perished at Shiloh than in all the engagements of the Revolution, the War of 1812–15 and the Mexican conflict put together – and were deprived of the respite that is necessary to discard obsolescent techniques and adopt and burnish new ones.

If, for instance, the romantic image of bayonet pushes and cavalry charges handed down from the 1700s and reinforced by the Mexican War had always been a misleading one, it was to have fatal repercussions on the Civil War's battlefields. Bayonets continued to be issued widely, but were as much for psychological effect as ever; of the 250 000 men treated in Union hospitals, less than 1000 had wounds that had been inflicted by edged weapons.[37] Indeed, the accuracy, volume, reach and lethality of fire that modern weaponry afforded made it extremely difficult for troops to get sufficiently close to engage in hand-to-hand combat at all. Swords and lances proved all but worthless; and, whilst horsemen continued to be of palpable value for screening, reconnaissance, raids and communication, they often fought on foot. The advantage clearly rested with the side that could stay on the defensive, tactically speaking. Whereas an oncoming foe was immensely vulnerable, the defender could dig in to reduce his exposure to the enemy's fire, be it from artillery or small arms. Soldiers were now habitually equipped with entrenching tools and would construct breastworks whenever possible. Hand grenades, which had first been developed in the 1700s but had quickly fallen into disuse for lack of dependable fuses, were reintroduced as a means of flushing ensconced troops from their positions, though they remained as temperamental as ever. Indeed, siege warfare, together with the techniques and means for conducting it, acquired new significance. Great lines of redoubts, trenches and other earthworks were constructed to protect important towns – notably Atlanta and Petersburg – and, in May 1864, at Drewry's Bluff, barbed wire made its first recorded appearance on the battlefield. Originally developed as an inexpensive fencing material for use by livestock farmers, it proved a formidable obstacle to attacking Confederate infantry and was denounced by their commanders as 'a devilish device that could only have been thought of by Yankees.'[38] Certainly, in this and other respects, disconcerting parallels were drawn between, on the one hand, the meat-processing industry that flourished in Chicago especially and, on the other, the conduct of modern warfare. Just as huge numbers of cattle, pigs and sheep were brought here and to other urban centres by rail to be systematically butchered in scientifically designed abattoirs, so too were scores of thousands of human beings herded onto trains to be sent to their deaths on clinically configured killing-grounds.[39]

So great were the advantages enjoyed by the defender that, under the guidance of somebody as adroit as Lee or General Thomas 'Stonewall' Jackson, as few as 3000 men might comfortably hold a front of 1000 metres. At Antietam, with, initially, just 25 000 troops, Lee, exploiting natural defences – notably a sunken lane in his left-centre and the bluff that, further south, dominated the stone bridge over the Antietam Creek – kept an army of three times that strength at bay in one of the goriest battles of the 1800s. Similarly, at Fredericksburg in December 1862, 12 500 Federal soldiers – some ten per cent of Ambrose Burnside's 'Army of the Potomac' – were mown down, mostly while mounting futile frontal assaults on the strong Confederate positions along Marye's Heights. Nevertheless, it is revealing that Lee, who never disposed of more than 78 000 men in this engagement, resisted the temptation to launch a counterstroke to try to push his shaken adversary into the River Rappahannock; he evidently feared that such a move, even if successful, might entail incurring casualties on a scale that he, unlike his adversary, simply could not afford.

Among other things, this highlights a crucial question: how was a tactical defence to be integrated into a successful strategic offensive? Both Beauregard, in the war's early days, and Lee subsequently advocated an invasion of the North with a view to terminating the conflict as rapidly as possible. However, for all the damage they inflicted on the Union forces, both Shiloh and Antietam left the Confederate army too battered to maintain the offensive. Likewise, after Chancellorsville in May 1863, where the rebels, despite being heavily outnumbered, again outmanoeuvred and outfought the 'Army of the Potomac' under, this time, General Joseph Hooker, Lee found that his army, which had suffered proportionately greater losses, had been left incapable of turning its tactical triumph into a strategic one; notwithstanding its 17 000 casualties, Hooker's force was still one to be reckoned with. At the same time, the Union strategy of maintaining pressure all along the front meant that Lee's divisions could not remain where they were: Grant had pinned down General John C. Pemberton's forces at Vicksburg; Rosecrans's 'Army of the Cumberland' was threatening Braxton Bragg's grip on Chattanooga; the maritime blockade was beginning to bite; and the Federal toeholds along the Confederacy's littoral were growing in number and size. If the Confederacy was not to lose the initiative altogether, resources would have to be scraped together for another advance onto Northern soil.

It was hoped that the ensuing encounter would deliver what Antietam had failed to. This time, however, Lee's offensive ended, not in stalemate, but in a sanguinary defeat. For all its importance, his mission had not been accorded the utmost priority by Richmond and he lacked sufficient men and *matériel*. Two years of war had claimed many of his best subordinates and, as a result, he experienced difficulties in trying to keep his forces on a tight rein. Moreover, once Jeb Stuart's cavalry, his army's eyes and ears, raced off on a raid, Lee found himself in the midst of hostile territory with little reliable information. Groping forward, his divisions bumped into the 'Army of the Potomac' at Gettysburg on 1 July 1863. Hooker had resigned the command of this force just days before and had been replaced by Meade, who, in contrast to his predecessor, proved hard to intimidate. Lee himself was not at his energetic best on this particular occasion and he gradually lost control of events, ultimately throwing Pickett's infantry into a frontal assault that was reckless if not desperate. After its many triumphs, he had perhaps persuaded himself that the 'Army of Northern Virginia' could do anything, and he was later to concede that he had asked too much of his devoted troops. Certainly, Lee's hopes went the way of his moral ascendancy as his attack was repelled by a Federal army that fought with dexterity and determination. However, that he had the humility and the honesty to confess to the survivors that the outcome was 'all my fault' reveals a great deal about both the man and the soldier.[40]

Just as the totality of warfare was growing,[41] so too was Napoleon's goal of securing victory with a single, crushing blow becoming increasingly difficult to fulfil. The day after the repulse at Gettysburg, Vicksburg capitulated and, within six months, the Confederates were to suffer a further heavy defeat, this time at Chattanooga. Yet it was not until 29 May 1865 that the war could officially be deemed to be over.[42] Lee himself gave up the struggle only on 9 April. Grant had sent him a message urging him to recognize 'the hopelessness of further resistance', which he did: 'There is nothing left for me to do,' he told his tearful staff, 'but to go and see General Grant, and I would rather die a thousand deaths.' He went, firmly rejecting one aide's suggestion that they should continue the fight by resorting to guerrilla warfare.[43]

Such resistance could only have prolonged the South's agony without doing anything to further her cause. Lee obviously understood the distinction between nobility and unpardonable vanity, and that war should be the continuation of policy, not irrational heroism. Grant evidently grasped this, too, for the parole and other concessions he extended to Lee and his troops went beyond the terms that Lincoln had formally endorsed, yet were in keeping with their spirit. This was an important precedent that helped end the fighting with remarkably little bitterness. It was also one of several episodes in the war that highlighted aspects of the often thorny relationship between the civil and military powers. When Grant pressed Lee, who had been belatedly appointed as the Confederacy's general-in-chief that February, to use his influence to get the whole of the South to surrender, he demurred, insisting that that was a decision for President Davis alone.[44] In seeking to secure an end to hostilities in North Carolina, Sherman, on the other hand, went so far as to conclude a convention with General Johnston that not only granted excessive concessions to the rebels, including an amnesty, but also, by its very nature, constituted an implicit if not explicit recognition of their government. Although Davis, predictably, readily approved the agreement, the Union's politicians just as swiftly repudiated it. Sherman was rebuked and Johnston compelled to surrender on terms similar to those offered to Lee.[45]

Sherman's leniency in this affair contrasts starkly with his ruthlessness in prosecuting military operations. As early as July 1862, McClellan had written to Lincoln expressing his horror at the turn the war was taking. Condemning the attempt to end slavery by force, the violation of citizens' rights and the confiscation of private property, he insisted that the conflict should be conducted in keeping with 'the highest principles known to Christian civilization ... [and] should not be at all a war upon

a population, but against armed forces and political organizations.'[46]
Sherman, above all, took the opposite view. Like the British in the
Anglo-American War of 1812–15, he concluded that in a conflict
between peoples, in this case democracies, the population as a whole
had to be made to suffer. 'We are not only fighting hostile armies', he
observed, 'but a hostile people, and we must make old and young, rich
and poor, feel the hard hand of war, as well as the ... [soldiers].'[47] The
most tangible manifestation of this reasoning occurred in the closing
weeks of 1864 and took the form of his infamous 'march to the sea',
when, having razed Atlanta, his army, 62 000-strong and advancing on
a 100-kilometre front, sliced through the heart of Georgia to Savannah,
living off the land and methodically destroying everything in its path
that might conceivably have been of use to the Confederacy.[48]

Many years later, Sherman was to tell a veterans' meeting that 'War is
hell.'[49] The American Civil War saw the belligerents employing, not just
military muscle, but also economic hardship, systematic destruction and
political propaganda to grind down the other side's morale. A conflict
between peoples rather than dynasties, it was often savage in the extreme.
The treatment of prisoners alone was a source of much bitterness and
controversy. After the Fort Pillow massacre in April 1864, the routine
exchange of captives was discontinued on Grant's orders. This resulted in
many prison camps – which, more often than not, were established with
inadequate sanitation, accommodation and other essential facilities –
being crammed full of men, many of whom had already been weakened
by wounds and the hardships encountered on campaign. Insufficient
shelter and bedding frequently left many captives exposed to the elements. Rations were normally lean – particularly in the Confederacy,
which often struggled to find sufficient food for its own soldiers, never
mind prisoners – while water, for drinking and washing, was rarely pure.

Under such circumstances, diseases like smallpox, tuberculosis and
typhoid spread like wildfire, claiming the lives of nearly 50 000 inmates
altogether. Some prisoners, however, fell victim to acts of deliberate
neglect or brutality by their captors. Henry Wirz, a Swiss-German immi-
grant and commandant of the most notorious of the South's camps, that
at Andersonville, Georgia, was hanged in November 1865 for war
crimes. Built to hold 10 000 prisoners, by August 1864 Andersonville
contained 33 000, most of whom lived in pits in the ground. Their suf-
ferings intensified by Wirz's cruel regime, all of 13 000 men perished
here, while many of those who lived to tell the tale – some of whom were
caught on camera – were hideously emaciated.

To this day, the number of fatalities sustained in the Civil War exceeds the total number of American lives lost in all the other conflicts the country has fought put together. Proportionally speaking, the price in dead – around two per cent of the then population – was greater than, for example, that incurred by Britain in the First World War.[50] Material destruction, particularly on the Confederacy's soil, was also immense, with, for example, much of South Carolina – which was regarded by the North as the original source of the rebellion – being deliberately laid waste by Sherman's troops in January and February, 1865.

Certainly, the plea made by McClellan in 1862 for a limited conflict prosecuted in keeping with Christian just-war theory proved pathetically anachronistic. Actual battles emerged as just part of a wider struggle that ineluctably sucked in whole populations and economies, and military and political imperatives repeatedly trampled over good intentions. Even the Churches of the North and South exploited their traditional divisions in the propaganda contest, depicting the struggle as a sacred one and portraying any setback as divine retribution for society's wickedness.[51] Indeed, it is noteworthy just how many prominent figures regarded themselves as instruments of Providence: John Brown, Lincoln, Lee and 'Stonewall' Jackson, to name but four, all referred to themselves in this way at various junctures. It was also in the war's midst that the first American coins to bear the words 'In God We Trust' were minted. Above all, the gist of Lincoln's Gettysburg Address of 19 November, 1863, was that the combatants had consecrated the battlefield, shedding their blood in atonement for, as he saw it, the sin of slavery, so 'that the nation might live' and, 'under God, ... have a new birth of freedom'. He was to return to this theme in his second inaugural address on 4 March 1865.[52]

For Lincoln was persuaded that this terrible conflict had to be for something more than just the Union, important though that was. And so it proved. The Civil War was second only to the Revolution in defining what the USA and being an American actually meant. It tested the letter and spirit of the constitution, and drew hitherto disparate peoples and regions into a far more intimate relationship. If it failed to end racial discrimination and intolerance, it abolished slavery's statutory foundations. Its outcome was, moreover, one of the great turning points of international history. Whilst we should resist the temptation to delve too far into speculation, what might have ensued had the South secured victory or a compromise peace is an intriguing thought. As things turned out, the North's unequivocal victory helped ensure that the twentieth century was dominated by the Americans, just as the nineteenth had been by the Europeans.

4

THE FRANCO-PRUSSIAN WAR

The outcome of the American Civil War transformed the balance of power in the western hemisphere. Under intense pressure from Washington, France withdrew her troops from Mexico in March 1867, leaving the luckless Maximilian to perish in front of a firing-squad – an event that Edouard Manet depicted on canvas in a subtle but bitter attack on Napoleon III's adventurism. Britain, too, once the effective enforcer of the Monroe Doctrine, grew more wary of provoking an armed confrontation with the USA, whose overwhelming military might gave her an unshakeable grip on the region, as the Spanish were to discover to their cost in 1898. Through the British North America Act, London established the Canadian Confederation in the same year that the French pulled out of Mexico and the Russians sold Alaska to the USA. All outstanding disputes with the Americans, notably the *Alabama* claim, were also settled quickly. Indeed, British foreign policy generally became more conciliatory and, wherever possible, was prosecuted with means other than violence, for the heady days of gunboat diplomacy and inexpensive empire-building were, it seemed, coming to an end. Whilst some comfort could be drawn from the USA's evident disinterest in deploying her new-found might far from her own shores, Britain's own ability to project military power was being eroded. Her army, and thus her capacity for land operations, remained weak at a time when the railway networks that her rivals were feverishly constructing to facilitate the deployment of their numerous soldiers were offsetting her maritime supremacy.

This was, moreover, a symptom of the growing industrialization and prosperity of Britain's competitors, not the least of which was the USA. The textile industry's reliance on American cotton, so graphically underscored during the Civil War; the USA's republican, democratic political system; the unchallengeable productivity of the grain and live-stock farmers of the Midwest, who, thanks to railways, steam ships and the onset of Free Trade, were able to export much of their surpluses beyond the Atlantic: all of these factors made the USA a formidable peacetime competitor for the UK in particular and Europe in general. Indeed, although the French and Russians, especially, welcomed the rise of the USA as a valuable counterpoise to the power of the British Empire,[1] the Union's victory in the Civil War accelerated or estab-lished trends that marked the beginning of the end of European global hegemony.

For instance, the novel recipes contained in *Mrs Beeton's Cookery Book*, which first appeared in 1861, give an indication of the changes in the diet of the British urban middle classes that were coincident with, and influenced by, the emergence of new international patterns of trade in foodstuffs. In the aftermath of the Corn Laws' repeal in 1846, British cereal farming, especially, enjoyed a period of tremendous prosper-ity. With their steam-powered threshing machines and huge storage barns, the grand, stone farmhouses built in, above all, East Lothian still bear witness to this golden age. It could not last, however, once the USA's expanding railways gave the virgin prairies access to the eastern seaboard. The decline of agriculture – and, with it, the traditional dom-inance of the landed nobility – throughout Europe was one of the most striking features of the 1800's closing decades. It helped push ever-more people into the cities and obliged young men, whose ancestors had tra-ditionally worked the land, to seek alternative careers in industry, com-merce and the armed forces.

If the outcome of the American Civil War heralded the end of European hegemony, it also marked the start of the rise of Anglo-Saxon dominance and helped ensure the continuation of the great liberal-democratic experiment. In waging the war, the Union had sought to protect and further its distinctive system of politics, as Lincoln empha-sized in his Gettysburg Address of November 1863: 'We here highly resolve that these dead shall not have died in vain – that this nation, under God, shall have a new birth of freedom, and that government of the people, by the people, for the people, shall not perish from the Earth.' In Europe, by contrast, although the violent conflicts of the mid-1800s owed much to a quest for a new liberal order, their outcomes proved disappointing to those who had persuaded themselves that rev-olution was the route to contentment. Nationalism, too, proved a mixed blessing. In Italy, the *Risorgimento* yielded the constitutional monarchy of Victor Emmanuel rather than a republic and was scarcely a bloodless affair. Alongside the wars of 1859 and 1866 were Giuseppe Garibaldi's invasions of Sicily and Naples and his two bids to seize Rome, the last of which was thwarted by the French garrison, whose commander, General Pierre de Failly, reported to Paris with grim satisfaction that '*Les fussils Chassepot ont fait merveilles.*'[2]

Meanwhile, Otto von Bismarck was dispelling pious notions of liberalism in Germany. He had been appointed as Prussia's chancellor in September 1862, with the initial task of implementing the military reforms devised by Albrecht von Roon, who had succeeded Edouard von Bonin as war minister in 1859. If Prussia was to remain a great power, Roon insisted, she needed larger armed forces. As, however, vast standing armies were a luxury that she could barely afford, any sustainable expansion could only be achieved through the use of reservists, who required no pay when on furlough. To this end, the Hegelian Roon envisaged changes to the conscription laws and the bringing of the *Landwehr* into a much more intimate union with Prussia's regular soldiers. Henceforth, conscripts would join the front-line forces for three years and then act as reservists for a further four. Thereafter, they would be attached to the *Landwehr* for five more years, during the first of which they would be liable for service with the reserves.

With its discrete, civilian organization replaced by a staff drawn from the regular army, the old *Landwehr* was thus transformed into a second-line reserve, while the size of Prussia's land forces as a whole increased considerably. Many German liberals harboured mixed feelings about these developments: on the one hand, they were mindful of the military's role in the suppression of the 1848 Revolution; on the other, they wanted to see Prussia develop the capability to contest Habsburg dominance in Germany. The ensuing argument reached its climax in September 1862, when the Prussian Assembly strove to block the reforms by refusing to grant the army any further funds. Bismarck, however, exploited a loophole in the constitution to raise the requisite taxes without parliamentary endorsement. Indeed, within 12 months the Assembly had been dissolved altogether.

Prussia's military build-up continued apace and was soon put to good use in the wars against Denmark and Austria. In September 1862, Bismarck had asserted that: 'The position of Prussia within Germany will be decided not by liberalism but by her power ... [N]ot through speeches and majority decisions are the great questions of the day decided – that was the error of 1848 and 1849 – but by blood and iron.'[3] Certainly, his vigorous foreign policy promised to yield what the German liberals themselves had failed to attain: national unification within a constitutional framework, and a uniform code of laws to regulate the economic and social life of the *Volk*. The doubters were won over by Prussia's victories and, by October 1867, the constitutional crisis was finally over. Meanwhile, as Bismarck coerced or enticed the states north of the River Main into forming the political union of the North German Confederation, Roon began the creation of a unified army by imposing Prussia's military system on her neighbours. Many of the various state contingents that made up the Confederation's armed forces retained an appreciable degree of autonomy and, as a result, had their own peculiarities in terms of regulations, armament, dress and organization. The Prussian model was followed for the most part, however. By 1870, Roon was able to count on having no fewer than 938 000 officers and men at his disposal in the event of hostilities, irrespective of whether the Confederation was assisted by the Germans beyond the Main or not.[4]

The attitude of the French high command and military educationalists to this huge force was one of scorn, the consensus being that 'It is a magnificent organization on paper, but a doubtful instrument for defence and would be very imperfect during the first period of an offensive war.'[5] Certainly, the Prussian mobilization of 1859 had exposed serious flaws in its conception and execution, and those of 1864 and 1866 had not proceeded without any hitches either. Nevertheless, whereas the catalogue of errors and breakdowns had merely strengthened French scepticism regarding Prussian military capabilities, Moltke, and the *Generalstab* he headed from 1857 onwards, had learnt from it. In any case, whatever the quality of the 12 *Armeekorps* at the Confederation's disposal, as late as 1866, France herself had just 288 000 troops with which to meet all of her commitments, including those in Rome, Algeria, Mexico and the Pacific. For all their perceived qualities, in the event of a confrontation with Prussia, France's professional soldiers risked being overpowered by sheer weight of numbers; their quantitative strength required augmentation as a matter of urgency.

Yet, in reality, the numerical inferiority of the French Army was just one of several grave deficiencies, as an investigative commission was to report in 1867. Supposedly highly confidential, the enquiry's findings were published anonymously as *L'Armée française en 1867*. Written by General Louis Trochu, one of the commissioners, this was highly critical, ridiculing, among other things, what was euphemistically referred to in military circles as '*Système D*', namely *débrouillage* – the tradition of muddling through. Trochu concluded that, however well spontaneous improvization had sufficed in the past, the waging of modern warfare demanded extensive and meticulous peacetime preparation. This had already been underscored by the shortcomings that had come to light in Russia and Italy. Victory is less likely to prove a catalyst for change than defeat, however; and the fact that those campaigns had proved success-ful in the end had only served to smother any thoughts of thorough-going reform. Despite the ineptitude that had surfaced in the military's attempts to exploit railways for the transport of men and *matériel* in 1859, for instance,[6] ten years were allowed to elapse before a new war minister, the able and diligent Adolphe Niel, established a central com-mission to delve into the minutiae of this crucial capability. Sadly, the ailing Niel died shortly after; and, although the committee outlived its creator, its work was neglected and its sittings were soon suspended by a cost-conscious and somewhat complacent administration. Similarly, the handful of limited measures that Neil introduced to overhaul the *État-Major*, which had barely altered since the days of Soult, were stifled by conservatism within the officer corps.

Indeed, the French Army was far from overawed by the rise of the German Confederation. It had, after all, taken seven coalitions involv-ing all of the great powers of Europe to subdue France under Napoleon I. What could Prussia and a few comic-opera allies expect to achieve on their own? French generals believed that *l'esprit militaire* with which their soldiers were imbued was the finest in Europe, as were their shoulder arms, the superb Chassepots, which were about to be supplemented with a new and seemingly deadly weapon, the Montigny *Mitrailleuse*. This crank-operated machinegun, which had been developed during the early 1860s and was put into full production in 1866, comprised a bun-dle of 25 barrels, each of which fired in turn, generating a stream of between 125 and 150 rounds per minute. With a maximum reach of 1800 metres, it promised to massacre any opponent and help offset any purely quantitative advantage that he might enjoy.

However, when subjected to the ultimate test, that of the battlefield, the *Mitrailleuse* was to have no more of an impact than machineguns had had on the engagements of the American Civil War. Although it was shrouded in secrecy as far as the French Army itself was concerned, articles about it had featured in several European military journals and a number of foreign observers had actually been permitted to see it.[7] When it was finally unveiled for use in the Franco-Prussian War, few

French soldiers had any idea how to operate it and still fewer had given any serious thought as to how such a device might best be used. Mounted on a gun carriage and, like the Gardner and Maxim machine-guns that Britain had purchased during the late 1860s, assigned to the artillery, these weapons were, despite their novel characteristics, not seen as requiring any special doctrine to underpin their employment in action. Instead of being used to give supporting or suppressive fire from carefully selected and protected positions within the French lines, they were simply regarded as just another type of ordnance and treated as such. Habitually deployed alongside batteries of field artillery which could not in any case match the range of the Germans' Krupp breechloaders, many of them were knocked out in the opening engage-ments of the war, often before they even had an opportunity to fire a shot.

Although the French generals were quite right in identifying morale as the single most important influence on warfare, in doing so they over-looked the significance of too many other factors, many of which, iron-ically, affect people's willingness to go on fighting. During the American Civil War, Lee especially had exploited his soldiers' firepower with a tac-tical skill that was as consummate as the casualties he inflicted on the Federal armies were heavy; as late as June 1864, Grant sustained some 5000 in a few minutes in a clumsy frontal assault at Cold Harbor. All of the Confederates' triumphs in this regard were to no avail, however, because the Union had both the physical and moral strength to over-come such losses; it was frequently left less drained by defeat than the rebels were by victory. Yet, when Niel strove to increase the amount of trained manpower available to the French Army, his proposals quickly ran into opposition. As well as seeking extensions to the periods of ser-vice undertaken by regulars and reservists, he suggested that the *Garde Nationale*, which had been abolished after the Bonapartist coup of 1851, be revived in the form of a *Garde Nationale Mobile*. The regular army was, however, sceptical about the military value of a mass of reluctant con-scripts who would, perforce, receive little equipment and training and whose political allegiances could render them troublesome; the old fear of *le péril intérieur* still lingered. Moreover, among the wider population were many who, in spite of Napoleon's adventurism, were tempted to believe the oft-repeated assurance that '*L'Empire, c'est la paix*'; that the great scientific and artistic accomplishments, the growth of interna-tional law as evinced by the Declaration of Paris, and the increasing prosperity and industrial development that were this period's hallmarks were indeed the harbingers of the perpetual peace predicted by so many of the Enlightenment's philosophers and, more recently, by the Manchester School of Cobden and John Bright.

Public opinion of this kind proved a powerful force, particularly in a political system that was in the throes of liberalizing itself. Dismissing the recent sanguinary contest between two democratic polities in North America as an aberration, many people simply could not bring themselves to believe that the France of *gastromonie*, of the Impressionists and François Rodin, of Camille Saint-Saëns, César Franck, Jacques Offenbach and Georges Bizet could sully itself by so much as contemplating another war. Others' objections to new military measures were more pragmatic than hedonistic. Commercial factions expressed misgivings about the possible effects on agriculture and industry if more manpower was diverted into the unproductive armed services. Other groups, mindful of the regime's Mexican and Pacific enterprises, were anxious to minimize the scope for the abuse of military power. Republican deputies in particular had an implacable dislike for standing armies of any description, rejected 'offensive' wars and wanted France's defence to be entrusted to the nation in arms, should she be attacked. Conservatives, by contrast, disliked raising additional taxes to finance an enlarged military establishment at a time when so many of their countrymen and women evidently regarded war as unthinkable or, at worst, avoidable.

Predictably, few of the details of Niel's proposals survived such an acrimonious debate intact. The reforms that were eventually implemented in February 1868 fell far short of what he had recommended, comparatively modest though his original suggestions were. For those liable, the maximum duration of military service was set at five years, to be followed by four years with the reserves. This, it was calculated, would yield a total force of around 800 000 personnel by 1875. Niel's proposal that the *Garde* be reconstituted was also adopted. Comprising those of military age who avoided the draft, it was expected to furnish another 500 000 men on mobilization. However, the few resources that were allocated to it were plundered from those of the regular army. The provisions for instructing and preparing the *Garde* were, moreover, diluted to a degree that was quite preposterous. Enrolled for five years, its members were to engage in annual exercises. Yet, whereas Niel wanted these to amount to three weeks per year, the law limited them to just two. These were, furthermore, to be completed a day at a time, with not more than 12 hours of training each day, and under conditions that permitted the men involved to travel home in the evening. There were even exemptions from these minimal obligations for those who satisfied certain criteria.[8]

Neil died in August 1869 and was replaced by Edmond Leboeuf, whose concerns about the political and military dependability of the *Garde* ran so deep that he deliberately slowed the implementation of his predecessor's scheme. In any case, money for the raising and equipping of new regiments became increasingly scarce, as, in keeping with the public mood, the *Corps Législatif* whittled down defence expenditure. Indeed, the liberal ministry led by Émile Ollivier that took office in January 1870 slashed military spending by all of 13 million francs and contemplated reducing the size of the draft in anticipation of moves towards general disarmament by the great powers. Only six months later, this selfsame administration was to declare war on Prussia, albeit with some hesitation at the last moment. Predictably, the small but vociferous Republican faction within the Chamber criticized the decision and vainly attempted to prevent the voting of war-credits, which was passed by an overwhelming majority on 15 July. Meanwhile, in the streets of Paris, the news of the outbreak of war was cheered by huge crowds who sang 'The Marseillaise' and chanted '*Vive la France! À Berlin!*' Some sections, at least, of *le peuple français* were evidently far more bellicose than their rulers had liked to believe.

Many of the lessons that might have been drawn from the American Civil War and Sadowa were lost on the French high command. In stark comparison to the seriousness with which it was treated in Germany, military education was somewhat neglected in France. Indeed, it is far from certain whether many officers had either the interest or the opportunity to examine any intellectual analyses of what had actually occurred in these recent conflicts and why. In any case, military thought was in a state of flux, with the result that conflicting views were on offer. Whereas Napoleon III himself and some '*Polytechniciens*' like Trochu stressed the pivotal role that general staffs fulfilled in contemporary warfare and the concomitant need for trained specialists who understood the minutiae of mass mobilization, railway operations, logistical loops and so on, the French Army's assignments in North Africa and Mexico had posed challenges that bore little resemblance to those that would be faced in the event of a European war.[9] Similarly, although the struggle in North America had been an attritional one and had been decided as much by events off the battlefield as on it, in 1866 it had taken Prussia just seven weeks and one major engagement to defeat the Austrians in a campaign not entirely dissimilar to that conducted by the great Napoleon 60 years earlier. Uncertainty about the future was, moreover, not confined to France alone, as the works of some foreign military authorities suggested. One very influential book in English that first appeared as late as 1866 was Edward Bruce Hamley's *The Operations of War*. This reverted to what, for many European and American soldiers, was a familiar perspective, that of Jomini; it largely neglected issues such as morale, entrenchment and fortifications, logistics, penetration in depth and the use of exterior, rather than interior, lines, all of which had been prominent features of the struggle between the Confederacy and the Union.

Recent naval operations had also emitted several contradictory messages, much to the bewilderment of some theorists. The American Civil War had witnessed the Union blockade, the duel between the *Virginia* and the *Monitor*, the use of mines, torpedoes and submersibles, and a number of engagements involving either a handful of ocean-going ships or flotillas of gunboats, many of the latter occurring on rivers, where mechanized vessels were that much more manoeuvrable than sailing ones. However, there was no sizeable sea battle to analyse and draw guidelines from. There had, moreover, been just one major maritime clash during the war of 1866, that between the Italian and Austrian fleets off Lissa. Here, the Austrians, with only 37 ships, only three-quarters of which were steamers, including just seven ironclads, confronted Admiral Carlo di Persano's squadrons. He disposed of 42 vessels, 33 of which were steam-driven, with 12 ironclads or partially armoured ships among them. The Italian advantage in firepower seemed no less overwhelming. To their 680 guns, which included several pieces of the latest heavy ordnance manufactured by Armstrong Whitworth, the Austrians could oppose only 550. In fact, as highlighted by one contemporary French authority, if added together, their broadsides amounted to little more than half the weight of shell that could be discharged from all the Italian guns simultaneously.[10] All of these disadvantages notwithstanding, however, the Austrians, under Admiral Wilhelm von Tegetthoff, won the engagement by recourse to a very old tactic, ramming. Shrugging off the gunfire from the enemy fleet, which was deployed in line ahead, Tegetthoff's most powerful steamers attacked in a wedge-shaped formation, deliberately targeting the Italian capital ships, three of which were sunk and others damaged. At this, the rest of Persano's fleet retreated.

What were naval strategists and tacticians to make of all this? There was little in the works of such contemporary writers as Captain Sir John

Colomb – who, as we shall see, was primarily concerned with sea power's role in the defence of the British empire – that was of much guidance to either French or Prussian naval strategists. As continental powers, both their states could and did rely primarily upon their land forces for security; naval strength could only play a subordinate role. Indeed, although, in the war of 1870, the French maintained undisputed control of their own territorial waters and even mounted a limited blockade of the German Confederation's coastline, their plans for an amphibious assault had to be abandoned once their marines were sucked into the increasingly desperate fight for the very heart of France.[11] With their littoral secure, the Prussians, who had set aside an entire *Korps* for coastal defence, were free to divert these soldiers from peripheral operations to the central missions of destroying the French armies and taking Paris. That, throughout this, the flow of France's maritime trade continued uninterrupted, facilitating the raising of foreign loans and the importation of armaments from abroad, was of course, a source of exasperation for the invaders and was to help stimulate Germany's later interest in building up her battle fleet. (It is indeed noteworthy that the young Alfred von Tirpitz served as an officer with the Prussian Navy during the conflict.) Nevertheless, a few gunboats on the Seine aside, France's warships could do nothing to directly influence the land battles that ultimately determined the struggle's outcome.[12]

For the war of 1866, Moltke, a disciple of Clausewitz rather than of Jomini, had employed a strategy of exterior lines, which had culminated in the concentration of the Prussian armies on the battlefield of Sadowa. His plans were controversial in the eyes of some of his colleagues and had encountered appreciable opposition. Nevertheless, although his success had vindicated him, it would be a mistake to attribute Prussia's victory purely to the quality of his strategic thought or to any other single element in the panoply of factors that can influence the outcome of a campaign. The Dreyse rifle gave the Prussians an important tactical advantage, but the Austrian artillery, on the other hand, had performed well, too. In any case, technology is only as good as the people employing it. Prussia's triumph can only be satisfactorily explained by the taking of a holistic view of the belligerents' forces, including their morale and the quality of their leadership, staff work and logistical support.

This approach is certainly essential in any analysis of the Franco-Prussian War. The French, who had an atavistic penchant for the offensive, envisaged mounting a thrust towards Berlin much as Napoleon had done in 1806 and confidently expected the same outcome. Yet, whereas Napoleon had secured the diplomatic isolation of his quarry before embarking on the Jena campaign,[13] in 1870 the situation was reversed. This time, France was goaded into waging war without the support of allies – slender hopes of eventual Austrian, Danish and Italian assistance were ended abruptly by the early reverses sustained at Spicheren and Froeschwiller in August – and it was exclusively on her territory that the fighting took place. As in 1859, 1864 and 1866, the Prussians' mobilization was not blemish-free, but it ran like clockwork when compared with that of their adversaries, who rashly merged their call to arms with the process of strategic concentration in an ultimately counterproductive bid to save time. Gaps in the French logistical loop also proved crippling.[14] Exploiting the resources of six principal railway networks, in the space of just three weeks the Lines of Communication Department of the Prussian *Generalstab*, by contrast, coordinated the *Aufmarsch* of some 480 000 Confederation troops to the Rhineland. The sheer speed and size of this movement proved fatal to what few plans the French staff had concocted. Having lost the initiative, they never really regained it, and were forced into a series of essentially defensive battles, too many aspects of which were mishandled.

Nevertheless, like Napoleon I, Moltke evinced an acute awareness of war's sheer intractability. 'No plan of operations can look with any certainty beyond the first meeting with the major forces of the enemy', he once emphasized. 'The commander is compelled ... to reach decisions on the basis of situations which cannot be predicted.'[15] As we have seen, Napoleon was extraordinarily successful at divining his opponents' reactions to a given state of affairs, but he would surely have agreed with Moltke's observation that 'You will usually find that the enemy has three courses open to him, and of these he will adopt the fourth.'[16] War is, after all, a reciprocal activity; that some French commanders and politicians might at times have posed an even bigger threat to their own side than they did to the enemy should not blind us to both the miscalculations and accomplishments of the belligerents as a whole. In the course of the campaign, many of Moltke's strategic plans unravelled as a result of the behaviour of insubordinate or headstrong commanders, misunderstandings, adverse weather, fatigue, breaks in his forces' logistical loop and other manifestations of what Clausewitz termed 'friction'. Indeed, generally speaking, the Germans won the war by committing fewer errors. This is for the most part to be attributed to the superior military education and organizational capabilities of Moltke and the *Generalstab* rather than to markedly better strategic or tactical thought.

The relative smoothness of the Germans' mobilization, coupled with the sheer size of their leading echelon, also gave them a quantitative superiority in the crucial, opening battles of the war. In the recent past the French Army's officer corps had, in any case, geared itself to the conduct of small-scale operations, which called for a high degree of initiative and a 'hands-on' approach to unit leadership. Timely mobilizations and the disposition of entire *corps d'armée* were undertakings that few generals had ever had to think about, let alone implement. Marshal Patrice MacMahon had distinguished himself at the taking of the Malakhoff and clinched the victory of Magenta, but had since spent several years acting as Algeria's governor-general; he was destined to be worsted at Froeschwiller and wounded and captured at Sedan. Canrobert, too, had fought in the Crimea and Italy, but, in spite of this or probably because of it, declined to shoulder any responsibilities greater than those of a *corps* commander during the war of 1870/1. In fact, once Napoleon began his descent into the torpor that first began creeping over him as early as 7 August and culminated in him abandoning his forces for Châlons nine days later,[17] the leadership of the 'Army of the Rhine' passed to Marshal François Bazaine by default; there was no other senior officer available who was able or willing to take on the job. Renowned for his personal bravery, he was a soldier's soldier, however. He found it difficult to be anything other than deferential towards the likes of Canrobert and failed to stamp his authority on proceedings. Moreover, his main claim to fame comprised his service in Mexico. Suddenly appointed to command a large force engaged in intensive operations against a formidable adversary, he soon found himself out of his depth. The Battle of Gravelotte-St-Privat, for instance, saw 188 000 Germans with 732 guns pitted against 112 000 French troops with 520 pieces of ordnance. In the light of their past experience, it is perhaps little wonder that, here and elsewhere, the French commanders struggled to coordinate their activities efficaciously.

Bazaine's conduct during the fighting at Vionville-Mars-la-Tour was redolent of that of one of his illustrious predecessors, Marshal Ney at Waterloo. Certainly, he behaved more like an ordinary soldier than a general.[18] He was later to be accused of, and tried for, treason. However, the principal burden of responsibility for the breakdown in the French high command in the war's opening stages more properly rests with Napoleon III. Having shamelessly exploited his famous uncle's martial reputation, he failed to fulfil the role of warrior-monarch to a degree that would have dismayed Napoleon I. The latter had always taken personal responsibility for the formulation of strategy. Indeed, if only because of this, in 1870 the French Army instinctively and unquestioningly looked to the emperor for definitive guidance in this regard, just as it had done in the years 1805–15. Little, if any, was forthcoming, however; Napoleon III lacked both the skill and the physical and mental energy to provide it. Nevertheless, having abdicated his responsibilities as commander-in-chief, he lingered with the forces that Bazaine nominally commanded, desperately hoping to be present at a victory that was to prove elusive. Thereafter, the same dynastic and political considerations motivated him to join MacMahon's ill-fated 'Army of Châlons', where, once again, his presence ineluctably compromised the authority of the man he had entrusted with supposedly supreme command. Nor was this all. As emperor, he also embodied the paramount civil power; yet, while dallying in the field, he handed responsibility for the exercise of this prerogative to a Council of Regency, headed by his wife, which, among other acts, dismissed Leboeuf.

This occurred on 9 August and was just part of a profound political crisis that engulfed France in the aftermath of her initial military reverses. Undeserved though it was, Leboeuf's removal was predictable once his now infamous assurance that the army was ready 'to the last gaiter button' had been perceived to be hollow. Ollivier's position also proved untenable and he resigned in favour of General Cousin de Montauban, Count of Palikao, who, as head of the French contingent in the amphibious expedition undertaken jointly with the British against Peking in 1860, had emerged as a hero from the Second Opium War. A talented soldier and able administrator, he was now asked to serve as both president of the council and as war minister.

Ollivier's last act prior to stepping down had been the announcement of several emergency measures. Approved by the *Corps Législatif*, these included the placing of Paris on a siege footing; the transfer of the marines and their ordnance from the Admiralty's control to that of the army; the doubling of the existing war-credits to 1000 million and the issuing of bank notes to the tune of 600 million francs; the immediate drafting of the entire conscript class for that year and the amassing of 450 000 reservists. Indeed, every able-bodied bachelor and childless widower between 25 and 35 years of age was deemed liable for military service. By dint of such drastic steps, Palikao was enabled to cobble together sizeable new forces to field alongside Bazaine's hard-pressed divisions around Metz, notably MacMahon's 130 000-strong 'Army of Châlons'. However, no sooner had this set out to make contact with the

'Army of the Rhine' than a formidable German force, specially put together for the task, confronted it. Far from the fighting, in Paris, Palikoa fatally misread the strategic situation and, fearful of the political consequences if Bazaine was not extricated at once, insisted that MacMahon proceed to his assistance without delay. This the marshal obediently tried to do, thereby playing right into Moltke's hands.[19] Napoleon, who was with the doomed army, might have saved it had he asserted himself and overruled the authorities in Paris. By failing to do so, he sealed both his own and MacMahon's fate. Intercepted by the advancing Prussians, the 'Army of Châlons' was herded into the frontier town of Sedan. Encircled by forces that outnumbered it by almost three to one and with little ammunition or food, it was in a hopeless situation. A two-day battle ensued, the outcome of which was as much of a foregone conclusion as anything can be in war. On 2 September, Napoleon III, together with all the remnants of his battered army, capitulated.

Sedan was one of the greatest humiliations in French history, as underscored by Émile Zola in his novel, *La Débâcle*. Unlike his uncle after Waterloo, however, Napoleon III did not abdicate, nor did his personal surrender constitute the capitulation of France in her entirety, even though it did precipitate the collapse of his regime. As the tidings of the emperor's defeat spread through Paris, plunging the city into uproar, the Left seized its opportunity to overthrow his dynasty. On 4 September, at the Hôtel de Ville, the Third Republic was proclaimed and a new government, consisting almost exclusively of deputies representing the Seine Departments, was improvised: Trochu, who, as we have noted, had incurred the displeasure of the Imperial authorities, was, as the only senior soldier acceptable to both the army and the Parisians, appointed governor of the metropolis as well as president of the council; Léon Gambetta became the interior minister; Jules Favre was entrusted with foreign affairs; while Charles de Freycinet, a civilian, took up the reins at the War Office, where he was assisted by a Military Council. Needless to say, none of these men had a mandate from the French electorate as a whole, but the holding of a countrywide ballot was out of the question as long as war bestrode the land. In any case, Gambetta – who, in the later stages of the conflict, assumed control of the War Ministry, too, becoming the principal advocate of further resistance – and his colleagues were only too aware that the rural peasantry and the *bourgeoisie* were as opposed to militant republicanism as ever. Indeed, when, in early 1871, the Prussians did permit a national ballot to take place, the French electorate returned Orléanist and legitimist candidates in overwhelming numbers, exchanging Gambetta and the war-party for an administration under Thiers that was willing to pay almost any price for peace.

In the interim, however, the political situation proved as perplexing for the belligerents as the conduct of the war itself. The Empress Eugénie had taken refuge in Britain, but, like her husband, had not abdicated; Napoleon was in captivity in Cassel; and Bazaine's army, which had sworn allegiance to the emperor, remained at large. Though cooped up in Metz and all but ignored by the self-styled Government of National Defence in Paris, it had yet to lay down its arms and was not in fact to do so until as late as 29 October. For weeks on end, the marshal remained, in Bismarck's eyes at least, a virtual plenipotentiary through whom a comprehensive peace might be arranged and who, in that event, would dispose of sufficient military power to have some prospect of enforcing it. The legitimacy of the Republican administration in Paris, by contrast, was less apparent. Perhaps more to the point, Gambetta and his ilk were only interested in concluding peace without yielding 'an inch of France's soil or a stone of her fortresses'.[20] However, a settlement along these lines was not going to satisfy either Bismarck or the *Generalstab* or the German public and press. It was imperative that the French not only be punished for having launched yet another aggressive war against the German people, but also that they guarantee that such a thing would never occur again. Any such safeguards could not, moreover, take the form of mere bits of paper; France's strategic options would have to be physically truncated through the surrender of territory and key border fortresses, notably Metz and Strasbourg.

However, even if the Government of National Defence could be compelled or induced to accept such terms, it was not clear whether it was in a position to uphold them. For 200 years, Germany had repeatedly fallen victim to French expansionism and adventurism, while France's endemic political instability had been a source of insecurity for the whole European continent for the past 80. Whereas a cardinal tenet of the reasoning espoused by the Enlightenment and the Manchester School was that a system of democratic politics promoted peace, in France's case it had all too often led to war; Ollivier's liberal ministry had proved indistinguishable in this regard from the *empire autoritaire* or, for that matter, the First Republic. Indeed, the essential validity of this point – frequently reiterated by Bismarck in the various meetings aimed at bringing the conflict to a conclusion – was to be demonstrated again only days after the preliminaries of the Peace of Frankfurt were finally

ratified. No sooner had the Prussian occupation force begun withdrawing from Paris on 3 March 1871 than the rioting that was to culminate in
the establishment of the Commune began. As had happened so often in
the past, many units of the *Garde Nationale* proved to be politically unreliable and, with his country descending into civil war,[21] Thiers was to
have to persuade Bismarck to amend the peace accord so as to permit
more regular troops to be brought into the metropolis. All of this was to
delay the longed for return of the German armies to their homeland,
much to Bismarck's chagrin. It did ensure, however, that the peace he
had laboured so long and hard for did not break down completely.

Peace, after all, albeit one with different characteristics from that
which it replaces, is the ultimate goal of any war. With the annihilation
of MacMahon's forces at Sedan and the encirclement of Bazaine's at
Metz, it became clear to Moltke that the most promising way to end hostilities was to capture Paris. By 20 September, he had sealed the city off
completely and started ringing it with batteries and entrenchments. Its
isolation from the outside world was further intensified a week later
when his troops fished the arterial telegraphic cable from the Seine's
depths and severed it. Nevertheless, Moltke had no intentions of storming or even bombarding Paris at this juncture. He knew that such a massive population centre could not fend off hunger and cold for very long
once its stocks of food and fuel were exhausted. The French authorities,
moreover, had taken certain steps that, however well intentioned, could
only make his tactics that much more efficacious. Motivated by the same
military and political logic as him, the Government of National Defence
had subordinated every other consideration to the retention of the capital. They had incorporated virtually every available soldier immediately
to hand into the city's garrison, expanding it to all of 260 000 men,
while enjoining whatever forces could be mustered in the provinces to
assail the besieging army's flanks and rear. Calling for *guerre à outrance*,
the city's many radical republicans were bent on emulating the defenders of Saragossa during the Peninsular War, the revolutionaries of the
early 1790s and other exponents of what they perceived to have been
successful popular resistance. Above all, they advocated the launching of
a *sortie torrentiale*. Trochu, however, feared that too many of the available
troops – large numbers of whom were either green conscripts just
summoned to the colours, or National Guards – lacked sufficient discipline, training and equipment to mount offensive operations. If they
remained in the city and waited to be attacked, on the other hand, their
weaknesses could be offset by its defences.

As we have seen, the process of fortifying Paris had been started under Louis Philippe, and a further 12 million francs were now lavished on improvements to the perimeter's walls and bastions which, extending for 60 kilometres, were designed to keep typical siege guns at a safe distance from the city's heartland. If manning such a huge boundary placed enormous demands upon the defenders, sealing it off was a commensurably greater task. Indeed, Moltke's investing forces occupied a front of 80 kilometres in length. Nevertheless, their blockade proved a tight one. On 12 September, a week before the siege commenced, the Government of National Defence had taken the precaution of relocating several of its members to Tours, from where they could more easily maintain contact with the foreign ministries of Europe and organize the war-effort in the provinces. In fact, Paris, always set apart from the rest of France by its distinctive political culture, was now increasingly dismissed as an irrelevance by much of the country's hinterland.[22] Anxious to counter this growing indifference and nip the Tours Delegation's plans for elections in the bud, Gambetta himself left the capital on 7 October.

He did so by balloon, which, together with carrier-pigeons, constituted the sole means of communication left to the inhabitants of the beleaguered city. Procured from a Monsieur Godard, the balloons were employed to ferry official couriers, dignitaries and post to beyond the German lines, while, to maximize the amount of information the pigeons could deliver, modern photographic and printing techniques were used to reduce messages to microscopic proportions.[23] However, Godard's balloons were inflated with coal-gas, of which, like so many other commodities, Paris had finite stocks. The Left, especially, advocated the introduction of a system of general rationing, but this was far easier said than done. As always, the weakest members of society were those who suffered most. Shortages of fresh milk, for instance, had dire repercussions for babies and infants, while, without fuel for heating, the old in particular perished from hypothermia as the winter set in. Increasingly, the Government of National Defence proved unable to reconcile its liberal idealism with military necessities and the need to maintain order in a city racked by social and political divisions.

For the Germans, the plight of the Parisians was as much a source of difficulty as it was encouragement. This was particularly so once Bismarck, understandably desperate to end the siege and, thereby, hostilities, persuaded his king to compel the reluctant Moltke to start bombarding the city. Indeed, in waging war in the midst of the nineteenth century, these men found themselves grappling with problems strikingly similar to those that were to confront Western politicians and military personnel at the end of the twentieth. Whereas soldier-monarchs like Napoleon I had embodied both the supreme military and civil authority, William I had to struggle to reconcile the sharply contrasting views of, on the one hand, his chancellor and, on the other, the army's chief of staff. However much they might have agreed with one another that war should be the continuation of policy, they were often at loggerheads over its detailed conduct. Moreover, with snooping newspaper correspondents reporting all that transpired – or, to be precise, what they perceived to be happening – international and domestic public opinion were powerful forces that could not be ignored. Bismarck rightly feared them.

Some three months before the bombardment of Paris began, Strasbourg capitulated after having endured weeks of indiscriminate shelling by German troops bent on coercing the beleaguered garrison into surrender. The city's capitulation finally took place on the 28 September, but, long before then, a delegation from Switzerland had materialized, seeking to arrange the evacuation of non-combatants. Such humanitarian sentiments conflicted with those of the vociferous German public and press, however, as well as with military imperatives. Whereas the war of 1866 had not been coloured by ethnic animosities, bad blood was bound to play a role in a conflict between peoples and during which the distinctions separating combatants from non-combatants ineluctably became nebulous. Whilst, among the soldiers of the opposing armies, a sense of shared hardships and dangers frequently mollified any enmity, there were episodes of shocking brutality, including the massacre at Passavant of a *Garde Nationale* battalion that had surrendered.[24] As is so often the case in war, however, the most implacable hatred was often evinced by those who were farthest from the fighting. Bismarck's wife, for instance, wanted all the French 'shot and stabbed to death, down to the little babies.'[25] Even the pious Moltke found himself sanctioning increasingly brutal reprisals against the *francs-tireurs* – to whom belligerent status was denied by the Germans and whose accountability to the French authorities was at best limited – and those French civilians who were either found to be resisting his troops or were perceived to be doing so. Although his objections to the bombardment of Paris were mostly inspired by his military pragmatism, there were those at home and abroad who attacked the policy on moral grounds. 'There hangs over this whole affair an intrigue contrived by women, archbishops and professors...', an exasperated Bismarck grumbled to his wife at the end of October.

> Meanwhile the men freeze and fall ill, the war is dragging on, the neutrals waste time discussing it with us, while... France is arming herself with hundreds of thousands of guns from England and America.... All this so that certain people may be praised for saving 'civilisation'.[26]

Like Lincoln during the American Civil War, Bismarck was fearful that, if the fighting dragged on, foreign intervention of one kind or another would ensue. Certainly, Russia's repudiation, on 29 October, of the Black Sea clauses of the Treaty of Paris did raise the prospect of an international conference that might seek to impose a settlement on Prussia and France, too. In any case, the former was fast falling victim to her own success as, in the eyes of the world, her victories over the fledgling republic transformed her from an avenger to an oppressor. At the beginning of December, Moltke wrote to Trochu advising him of the defeat of the 'Army of the Loire' and the fall of Orléans. Regardless of whether, as Bismarck suspected, this was a surreptitious peace overture, it persuaded the French high command that the relief of the capital was now becoming improbable. It coincided, moreover, with the gory failure of a bid by Paris's defenders to break out. Thereafter, Trochu agreed to make one more attempt to do so, if only to demonstrate to the radical republicans that their vaunted tactic of a *sortie en masse* could not succeed against such disciplined, well-equipped adversaries. The Battle of Buzenval, as it is known, certainly made the point for him, ending as it did in another sanguinary check. Expecting this to spark off riots or even a rebellion, the government now relieved the hapless Trochu of command of the garrison and appointed General Joseph Vinoy in his stead. Sure enough, on 22 January 1871, shots were exchanged around the Hôtel de Ville as a few left-wing extremists, including some members of the *Garde Nationale*, were dispersed by troops loyal to the administration. But the mass rising that had been feared did not occur. With the food stocks all but exhausted and with no prospect of salvation, the whole of Paris's population had to acknowledge, however grudgingly, that the end was nigh and that the government would have to sue for terms.

The signing of an initial armistice followed on 28 January. By this stage, the Republic's armies had been as comprehensively defeated as had those of the Empire before them. Though overwhelmed on the strategic plane, at the tactical level the latter especially had fought with some distinction. Indeed, the successes enjoyed in this regard, the most notable being at Mars-la-Tour and Borny, proved cruelly deceptive. 'It is fire effect, nowadays so powerful, which will determine the issue', Moltke had predicted on the eve of the war.[27] Yet, from the outset, actual events on the battlefield showed this to be too much of a simplification. Indeed, a pattern emerged at Froeschwiller that was to be repeated several times. Here, the French found themselves confronted by greatly superior numbers of enemy troops who attacked not so much in depth as on a broad front, enveloping their prey. Although the greater reach and rate of fire of Krupp's ordnance offered significant tactical advantages, the Chassepot was appreciably superior to the Dreyse rifle in both these respects. In fact, the infantry units of the Confederation and its allies were often checked by their French counterparts, eventually advancing to occupy ground that the German artillery had effectively conquered through remote bombardment. French technological failures occasionally contributed to the outcome, too, as did the use of outdated doctrines. The percussion fuses of the German shells evidently proved more reliable than the timing mechanisms used by the French up to the Battle of Coulmiers (November, 1870); the latter devices, if they exploded at all, could only be set to certain ranges.

Whereas this effectively created safe havens for the enemy, at Froeschwiller, MacMahon allowed the German infantry to get too close to his own guns. Clinging to the French Army's traditional practice, he kept much of his artillery in reserve, intending to commit it at the climactic moment. His timing and *coup d'oeil* failed him, however, and his gunners were driven back by a hail of rifle-fire. Attempts by both sides to use cavalry for shock-action were similarly flawed. For example, at Froeschwiller, the nine squadrons of General Michel's *cuirassier* brigade were virtually wiped out executing charges that were as futile as they were courageous, while, at Sedan, General Margueritte's squadrons met the same fate. Although the Prussian king himself was moved to remark on the bravery of the latter group of horsemen,[28] it is improbable that they came within a sword's length of a single enemy soldier, so intense was the fire directed against them. Even the success of Bredow's charge at Vionville – which, perfectly timed and carefully screened, managed to catch Canrobert's batteries on the hop, throwing them into chaos at a critical moment – was only gained at the cost of 50 per cent casualties among the attacking cavalry.[29]

Similarly, the premature attack by the Prussian Guard *Korps* at St Privat bears witness to the destructive effects of modern firepower;

8000 men were killed or wounded, mostly in the space of 20 minutes. A small indication of the extraordinary dedication of France's better troops is also provided by the losses they endured. One regiment that entered the battle at Froeschwiller 2300-strong emerged with just three officers and 250 men. In the same engagement, the 3rd *Zouaves* lost 45 out of their 66 officers and 1775 out of 2200 rank and file.[30] That they continued resisting to such extreme lengths suggests that their morale was all that had been claimed on the eve of hostilities. Certainly, the war was not lost for lack of courage. Indeed, the French infantry generally lived up to their reputation for resilience and aggressive spirit, not least at Borny, where their savage, dashing counter-attacks confirmed the Germans' evaluations of their tactical prowess.

Other traditions of the French Army, however, contributed to its ultimate defeat. Besides the ubiquitous '*Système D*', practices and equipment developed for the recent campaigns in Mexico and Africa proved ill-suited to large-scale operations undertaken on friendly soil in the heart of Europe. Whereas the Prussian uhlans and hussars roamed almost at will, the French light cavalry, reluctant to venture far without infantry support, proved inept at reconnaissance, screening and the penetration of enemy-held territory; it soon became more of an encumbrance than an asset. Similarly, instead of simply resting by the roadside, French columns insisted on coiling up at the end of each day's march, with the result that units, groping through the darkness, would continue to trickle into the camps throughout the night. Many soldiers, moreover, slept, not in billets as the Germans usually did, but in flimsy tents intended for use in warmer, drier climes. Freezing temperatures and heavy rain often combined with hunger in undermining morale.

The sudden influx of reservists and raw recruits into units of the standing army also undermined the French forces' cohesion, just as theorists like Du Picq had feared it might. This problem became particularly acute once the Republic began drafting roughly a million men into the army in the aftermath of Sedan. By the time of the armistice, the first of these, some 578 000 bachelors, had been mobilized. Yet, like the Americans in 1861, the French struggled to furnish such a mass of raw levies with sufficient training and equipment, let alone a leavening of seasoned troops. Technicians, such as engineers and gunners, and officers were in particularly short supply. That the Republic had to turn to Catholic, royalist generals like Vinoy, Claude d'Aurelle de Paladines and Auguste Ducrot, an authoritarian who loathed revolutionaries, to command its armies was not only somewhat ironic, but also exerted a malign influence over civil-military relations; too many radicals eyed these professionals with intense suspicion.[31] Efforts to overcome the dearth of regimental officers also caused difficulties. Former soldiers had to be granted commissions, while units of the *Garde Nationale Mobile* were permitted to elect their leaders. However, as the latter scheme led to the dislodgement of presiding officers without due regard to the provisions of military law, it proved short-lived. Thereafter, the expedient of doubling the size of companies was resorted to, whereby the demand for officers was halved.

This did nothing to improve the discipline and tactical manoeuvrability of units that were deficient in both. Control, both military and political, over the *francs-tireurs* who fought, at least nominally, for France was also shaky. Largely foreign volunteers, many of them had their own political agendas. Garibaldi's cause, for instance, was that of the universal republic envisaged by Mazzini, which made him and his Italian mercenaries as big a threat to French conservatives as they were to Moltke's armies. As had happened in the Iberian Peninsula 60 years before, guerrilla warfare's very nature exacerbated the social and political rifts that international conflict had highlighted.[32]

Indeed, both the Germans and French found that for every possibility in modern warfare there was a corresponding problem. The shortages of trained specialists to support and lead them reduced the potential of the Republic's massive armies, as did the lack of up-to-date armaments with which to equip them. There were insufficient Chassepots to go round, but few of the shoulder arms purchased abroad were as deadly. One consignment of rifled muskets imported from the USA that had been gathering rust in an arsenal since the Civil War was issued to the Breton *Gardes Nationales*, who, as fate would have it, were then entrusted with the defence of a key sector of the French position at Le Mans; untroubled by their ineffectual fire, it was here that the Germans broke through. The importation of armaments, often of differing designs and calibres, also complicated maintenance and ammunition requirements, while the encirclement of Paris deprived the provincial forces of the services of so much of France's manufacturing industry.

On the other hand, the prosecution of that selfsame siege presented Moltke with huge practical difficulties, not the least of which was that of keeping the investing units adequately supplied with food and ammunition. Much of this had to be imported from Germany, but there were only two railway lines available, both of which were menaced by neighbouring strongholds that remained in enemy hands. Aggravated by the ravages of war, including the destruction of tunnels and other acts of sabotage, the shortcomings of France's railway network impeded the Germans' operations, just as they had hampered those of her own troops. Although they employed captured rolling stock and, much to the detriment of domestic services, brought in some 3500 railway workers and 280 locomotives from Germany, the invaders experienced real difficulties in constructing and preserving a continuous logistical loop, particularly once their armies penetrated deep into France and the bombardment of Paris began. If Gambetta ultimately lost the war through his failure to win the hearts and minds of the French people, there were moments when it seemed as though the Germans, for all their victories, might fall at the last hurdle for want of adequate supplies.

5

FROM THE TREATY OF FRANKFURT TO THE RUSSO-JAPANESE WAR

The *Triumphlied* composed by Johannes Brahms was but one of many artistic and more enduring manifestations of the rejoicing that swept through Germany following the signing of the Treaty of Frankfurt in May 1871. The shift in the European balance of power that this accord confirmed was, however, not universally welcomed. If the Vienna settlement of 1815 had survived largely intact up to 1854 because no state had sufficient strength or will to overturn it, since then the great powers had been chipping away at it in a process that had now led to the crushing of France and the emergence of a united Germany under Prussian leadership. Italy, too, had been forcefully combined into a single monarchy, further eroding Austria's prestige, already much weakened by the demise of the Romanov–Habsburg alliance and the events of 1866. For her part Russia had, by 1871, regained most of what she had lost 15 years earlier and had reverted to exerting pressure directly on Turkey and, thereby, indirectly on Britain. Overall, it was a less satisfactory balance of power than the one it replaced and appeared to contemporaries to be that much more precarious. Yet, although the last three decades of the 1800s were punctuated with crises and war-scares, hostilities between Europe's leading nations were avoided. In fact, the peace that prevailed between 1871 and 1914 remains one of the longest in the continent's history.

Some historians have suggested that this phenomenon is to be explained by the 'New Imperialism' that allowed the great powers to play out their rivalries in far-flung corners of the world and so acted as a safety-valve whenever tension reached dangerous levels within Europe.

Whilst there is some truth in this, the fact that they felt sufficiently secure at home to indulge in adventurism abroad is surely testimony to the underlying robustness the powers perceived the *status quo* as having. Indubitably, France was burning to avenge the humiliations of 1870/1, but Bismarck's skilful diplomacy kept her too isolated for her to try. In the interim, she sought to console herself with fresh gains in Africa, and took the lead in making colonialism a state affair rather than a private one. A methodical, rapid process replaced the gradualism of earlier decades as states sought assured markets and sources of raw materials abroad to help underpin the existing political and social order at home. Colonial aggrandizement also seemed the sole way in which the Western European states, physically hemmed in by the emerging giants of the USA and Russia, might remain major powers in a world of new alignments and blocs.

By 1883, this policy, however, had embroiled the French in bitter domestic wrangles and in conflicts with the Tukulor and Samorian Empires, which were to drag on for 10 and 15 years, respectively. The British, too, had their strategic problems, not the least of which was the incipient, relative decline of their maritime supremacy as a consequence of technological, industrial, social and doctrinal change. The Royal Navy's professionalism commanded the respect of sailors throughout the world, yet its admirals were still obsessed with the doctrine that had been formulated in Nelson's day. Despite the switch from sail to steam and from wood to metal, little thought had been given to the evolution of maritime strategy. This intellectual stagnation can be at least partly explained by a loss of confidence in what, for centuries, had been Britain's first line of defence, as, between the end of the Crimean War and the grand Spithead review that marked Queen Victoria's Diamond Jubilee in 1897, the utility of naval might in general, and that of Britain in particular, was gradually undermined.

Battleship construction had always proved a costly, time-consuming affair that called for skilled workforces, dockyards and other specialist infrastructure. In the course of the 1800s, however, Britain's shipbuilding industry – like so many other sectors of her economy – underwent relative decline as industrialization spread to her competitors and they began exploiting ever more of their latent potential. The construction of railways especially not only played a major part in this process, but also, by transforming overland communications in many regions of the world, tilted the military balance to the detriment of small, essentially maritime powers like Britain and the Netherlands. Peripheral strategies based on the exploitation of the sea could now be countered through the rapid movement of large armies by rail.

In any case, Britain's capacity to maintain the quantitative and qualitative strength of her fleet was also waning. Designing a modern warship could be difficult enough in so far that it called for the achievement of the optimal mixture of firepower, armoured protection and mobility, with the precise distribution of the first two elements being a further consideration. The very sophistication of the screw-driven, metal warships that emerged in the second half of the 1800s led to a dramatic increase in the cost of building such vessels during a period when *laissez faire* was in retreat, popular participation in government was expanding and many rulers, not least successive British premiers, were being pressed to increase spending on social and economic development. Moreover, in the past Britain had enjoyed a crucial advantage in terms of her ability to produce warships comparatively swiftly, since this had enabled her to draw on emerging technologies and react to other innovations that much more quickly than her rivals. Yet, if the rise of the US Navy was not to prove a pressing problem until the early 1900s, the size and sophistication of the fleets of Britain's more immediate neighbours, notably France, were becoming troublesome as early as the 1860s. At the end of that decade, her's amounted to 49 ironclads, among which were 14 frigates, all heavily armed and capable of speeds of up to 14 knots.

The English Channel was being bridged by steam, intensifying existing concerns that the Royal Navy could no longer be relied upon to fend off an invasion that might come out of the blue. Such anxieties were already beginning to focus attention on the British Army's plight when the wars of Prussian supremacy exacerbated them. Was it strong enough to protect the homeland? Should resources be diverted from the Navy to it and to the construction of more coastal fortifications? Indeed, what should the balance between maritime and land forces now be? The former might influence a continental war, but, in isolation, could not decide one; the Polish and Danish crises of 1863 and 1864 respectively had again revealed Britain's virtual impotence when confronted with adversaries that were willing and able to sacrifice their seaborne trade and coastal settlements. On the other hand, the troops of any expeditionary force remained dependent on the fleet for their transportation and supply.

The question of the respective roles that the British land and sea forces should fulfil was one that increasingly exercised the mind of Captain Sir John Colomb, author of *The Protection of our Commerce and Distribution of our Naval Forces Considered* (1867) and other pieces on imperial defence. He depicted the Royal Navy as Britain's shield and the army as her spear. The protection of Britain and her colonies, he stressed, ultimately rested on her retaining control of the sea-lanes. If this were to be lost, then, in the light of her growing dependence on imported foodstuffs, Britain could be starved into submission. If, on the other hand, it were retained, the army could be used at will.

But it was far from certain whether Britain's comparatively tiny land forces could hope to make much headway against the vast armies at the European continental powers disposal. The sheer size of the Russian Army, for example, profoundly affected British plans for the active defence of India in particular. Russia acted as a counterweight to Berlin's might, too. Up to 1871, Bismarck had been able to exploit her ambitions in the Black Sea, but, thereafter, she became less malleable, concerned by the growth in Germany's strength. As any conflict with Russia in the East would almost certainly tempt France into starting hostilities in the West at the same time, Berlin had an overriding interest in preserving the *status quo*. Accordingly, in an effort to gain leverage over Russia and to maintain France's isolation, Bismarck entered into the 1879 Dual Alliance, the 1882 Triple Alliance and the 1887 Reinsurance Treaty. However, Germany's endeavours to shore up Austria–Hungary ineluctably thwarted Russian ambitions in the Near East and, by the late 1880s, Russo-German relations had deteriorated to the point where war seemed likely. Although fighting was ultimately avoided, the situation did present a window of opportunity to the French, who, with the secret military convention of 1894, formalized the possibility of them taking joint action with the Russians against Germany.

Clearly, there were potential trouble spots both within Europe's heartland and on its periphery. However, in the late 1800s, the process of colonization that had first been started by the European states in the 1400s reached its climax as ten per cent of the Earth's population and some 16 million square kilometres of territory were added to their acquisitions in the space of a few years. As the influence and interests of the European powers spread ever further across the world, several arcs of potential or actual conflict developed. One of these ran along the upper Nile, another along Britain's primary line of communication with India through the Suez Canal and the Red Sea, while a third stretched from Constantinople to Afghanistan.

One was also to emerge in the Far East, between Korea and Manchuria. Still riven by the Taiping rebellion that had begun ten years before, no sooner had China been defeated by the British and French in

1860 than she faced further demands for concessions from the great powers. For a time it seemed that she might disintegrate completely. However, the Qing dynasty's forces – including the 'Ever-Victorious Army' that was ably led by, first, an American soldier of fortune, Frederick Ward, and, later, Britain's Charles 'Chinese' Gordon – finally succeeded in quelling the Taiping rebellion and thus won China a breathing-space. By the 1880s, she had acquired a few of the trappings of a modern state, including some sophisticated armaments. But the changes introduced by the so-called 'self-strengthening movement' to the old Confucian system of government and values were essentially cosmetic. The Chinese were neither able nor willing to embrace Western methods to the same extent as the Japanese, who established a strong central government, backed by powerful armed services, reformed their legal and taxation systems, and embarked on an ambitious industrialization programme. When China and Japan crossed swords over Korea in 1894/5, so complete were the latter's victories that the collapse of the former again seemed to be imminent.

Indeed, after the signing of the Treaty of Shimonoseki in 1895, events in the Far East were to acquire mounting significance in the relationship between the European states, not least because of their implications for the 'great game' that, since the Crimean War, the Russians and the British had been playing across an ever-larger swathe of Asia. Although the inroads made by the former into the Ottoman Empire in 1877/8 were checked by diplomatic pressure at the Congress of Berlin, her steady advance through the khanates of Central Asia led to an alarmed Britain embarking on the Second Afghan War. Nevertheless, fearful of a blow against India and despairing of ever being sufficiently strong to ward off any determined Russian offensive here, not to mention all the other points along the Constantinople–China axis where an attack might materialize, the British hoped to counter any threat by menacing Russia's soft underbelly in the Black Sea. However, Turkey's Armenian pogroms, which alienated the British public, and her continuing frailty rendered this time-honoured policy unsustainable. The Suez Canal, in which Disraeli had acquired the controlling share in 1875, became the principal focus of British concern in the eastern Mediterranean. With the transition from sailing ships to steamers, the traffic passing through it was on the increase, and it had already established itself as the primary route to and from India, cutting all of 9000 kilometres off the journey. Around 80 per cent of the vessels utilizing the waterway were British even before Gladstone ordered the occupation of Egypt in 1882.

Indeed, fears for the sea-lanes to India had a major impact on British policy in both the northern and southern reaches of Africa. Mastery of the upper Nile was regarded as essential for Egypt's security and helps explain the willingness of the British to confront the French at Fashoda in 1898 while conciliating them in western Africa.[1] Up until the September of that year, however, Mahdism posed a more immediate threat to Britain's grip on the region and was the target of the lengthy campaign that culminated at Omdurman.

Here, the Khalifa's men fought with great bravery, but, attacking across open terrain against disciplined troops with modern armaments, were never likely to succeed. Around 11 000 were killed, and thousands more injured. Although they possessed shoulder arms, too, at least 15 000 of them, many were in a poor state of repair. Moreover, they were not deployed *en masse*, but dispersed throughout their army to provide covering fire for its hordes of spearmen and swordbearers. Few of these ever got sufficiently close to use their weapons, though the fighting did include a celebrated, if reckless, charge by 320 men of the British 21st Lancers against a group of 2000 dervishes. The latter inflicted proportionately heavy losses on their assailants before breaking, the lancers dismounting to rout them with carbine-fire.[2]

Like that of any battle, Omdurman's outcome was determined by a blend of factors, including morale, tactics and technology. The Mahdists, however, did face firepower of a particularly formidable kind, employed under optimal conditions. By the 1880s, smokeless propellants were being used in munitions, greatly improving visibility in fire-fights. This raised the effective range of shoulder arms to 800 metres. At Omdurman, although some infantry units of the Anglo-Egyptian army tried to exploit the maximum reach of their weaponry by opening fire from nearly double this distance, the real damage was evidently done at around 800 metres. Indeed, few Mahdists seem to have penetrated to within 500 metres of their opponents' lines, and no dervish got closer than 50.[3] Moreover, anything that the defenders' shooting lacked in precision was probably offset with sheer volume, since the Mahdists attacked in vulnerable, dense formations against infantry who enjoyed an unprecedented capacity to generate firepower. In 1889, the British had replaced the Martini-Henry single-shot breechloader introduced by Cardwell with the Lee-Metford. This was fitted with a magazine, as was the short, light, but hard-hitting Gras-Kropatschek rifle, which was employed by the French and Portuguese, the Lebel which, added to the French inventory in 1886, was the first smallbore, smokeless shoulder arm adopted by a major power, and the Mauser mark 98, issued to the German Army in 1885 and favoured by the Boers in the war of 1899–1902. The 1880s also saw much more efficacious use being made of machineguns in land warfare. Because of their bulky design and the weight of ammunition they consumed, they had initially proved more popular with navies than armies, and were often mounted on riverboats. The British, however, were among the first to recognize the wider potential of such armaments. They made good use of Gatlings in the Ashanti War of 1873/4 and were quick to adopt the new lighter designs, notably the Maxim, which superseded the earlier hand-cranked models. Certainly, the British Maxims did terrible execution at Omdurman, as did 50-pounder shells filled with lyddite, a new and formidable high explosive.

In case control of the eastern Mediterranean was ever lost, Britain was also eager to retain the Cape. However, the discovery of valuable gold reserves in the Rand in the 1880s threatened to make this that much harder. This fabulous wealth not only caught many a covetous British eye, but also attracted the attention of foreign powers and incited Afrikaner nationalism. In striving to reassert their dominance of the region, the British – who, following a small but humiliating setback at Majuba Hill, had recognized the independence of what had been a poverty-stricken Transvaal as recently as 1881 – were to precipitate the Boer War of 1899–1902, the longest, goriest and most expensive armed conflict they had participated in since the struggle with Napoleon.[4] While its spiralling costs in men and money jeopardized her capacity to keep her guard up elsewhere, the reverses she sustained in the opening months of the war and the tactics she resorted to during its final stages – which were dominated by guerrilla warfare – also inflicted terrible damage on Britain's international standing and national unanimity.

Coupled with the use of concentration camps, the destruction of Afrikaner farmsteads in a bid to deprive guerrillas of horses, supplies and shelter proved particularly controversial. In order to secure cleared areas of territory and key communication routes, the British also constructed colossal barbed-wire entanglements and a network of over 8000 blockhouses, each of which was linked to the next by telephone, a device that had acquired an ever greater role in military operations since Bell developed it in 1872. Spain had recently employed similar measures against Cuban rebels – a practice that helped propel the USA into war with her in 1898. Yet, brutal though they were, it is not apparent what alternative policies either of these colonial powers might have used to quash resistance mounted from within a civilian population. Guerrilla warfare ineluctably clouds the distinctions between combatants and non-combatants and is frequently as socially divisive as it is savage. Many Afrikaners actively aided the British, who had also enlisted the support of thousands of blacks. Seen by the Boers as racially inferior, the latter in particular could expect no mercy. Those whites who collaborated, surrendered or merely advocated peace often had to be protected by the British from Boer reprisals, too.

Although the British Army had, by the time of the South African conflict, at long last undergone some change as a result of Cardwell's programme of 1871, it lagged far behind its continental counterparts, most of which, alarmed or inspired by the outcome of the Franco-Prussian War, had quickly embraced the structures and methods employed by the Germans. Cardwell's abolition of the purchasing of commissions and his introduction of new weaponry, regional recruitment, 'linked' battalions and short-service enlistment went some way towards creating a more professional and efficient force. However, as conscription was not adopted and the supply of volunteers never kept pace with demand, the army's reserves remained disturbingly weak. In 1886, a start had been made on the organization of a dedicated expeditionary corps, but few of the recommendations of the Hartington Commission, which was established two years later, had been implemented in full, leaving the army lacking a modern general staff and a political and bureaucratic machine that might have proved capable of coordinating imperial defence effectively. An intellectual foundation for warfare on a large-scale was also lacking; Charles Callwell's *Small Wars* (1896), which drew its lessons primarily from the Indian Mutiny and French experience in Algeria, was very influential at this juncture, having an obvious appeal for soldiers whose daily lives revolved around constabulary operations. The Boers' use of dispersal, entrenchment and the latest weaponry, notably the Mauser and smokeless propellants, also perplexed the British, not least at Colenso in 1899. One officer who had also fought at Omdurman just 15 months before noted that 'Few people have seen two battles in succession in such startling contrast .... In the first, 50 000 fanatics streamed across the open regardless of cover to certain death, while at Colenso I never saw a Boer all day till the battle was over, and it was our men who were the victims.'[5] Certainly, notwithstanding the tremendous courage frequently exhibited by its personnel, the British Army's performance in the South African War was on the whole lamentable.[6]

Similarly, although its ships and crews remained among the best in the world, the Royal Navy, despite its importance for imperial defence

and power-projection operations, was slow to develop educational institutions and doctrines for the age of the triple expansion steam engine.[7]
Indeed, the Royal Naval College at Greenwich only opened in 1873,
and the debate about precepts evolved only gradually. In seeking to
identify basic principles of maritime strategy, Vice-Admiral Philip
Colomb, an instructor at Greenwich from 1892, made a noteworthy contribution to the filling of this intellectual void. His theoretical and historical studies, originally serialized in a magazine, were compiled and
republished in 1891 as *Naval Warfare*. His examination of Britain's
strategic naval problems, *Essays on Naval Defence*, appeared two years
later, close on the heels of Alfred Mahan's *The Influence of Sea Power Upon
History*. Echoing Mahan, the objective of maritime warfare, Colomb
insisted, was control of the sea, which could only be secured by a navy
capable of fighting major engagements with an adversary's fleet and of
conducting a close or distant blockade of his ports; coastal fortifications
and gunboats were essentially an expensive irrelevance once naval
supremacy was lost.

However, historical rather than technical and with broader horizons,
Mahan's work, though of less didactic and thus enduring value, over-
shadowed *Naval Defence*, catching the public's imagination at a time
when maritime competition was one of the most prominent dimensions
of the assertive nationalism evinced by the world's leading states.[8] The
most tangible manifestation of that mood in Britain's case was the Naval
Defence Act of 1889, which established the two-power standard she was
to apply to the maritime strategic balance for years to come. Indeed,
Mahan did not so much start a new trend as justify an existing one, further undermining latent opposition to the US Navy's expansion, for
instance. After 1865, that force had been reduced in size. Moreover, with
global trading interests to protect but lacking overseas bases, until the
end of the 1870s it continued to put its faith in wooden-hulled ships that
were driven primarily by sails. Though slower and less manoeuvrable
than steamers, such vessels were regarded as being more flexible
because they were easier to repair and less reliant on coaling-stations.
Partly as a consequence of this reasoning, the adoption of seemingly
superior technology was deliberately rejected, as occurred with the USS
Wampanoag in 1869. Originally designed during the Civil War, this
propeller-driven frigate combined a clipper-style hull with an exceptionally efficient steam engine, endowing her with both speed and
endurance. In a sense, however, she fell victim to her own success. The
evolution of warships was proceeding at such a pace as to render any

new design obsolete within a few years, as an 1877 report by the US Navy's chief engineer highlighted. Citing problems experienced by the French and Austrians with their ironclads, 'The decay of the wooden hulls ... and the advancement made in ... modern fighting-ships [has]', he concluded, 'rendered these vessels useless.'[9] The policy of allowing other powers to pay the price for such experimentation seemed, to the Congress and many American sailors, to have much to recommend it.[10]

Indeed, potent new technology, notably mines, torpedoes and submarines, had implications for classical maritime warfare that, from the 1880s, fascinated theorists such as the Russian Admiral Stepan Makarov and the French *Jeune École*.[11] By threatening the supremacy of the battleship, such devices seemed to herald a revolution in the composition and tactics of fleets. The earliest locomotive torpedoes – self-propelled weapons that travel underwater and which, like submerged mines and spar torpedoes, are designed to detonate against or close to the underside of a target – date from the 1860s. The invention of a Captain Luppis of the Austrian Navy, the concept was developed between 1864 and 1866 by Robert Whitehead, a British engineer who managed a factory at Fiume in Hungary. Initially known as the 'Luppis-Whitehead Fish Torpedo' but, later, simply as the Whitehead Torpedo, this device carried a high-explosive warhead in its nose and was powered by compressed air. In 1868, an important refinement was made to it through the incorporation of 'The Whitehead Secret', a depth-controlling mechanism that ingeniously combined a pendulum with a hydrostatic valve. Further improvements to the size, speed, range and payload of such torpedoes were achieved during the next three decades, while the addition of gyroscopic steering systems – the first of which was developed by an Austrian engineer, L. Obry of Trieste, around 1898 – greatly enhanced their accuracy. Indeed, by 1900, torpedoes that could propel a 100-kilogram, gun-cotton warhead at up to 29 knots over a range of 800 metres had been perfected.

A Whitehead Torpedo was first used in anger by the British frigate *Shah* in 1877. Its quarry, a Peruvian rebel vessel, the *Huascar*, managed to evade the weapon, which, at this juncture, was too lacking in pace and reach. The following year, however, the Russians sank a Turkish ship in Batum harbour with two torpedoes fired from some 80 metres away. This success helped highlight the potential of these novel armaments and, during the 1880s, they were adopted by almost all navies. Tremendously destructive, they seemed to threaten even the sturdiest of warships and precipitated extensive changes in the structure of fleets and individual vessels alike. Naval architects began to add dense belts of armour to the waterlines of capital ships, while some theorists called for radical alterations to the composition of fleets in the light of the apparent vulnerability of large, expensive vessels. Above all, in *Les Torpilleurs autonomes* (1885) and *La Reforme de la Marine* (1886), the bible of the *Jeune École*, Gabriel Charmes advocated a division of labour within the French Navy. Instead of investing its resources in a comparative handful of sizeable, armoured ships bearing a multiplicity of weapons, the fleet should, he argued, comprise lots of units made up of small vessels that would rely less on metal plating than on numbers, elusiveness, speed and manoeuvrability for their protection. Geared to particular combat roles, some should carry either guns or torpedoes, while others should be primarily designed as rams. Whereas part of the fleet should be geared to operations on the high seas, the rest should be custom-built for patrolling coastal waters.

Although the principle of the division of labour was gradually adopted by navies, it was not to be along the lines envisaged by Charmes. However, the advent of effective mines and torpedoes certainly necessitated changes to maritime strategy and tactics, as well as inspiring the creation of entirely new classes of naval platforms and other innovations. Not only was the waterline armour on many ships greatly enhanced, but also their interiors were reinforced through the adoption of cellular structures built around water-tight bulkheads. Special nets were also devised to screen harbours and moored vessels from torpedo attacks. Besides such passive defences, a new type of platform had to be developed that could actively counter the novel threat posed by torpedo-boats. The destroyer, as it became known, was a sleek, fast vessel armed with guns and torpedo tubes. Britain's first, HMS *Havock*, which was finished in 1893, was capable of 26 knots, while HMS *Viper*, completed six years later, could, thanks to her steam turbines, a propulsion system first exhibited by Charles Parsons at the 1897 Spithead review, achieve 34 knots.

Speeds of this magnitude enabled destroyers to threaten small and large vessels alike; even capital ships could prove vulnerable to audacious torpedo strikes. However, the coupling of locomotive torpedoes – which could be fired either from above the water-level, usually from swivel-mounted pods, or from fixed, underwater tubes – with submersibles created unprecedented possibilities for the mounting of insidious attacks. The notion of a submarine was an old one: as early as 1776, during the American Revolution, a submersible devised by David Bushnell had been used in an unsuccessful mine-laying attack on HMS *Eagle*; while the *Nautilus*, a craft devised 21 years later by Robert Fulton, had briefly caught the imagination of Napoleon. We have noted, too, how in 1864 the Confederates' hand-cranked *Hunley* sank the USS *Housatonic* with a spar torpedo. By the 1890s, however, sizeable, mechanically powered submarines were being perfected, not least by John Philip Holland, an American engineer who was eager to create a weapon that might weaken Britain's domination of the seas. Somewhat ironically, the Royal Navy ultimately acquired his patented, 1898 design for a submarine that was driven by electrical storage cells when submerged and a petrol engine when cruising on the surface.

While the debate about their value in blue water operations raged on, smaller, faster craft played a major part in the 'Scramble for Africa', notably in the Sudan, the Belgian Congo and in Portuguese Mozambique. Here, as in the American Civil War, river-going vessels served as a means of projecting power and moving, not just troops and supplies, but also heavy ordnance into areas that would otherwise have remained inaccessible. Indeed, a flotilla of gunboats added to the fire-power of Kitchener's forces at Omdurman, as well as providing crucial logistical support.

He was also able to make use of a military railway. This ultimately stretched as far as Atbara and, along with an adjoining telegraph, would later be described as 'the deadliest weapon' employed against Mahdism.[12] Meanwhile, the Russians had begun the Trans-Siberian railway, which would enable them to reinforce their Pacific-rim garrisons within a fort-night without having to slip troopships past the British or other poten-tially hostile fleets; though not finished until 1917, it gave an early indication of its potential in the 1904/5 Russo-Japanese War. Similarly, by 1900, the USA had laid some 308 800 kilometres of track, including four transcontinental lines, which had obvious strategic utility. Germany, too, continued to develop her railway network for military purposes. In a process of gradual nationalization, her Imperial Railroad Office bought up 12 000 kilometres of track belonging to independent compa-nies between 1879 and 1884, and the remaining 3400 kilometres over the next 20 years.

However, whilst their superior and improving technology enabled the Americans and Europeans to expand their dominions at the expense of backward or declining people – be they the Chinese, the Ottoman Turks, or African or American Indian tribes – there were incidents that under-scored the insufficiency of technology alone: much of Custer's 7th Cavalry was obliterated at the Little Big Horn in 1874; British columns were exterminated at Isandlwana in 1879 and at Maiwand in 1880; and the Italians were crushed at Adowa in 1896. War remained an intractable business. Furthermore, technological advances did not always enhance people's sense of security. The triumphs of Moltke's military machine had suggested that the delivery of a sudden, knock-out blow was feasible if properly prepared for. This increased the pressure to act quickly and resolutely in any crisis. By March 1892, Alexander III of Russia, for instance, had concluded that 'We really must come to an agreement with the French, and, in the event of a war between France and Germany, throw ourselves immediately upon the Germans so as not to give them time to beat the French first and then turn on us.'[13] Similarly, the creeds of the *Jeune École* called for unheralded torpedo attacks on merchant shipping and the bombardment of coastal towns by night, all of which contradicted attempts both to give non-combatants more protection during hostilities and to limit the peacetime accumulation of armaments through international law.

Indeed, the very sophistication and size of contemporary armed services intensified the ongoing debate about the utility and purpose of war and whether industrialization was a force for good or ill. In *Anti-Dühring* (1878), Friedrich Engels argued that the technical progress that had altered warfare's nature over the centuries had, in the Franco-Prussian War, reached its apogee. Further advances were now possible only through the militarization of society, which seemed to be happening through the proliferation of rifle clubs and reservist units and through the indoctrination of boys in public and private schools. Certainly, both Karl Marx and Engels, who had to assume sole responsibility for the completion of *Das Kapital* after the former's death in 1883, were fascinated by the events of 1870/1, not least the rise of the Commune, which seemed to bear out aspects of their cyclical theory of class war. Socialism, they believed, could only benefit from the raising of mass armies through conscription and from attempts by states to mobilize the whole of society in pursuit of a common goal. By contrast, John Ruskin, who, in 'War' in *The Crown of Wild Olive* (1866), had depicted warfare as the fountainhead of art, was horrified by the corrupting effects of industrialization on his Utopian vision of chivalrous conflict.

Ivan Bloch, on the other hand, thought that war's utility was being undermined by, among other things, that very process. A retired Russian banker and railway magnate, this wealthy pacifist could claim no professional expertise in the field of military affairs. However, after spending eight years subjecting warfare's emerging trends to sociological, economic and technical analyses, in 1898 he produced *War of the Future*, a study that was as impressively detailed in terms of its content as it was provocative in its message. Translated into French, German and – as *Is War Now Impossible?* (1899) – English, the basic thesis of his book was that, in the face of modern firepower, decision on the battlefield between similarly equipped forces was destined to prove elusive. With armies unable to mount successful offensives, an attritional stalemate would ensue that could only threaten to end in financial and social collapse. Indeed, the Occidental world's interdependent economies would barely be able to cope with the disruption caused to labour and trading markets by any general conflict. War, therefore, was not to be dismissed as impossible, but was certainly likely to prove, at best, counterproductive.

Whilst anxieties about the growing volume, accuracy and lethality of fire on the battlefield were shared by all armies and had been for 50 years at least, Bloch's emphasis on technology and his neglect of the single most important consideration, morale, was seen as a weakness in his argument. Certainly, actual experience in the Boer and Russo-Japanese Wars, both of which followed soon after his book's appearance, seemed to contradict too much of his theory. If the first of these conflicts could be discounted as an atypical illustration – as a clash between forces essentially designed for, and accustomed to, colonial warfare and opponents that lacked even the trappings of regular troops – the Russo-Japanese War of 1904/5 seemed highly revealing, pitting, as it did, the Japanese Army and Navy against the tsar's soldiers and sailors. The former had been trained by German and British officers respectively, while the Russian forces were regarded as some of the most formidable in Europe. Moreover, a few exceptions aside, notably chemical weapons, powered aircraft and tanks, both sides possessed every form of technology that was later to be employed in the First World War. Although the fighting for Port Arthur and Mukden, especially, underscored the advantages that modern armaments, barbed wire and deep entrenchments bestowed on the defender, the Japanese demonstrated that successful offensives were still possible, providing the attacker showed initiative, his planning was meticulous and his morale sufficiently high to endure heavy casualties.

By challenging much of the philosophy that underpinned war (and much else besides), Bloch's reasoning was politically and militarily unpalatable. It had no discernible, immediate impact within official circles, though his views were to have some effect on several later writers, not least the French soldier-theorists Émile Mayer and François de

Négrier. By contrast, other, more influential Frenchmen – notably Hippolyte Langlois, the École de Guerre's commandant at the turn of the century, and Ferdinand Foch, who was then that institution's professor of military history, strategy and applied tactics – espoused the doctrine of the offensive, often invoking Ardant du Picq's *Battle Studies* in support of their theories. With an introduction written by Ernest Judet, a right-wing, anti-Dreyfusard journalist, the second edition of this work appeared in 1903, when the French Army was faced with political persecution at home and an ever stronger Germany abroad. The Dreyfus *Affaire*; the anti-militarism and pacifism of the socialists; the individualism of the *bourgeoisie*; the support, not least among republican and egalitarian parliamentarians, for new conscription measures that would create a nation-in-arms by ending all social and educational exemptions: all of these factors had a dispiriting effect on an army that was still haunted by the humiliations of 1870/1. In these circumstances, *Battle Studies*, with its emphasis on morale, *esprit de corps* and the offensive, seemed to many officers to have both martial and political utility.

Japan's victory over Russia just a couple of years later intensified the debate in France and elsewhere about the merits of the offensive. Furthermore, her success, bought at terrible cost, acquired Japan greatpower status. For a world strongly influenced by Darwinian notions of competition, these developments had a clear, if unsavoury, message that shook the convictions of many liberal intellectuals. Herbert Spencer, for instance, in the course of writing his *Principles of Sociology* (1876–96), lost faith in the Cobdenite creed of inexorable human progress and began, however reluctantly, to echo Max Weber's view that world politics was becoming a perpetual contest between autonomous cultures. For his part, Moltke insisted that

> Permanent peace is a dream and not even a beautiful one, and war is a law of God's order in the world, by which the noblest virtues of man, courage and self-denial, loyalty and self-sacrifice, even to the point of death, are developed. Without war the world would deteriorate into materialism.[14]

Friedrich Nietzsche would have approved of the traces of Darwinism in this thinking and ridiculed Moltke's faith in 'God's order'. Whereas most of his intellectual contemporaries either wanted to save or conquer the world, as a radical philosopher, he struggled to understand it. A professor at Basle University, he had served as a medical orderly during the Franco-Prussian War – an experience that further undermined his already frail health and intensified his obsession with theodicy. Deeply influenced by Arthur Schopenhauer's aetheistic thought, he found life painful and sought an escape from it through music, particularly Richard Wagner's, in whose works, notably *Lohengrin*, Nietzsche discerned a pre-Christian order. Although eventually alienated by Wagner's nationalism – and, indeed, the composer's growing fascination for sacred, Christian music-dramas, which culminated in the writing of *Parsifal*, his last opera – he clung to this vision, elaborating it in his philosophical works of the 1880s, notably *Menschliches, Allzumenschliches, Also Sprach Zarathustra, Die Fröliche Wissenschaft* and *Jenseits von Gut und Böse*. In the parable of *The Madman*, Nietzsche proclaimed the death of God, leaving humankind as the sole arbiter. The 'Will to Power', derived from Schopenhauer, was the source and meaning of life. People should, Nietzsche's nihilism dictated, think for themselves and become what they really were, transcending the imposed values of theistic doctrines, particularly the humanitarianism, tolerance and compassion espoused by Jesus of Nazareth. Indeed, persuaded that war had achieved far more than love of one's neighbour ever could, Nietzsche delineated the concept of the *Übermensch* – a leader who, shaking off all sentimental and moral inhibitions, would employ violence to create a new, better world.

Nietzsche succumbed to insanity in 1889 and had to be nursed by his sister, Elisabeth, until his death 11 years later. In completing his unfinished works, she wilfully distorted his ideas, injecting her own fanatical nationalism and the anti-Semitism of her husband. *Der Wille zur Macht*, especially, was destined to have a profound impact on, among others, Hitler and Mussolini. For them, Nietzsche's views, actual or perceived, offered an answer to what is perhaps the central question of human existence and which only arises because of our capacity for conceptual thought: what are we supposed to be? The widespread decline in religious observance that occurred in the Western world during the 1800s reflected a wider uncertainty in this respect. Whereas the great social movements advocating education, temperance, feminism, or better treatment of convicts, the mentally ill or the handicapped all believed in progress, human perfectibility and the individual's capacity to discern his or her own salvation, many people were overwhelmed by the sheer pace of change and the reasoning it spawned. There was just too much technology, too many ideas, books and political movements. Modernity and industrialization had reduced life to a rat-race in which Utopian codes of honour, chivalry and self-sacrifice seemed sadly anachronistic. At both national and individual levels, strength and skill were now to be equated with goodness; and the ultimate competition had to end in death.

There were those, of course, who, in spite of or sometimes because of the implications of all of this, sought to reassert their faith in alternative values. Science might explain how the universe functioned, but could not adequately answer the question of why. Reason alone was incapable of furnishing the romantic, non-utilitarian significance that human beings crave. To many members of the French Right, for instance, the *débâcle* of 1870/1 appeared to be the result of the laxity of morals that had characterized the Second Empire. Overcome by a 'passionate desire for virtue', the National Assembly voted in 1873 for the construction of the Sacré-Coeur Basilica which, to this day, dominates Paris's skyline.[15] Similarly, the pious avant-garde architect Antoni Gaudi was persuaded that his Sagrada Familia Cathedral, begun in 1883, in Barcelona could save his city from secularism's evils. In Britain and some of the other European states, the late 1800s also witnessed the growth of temperance and evangelicalism, not least within the armed forces. The number of chaplains, many now in uniform, rose, too.

Moreover, if much of the music of this period – notably Tchaikovsky's *1812 Overture*, Louis Ganne's *Marche Lorraine* and *Le Père la Victoire*, Suppé's *O, Du, mein Österreich*, the great anthems of Wagner and Verdi, and Elgar's *Pomp and Circumstance Marches* – reflected the military bluster and national and imperial confidence of the late 1800s, in Britain, for instance, Rudyard Kipling's *Tommy Atkins* and the work of Agnes Weston's Sailors' Rests helped highlight the poverty and neglect suffered by many veterans. Whereas the navvies employed to build the Crimean military railway had been better paid than the troops,[16] those who had 'devoted the best part of their lives, sacrificed their health, and cheerfully scattered their limbs in rolling the tide of battle from … [their country's] door',[17] were now increasingly regarded as deserving poor, not outcasts.

If the treatment of soldiers and sailors had improved somewhat in this regard by the end of the 1800s, in other respects little had changed. Medical care and hygiene in the field was often flawed, despite the discoveries of Louis Pasteur and Joseph Lister. Indeed, in the Boer War, more British troops fell victim to disease than to the enemy's fire. Nevertheless, men continued to see military service as, at worst, a way to avoid the drudgery and anonymity of Civvy Street. Recalling his experiences at Waterloo, one British officer confessed that he would 'rather have fallen that day as a British infantry-man, or as a French cuirassier, than die ten years hence in my bed. I did my best to be killed ....'[18] Some 85 years later, this sentiment was echoed by Field Marshal Wolseley, Commander-in-Chief of the British Army, who wanted to end his career in battle rather than die in bed 'like an old woman.'[19] Within months of his passing in 1913, the European powers embarked on a conflict of unprecedented totality. The type of war predicted by Bloch, it was to prove as impersonal as it was attritional.

NOTES

1 THE NAPOLEONIC ERA AND ITS LEGACY

1. In this respect, Jomini echoed Machiavelli. See A. Gat, *The Origins of Military Thought* (Oxford: 1989), pp. 6–7. For the essence of Jomini's reasoning about Napoleonic warfare, see ibid., pp. 119, 122.
2. Moreover, armies tended to acquire stocks of muskets from various sources. The British, for example, provided their continental allies with large numbers during the Napoleonic Wars, many of which then fell into French hands.
3. G. Hanger, *A Letter to Lord Castlereagh*, (London: 1808), p. 78.
4. Leaving aside the issue of speed of reaction, the naked eye's limitations pose a dilemma in this regard. As Major F. A. Griffiths, pointed out in his *Artillerist's Manual and British Soldier's Companion*, eight editions of which appeared between 1839 and 1859:

   > A single individual may be seen at a 1,000 yards, but his head does not appear as a round ball until he has approached up to 700 yards.... At 500 yards the face may be observed as a light coloured spot; the head body, arms and their movements, as well as the uniform ... can be made out. At between 200 and 250 yards all parts of the body are clearly visible ... and officers may be distinguished from the men.

5. *Instructions for the Drill, Manual and Platoon Exercise* (Edinburgh: 1800 edn), p. 23.
6. See D. Gates, *The British Light Infantry Arm* (London: 1987), pp. 138–48.
7. This crucial qualification is frequently overlooked. Rothenberg, for instance, remarks that 'Napoleon, a trained gunner, ... failed to grasp the possibilities of reverse-slope fire by howitzers, perhaps a major factor in his defeat at Waterloo.' See G. E. Rothenberg, *The Art of Warfare in the Age of Napoleon* (Staplehurst: 1997 edn), p. 74.
8. B. P. Hughes, *Firepower: Weapons Effectiveness on the Battlefield*, 1630–1850 (London: 1974), pp. 34, 38; O. F. G. Hogg, *Artillery* (Camden, CT: 1970), pp. 180–1.
9. E. Baker, *Remarks on Rifle Guns* (London: 1829 edn), p. 9.
10. F. Seymour Larpent, *The Private Journal of F. Seymour Larpent* ... (G. Larpent, ed., London: 1852), II, pp.113–4.
11. W. Krimer, *Errinerungen eines alten Lützower Jägers* (Stuttgart: 1913), II, p. 66.

12. H. von Boyen, *Denkwürdigkeiten und Errinerungen* (Stuttgart: 1899 edn), II, pp. 383–4.
13. C. Mercer, *Journal of the Waterloo Campaign* (London: 1985 edn), p. 153.
14. See, for instance, *The Napoleonic War Journal of Captain Thomas Henry Browne* (R. N. Buckley, ed., London: 1987), p. 53.
15. See R. W. Phipps, *The Armies of the First French Republic* (Oxford: 1926–39), I, p. 184.
16. C. von Clausewitz, *On War* (M. Howard and P. Paret, eds, Princeton, NJ: 1976), pp. 91–2.
17. T. Pakenham, *The Boer War* (London: 1997 edn), pp. 41, 258, 401.
18. Britain's transport assets frequently fell under scrutiny in this regard. For instance, when confronted with a looming deficit in 1809, the Treasury proposed reductions in the Royal Wagon Train and troopship numbers as ways of lowering expenditure 'without any diminution of real efficiency'. Yet, had they been implemented, these cuts could only have compromised Britain's ability to sustain her army in the Iberian Peninsula and execute amphibious raids. See C. D. Hall, *British Strategy in the Napoleonic War* (Manchester: 1992), p. 22; R. Muir, *Britain and The Defeat of Napoleon* (New Haven, CT, and London: 1996), pp. 110–13.
19. Quoted in A. Brett-James, *Life in Wellington's Army* (London: 1972), p. 111.
20. Examples of cuirassiers can still be seen in the ceremonial cavalry of the British Household Cavalry Regiment and the French *Garde Républicaine*. When wearing full attire, such a soldier will have an average weight of some 108 kilograms and will require a horse of around 450 kilograms to carry him. Although armies could achieve economies of scale in the 1800s and thereby reduce the expenditure involved in procuring heavy cavalry, today the cost of a cuirassier's equipment, excluding his mount, is still daunting, being estimated at £33 000 by the British Ministry of Defence.
21. See F. L. Petre, *Napoleon's Conquest of Prussia, 1806* (London: 1972 edn), pp. 204–11.
22. See *Oeuvres de Frédéric le Grand* (J. D. E. Preuss, ed., Berlin: 1846–57), XXXVI, pp. 83–4.
23. Quoted in H. Delbrück, *History of the Art of War: The Dawn of Modern Warfare* (Westport, CT: 1985 edn), p. 388.
24. P. H. (Fifth Earl) Stanhope, *Notes on Conversations with ... Wellington, 1831–51* (Oxford: 1938 edn), p. 12.
25. See Gates, *Infantry*, plates 16 and 17.
26. See *A Short History of Signals in the Army* (London: 1927), p. 27; and T. Pakenham, *War*, p. 180.
27. G. Simmons, *A British Rifleman* (London: 1986 edn), p. 5.
28. See H. C. Robbins Landon, *Beethoven* (London: 1970), pp. 272, 282–3.
29. See, for example, J. B. F. Bourgogne, *Memoirs of Sergeant Bourgogne* (R. Partridge, ed., London: 1996 edn), pp. 6, 153.
30. Quoted in *Ludwig van Beethoven* (J. Schmidt-Görg and H. Schmidt, eds, London: 1970), p. 175.
31. F. Kerst, *Erinnerungen an Beethoven* (Stuttgart: 1913), II, p. 196.
32. O. Levasseur, *Souvenirs militaires d'Octave Levasseur ... 1802–15* (Paris: 1914), pp. 303–4.

33. See P. de Ségur, *An Aide-de-Camp of Napoleon: Memoirs of General Count de Ségur* (London: 1995 edn), p. 219; E. Blaze, *Life in Napoleon's Army* (London: 1995 edn), p. 39.
34. J. Coignet, *The Note-Books of Captain Coignet* (London: 1986 edn), pp. 123–4.
35. R. H. Gronow, *The Reminiscences ... of Captain Gronow* (London: 1892), I, p. 188.
36. J. B. Atkins, *The Relief of Ladysmith* (London: 1900), pp. 193–5.
37. See, for instance, R. Muir, *Tactics and the Experience of Battle in the Age of Napoleon* (New Haven, CT, and London: 1998), pp. 193–216.
38. See J. R. Elting, *Swords Around A Throne* (London: 1988), pp. 429–37.
39. Quoted in Petre, *Prussia*, p. 140.
40. *A Dorset Soldier: The Autobiography of Sgt William Lawrence, 1790–1869* (E. Hathaway, ed., Staplehurst: 1995 edn), p. 110.
41. Blaze, pp. 53–4.
42. Quoted in W. von Unger, *Blücher* (Berlin: 1907–8), II, p. 281.
43. In 1813, the Allies concluded the Trachenberg Convention, which sought to neutralize Napoleon's martial skill: whenever he advanced against one of their armies, it would retire while the others moved against his strategic flanks. See D. Gates, *The Napoleonic Wars* (London: 1997), pp. 245–6.
44. Stanhope, pp. 8–9, 80–1.
45. See Baron E. I. O. von Odeleben, *A Circumstantial Narrative of the Campaign in Saxony* (London: 1820 edn), I, p. 72–3.

2 FROM WATERLOO TO THE CRIMEA AND SOLFERINO

1. One such ship, HMS *Unicorn*, survived and now lies in Dundee.
2. C. Trebilcock, *The Industrialization of the Continental Powers, 1780–1914* (London: 1991), p. 56.
3. Ibid., p. 144.
4. R. Holtman, *The Napoleonic Revolution* (Philadelphia, PA: 1967) p. 111.
5. R. Fremdling, *Eisenbahnen und deutsches Wirtschaftswachstum, 1840–79* (Dortmund: 1975), p. 28.
6. See *Economic Development in the Long Run* (A. J. Youngson, ed., London: 1972), pp. 87–8.
7. Quoted in M. Howard, *The Franco-Prussian War* (London: 1981 edn), p. 2.
8. E. A. Pratt, *The Rise of Rail-Power in War and Conquest* (London: 1915), I, p. 1.
9. See G. E. Rothenberg, *Napoleon's Great Adversaries* (London: 1982), pp. 127–9, 148, 159–61.
10. Odeleben, *Narrative*, pp. 145–52.
11. Ibid., p. 150.
12. Quoted in Petre, *Prussia*, p. 31.
13. See Gates, *Wars*, p. 116.
14. Rothenberg, *op. cit.*, p. 168.
15. Quoted in B. D. Gooch, *The New Bonapartist Generals in the Crimean War* (Den Hague: 1959), p. 218.
16. Quoted in B. Vandervort, *Wars of Imperial Conquest in Africa, 1830–1914* (London, 1998), p. 162.

17. Quoted in J. P. T. Bury, *France, 1814–1940* (London: 1969 edn), p. 60.
18. See R. F. Leslie, *Age of Transformation* (London: 1969), pp. 229–30; Bury, *op. cit.*, p. 79.
19. See *The War Correspondents: The Crimean War* (A. Lambert and S. Badsey, eds, Stroud: 1994), p. 110. Also note Russell's report on the instruction of British troops in the use of the Minié, ibid., p. 17.
20. Quoted in ibid., p. 127.
21. See M. S. Partridge, *Military Planning for the Defence of the United Kingdom, 1814–1870* (London and New York: 1989).
22. See Gooch, *Generals*, p. 107.
23. See C. J. Bartlett, *Great Britain and Sea Power, 1815–53* (Oxford: 1963); and A. D. Lambert, *Battleships in Transition: The Creation of the Steam Battlefleet, 1815–1860* (London: 1984).
24. Fully restored, HMS *Warrior* lies at Portsmouth, England.
25. K. Chesney, *Crimean War Reader* (London: 1960), p. 42.
26. See J. Ellis, *The Social History of the Machine Gun* (London: 1975), pp. 15–16.
27. E. V. E. B. Castellane, *Journal du Maréchal de Castellane* (Paris: third edn, 1897), V, p. 40.
28. Quoted in A. Seaton, *The Crimean War: A Russian Chronicle* (London: 1977), p. 101.
29. See J. A. von Hübner, *Neun Jahre der Erinnerungen eines Österreichischen Botschafters in Paris…* (Berlin: 1904), I, p. 131.
30. See Gooch, *Generals*, pp. 95–6.
31. See B. Greenhill and A. Griffard, *The British Assault on Finland, 1854–55* (London: 1988).
32. *The Crimea Diary and Letters of Sir Charles Windham* (H. Pearse, ed., London: 1897), pp. 98–9.
33. Quoted in Gooch, *Generals*, p. 159.
34. Also see H. Strachan, *Wellington's Legacy: The Reform of the British Army, 1830–1854* (Manchester: 1984).
35. See note 18 of Chapter 1 above.
36. See Gooch, *Generals*, pp. 180–8.
37. Quoted in R. L. V. Ffrench Blake, *The Crimean War* (London: 1971), pp. 131–2.
38. *Panmure Papers* (Sir George Douglas and Sir George Dalhousie Ramsay, eds, London: 1908), I, pp. 46–51.
39. See Trebilcock, *Industrialization*, pp. 206–7.
40. See p. 187 above, and A. Gat, *The Development of Military Thought* (Oxford: 1992), pp. 39–42 and 114–72.
41. For Napier's views, see J. Luvaas, *The Education of an Army* (London: 1965), pp. 34–5.
42. Vandervort, *Wars*, p. 102.
43. Ibid., pp. 85–6.
44. See ibid., pp. 127, 132–3.
45. The larger of the two models is currently housed in the National Army Museum, London; the smaller in the Royal Armouries, Leeds.
46. See C. D. Eby, *The Road to Armageddon: The Martial Spirit in English Popular Literature, 1870–1914* (Durham and London: 1988); J. M. Mackenzie,

Propaganda and Empire (Manchester: 1984); J. Hichberger, 'Old Soldiers', in *Patriotism: The Making and Unmaking of British National Identity* (R. Samuel, ed., London: 1989).

47. See Trebilcock, *Industrialization*, pp. 446–7.
48. N. Stone, *Europe Transformed, 1878–1919* (London: 1984 edn), p. 33.
49. See D. G. Charlton, *Positivist Thought in France During the Second Empire* (Oxford: 1959).
50. See C. J. Arthur, *Dialectics of Labour* (Oxford: 1986); *The Philosophy of Thomas Hill Green* (A. Vincent, ed., London: 1986); I. M. Greengarten, *Thomas Hill Green and the Development of Liberal-Democratic Thought* (Toronto: 1981).
51. See Gates, *Infantry*, pp. 26–7.
52. R. Cobden, *Speeches on Questions of Public Policy* (J. Bright and J. Thorold Rogers, eds, London: 1870), II, p. 167.

3   THE AMERICAN CIVIL WAR

1. *The Complete Lincoln-Douglas Debates of 1858* (P. M. Angle, ed., Chicago, IL: 1991 edn), p. 117.
2. See W. W. Freehling, *The Road to Disunion* (New York and Oxford: 1990); B. Collins, *The Origins of America's Civil War* (London: 1981); R. H. Sewell, *A House Divided* (Baltimore, MD: 1988).
3. Also see R. N. Current, *Lincoln's Loyalists: Union Soldiers from the Confederacy* (Boston, MA: 1992).
4. See M. Fellman, *Inside War: The Guerrilla Conflict in Missouri*... (New York and Oxford: 1989).
5. See B. I. Wiley, *Southern Negroes* (Baton Rouge, LA: 1974 edn).
6. *Speeches and Letters of Abraham Lincoln* (M. Roe, ed., London: 1907), p. 195.
7. See D. T. Cornish, *The Sable Arm: Negro Troops in the Union Army, 1861–5* (New York: 1956), pp. 173–6.
8. Ibid., pp. 229–30.
9. See C. B. Dew, *Ironmaker to the Confederacy* (New Haven, CT: 1966).
10. See R. Andreand, *The Economic Impact of the American Civil War* (second edn, Cambridge, MA: 1967).
11. See B. Hammond, *Sovereignty and an Empty Purse: Banks and Politics in the Civil War* (Princeton, NJ: 1970).
12. See F. L. Owsley, *King Cotton Diplomacy* (Chicago, IL: 1959).
13. See S. E. Morison et al., *A Concise History of the American Republic* (New York and Oxford: 1977), pp. 314–15.
14. See J. M. McPherson, *What They Fought For, 1861–65* (Baton Rouge, LA: 1994).
15. See E. Foner, *Politics and Ideology in the Age of The Civil War* (New York and Oxford: 1980); *A Crisis of Republicanism* (L. E. Ambrosius, ed., Lincoln, NE: 1990).
16. See I. Bernstein, *The New York City Draft Riots* (New York and Oxford: 1990).
17. See P. S. Paludan, *A People's Contest: The Union and The Civil War, 1861–65* (New York: 1989).
18. See W. S. McFeely, *Grant* (New York: 1981).

19. See L. Lewis, *Sherman* (Lincoln, NE: 1993).

20. See E. C. Murdock, *Patriotism Limited, 1862–5: The Civil War Draft and the Bounty System* (Kent, OH: 1967).

21. See F. P. Prucha, *The Sword of the Republic: The US Army on the Frontier, 1783–1846* (Lincoln, NE: 1986).

22. Also see P. W. Gates, *Agriculture and The Civil War* (New York: 1965).

23. Quoted in G. C. Ward, R. Burns and K. Burns, *The Civil War* (London: 1991), p. 149.

24. See G. C. Rable, *Civil Wars: Women and the Crisis of Southern Nationalism* (Urbana, IL: 1989); W. H. Venet, *Neither Ballots Nor Bullets* (Charlottesville, VA, and London: 1991).

25. Quoted in Ward et al., *War*, p. 149.

26. See L. M. Starr, *Bohemian Brigade: Civil War Newsmen in Action* (Madison, WI: 1987).

27. See *The Long Road Home: The Civil War Experiences of Four Farmboy Soldiers...* (H. C. Lind, ed., Cranbury, NJ: 1992); *A Grand Army of Black Men* (E. S. Redkey, ed., Cambridge: 1992).

28. Quoted in Ward et al., *War*, p. 106.

29. See A. M. Josephy, *The Civil War in the American West* (New York: 1991).

30. See H. A. Gosnell, *Guns on the Western Waters* (Baton Rouge, LA: 1993).

31. *The Collected Works of Abraham Lincoln* (R. P. Basler, ed., New Brunswick, NJ: 1953), V, p. 98.

32. Quoted in R. F. Weigley, *The American Way of War* (London: 1973), p. 493.

33. Quoted in L. A. Coolidge, *Ulysses S. Grant* (Boston, MA: 1922), p. 54.

34. For a fuller discussion of Jomini's influence in this regard, see: D. Donald, *Lincoln Reconsidered: Essays on the Civil War* (second edn, New York: 1961), pp. 88–102.

35. See J. Ellis, *Machine Gun*, pp. 25–31.

36. See ibid., pp. 62–3.

37. D. Welsh, *American Civil War* (London: 1981), p. 161.

38. Ibid., p. 182.

39. See D. Pick, *The War Machine* (New Haven, CT, and London: 1996 edn), pp. 106, 178–88.

40. See *The Fremantle Diary* (W. Lord, ed., London: 1956), p. 215.

41. See, for instance, E. Hagerman, *The American Civil War and the Origins of Modern Warfare* (Bloomington and Indianapolis, IN: 1988); *On The Road to Total War* (S. Forster and J. Nagler, eds, Washington DC and Cambridge, 1997).

42. Also see M. C. Adams, *Fighting for Defeat: Union Military Failure in the East* (Lincoln, NE: 1992).

43. See D. S. Freeman, *R. E. Lee* (New York: 1935), IV, pp. 120, 122–3, 134–43.

44. See B. Catton, *Grant Takes Command* (Boston, MA: 1968), pp. 463–71.

45. See R. N. Current, *The Lincoln Nobody Knows* (New York: 1958), pp. 247–50 and 260–5.

46. *Documents of American History* (New York: 1949 edn), I, pp. 413–14.

47. W. T. Sherman, *Memoirs* (New York: 1875), II, p. 227.

48. See J. T. Glatthaar, *The March to the Sea and Beyond* (New York: 1986).

49. See Lewis, *Sherman*, pp. 635–6.

50. Ward et al., *War*, p. 398.
51. See V. B. Howard, *Religion and the Radical Republican Movement* (Lexington, KY: 1990); M. Snay, *Gospel of Disunion* (Cambridge: 1993); J. H. Moorhead, *Yankee Apocalypse* (New Haven, CT: 1978).
52. See G. Wills, *Lincoln at Gettysburg* (New York: 1992); J. M. McPherson, *Lincoln and the Second American Revolution* (New York and Oxford: 1991).

4   THE FRANCO-PRUSSIAN WAR

1. See *The United States and France* (L. M. Case and W. F. Spencer, eds, Philadelphia, PA: 1970); and *Europe Looks At The Civil War* (B. B. Sideman and L. Friedman, eds, New York: 1960).
2. Quoted in P. Howes, *The Catalytic Wars* (London: 1998), p. 430.
3. Also see J. J. Sheehan, *German Liberalism in the Nineteenth Century* (Chicago, IL: 1978).
4. See F. Kuhlich, *Die deutschen Soldaten im Krieg von 1870–71* (Frankfurt: 1995).
5. Quoted in J. Monteilhet, *Les Instiutions Militaires de la France, 1814–1932* (Paris: 1932), p. 39.
6. For an outline of this and other breaks in the French logistical loop, see Howard, *War*, p. 17.
7. Ellis, *Machine Gun*, p. 63.
8. Howard, p. 34.
9. See P. G. Griffith, *Military Thought in the French Army, 1815–1851* (Manchester: 1989), pp. 117–22.
10. See F. S. Lecomte, *Guerre de la Prusse et de l'Italie … en 1866* (Paris: 1868) II, pp. 46–7.
11. See T. Ropp, *The Development of a Modern Navy: French Naval Policy, 1871–1904* (London: 1987), p. 25.
12. See E. Chavalier, *La Marine française et la Marine allemande pendant la Guerre de 1870–71* (Paris: 1873).
13. See Gates, *Wars*, pp. 50–3.
14. See Howard, especially pp. 67, 70–1, 78, 129 and 162.
15. *An Anthology of Military Quotations* (M. Dewar, ed., London: 1990), p. 110.
16. Ibid., p. 85.
17. See Howard, pp. 122–5, 133–6, 148, 151.
18. See ibid., pp. 154–6.
19. See ibid., pp. 196–7.
20. See J. P. T. Bury, *Gambetta and the National Defence* (London: 1936).
21. See Bury, *France*, pp. 133–7.
22. See S. Audoin-Rouzeau, *1870: La France dans la Guerre* (Paris: 1989).
23. See G. Brunel, *Les Ballons du Siège de Paris* (Paris: 1933); F. F. Steenackers, *Les Télégraphes et les Postes pendant la Guerre de 1870–71* (Paris: 1883).
24. See Howard, p. 379, note 1.
25. Quoted in M. Busch, *Bismarck: Some Secret Pages of His History* (London: 1898), I, p. 273.

26. O. E. von Bismarck, *Bismarck's Letters to his Wife from the Seat of War, 1870–1* (London: 1915), p. 74.
27. Quoted in A. Jones, *The Art of War in the Western World* (Oxford: 1987), p. 401.
28. See Howard, p. 216.
29. Ibid., p. 157.
30. Ibid., pp. 114, 116.
31. Also see W. Serman, *Les Origines des Officiers français, 1848–70* (Paris: 1979).
32. See Gates, *Wars*, pp. 11–13, 171–5, 185–8.

5 FROM THE TREATY OF FRANKFURT TO THE RUSSO-JAPANESE WAR

1. Also see *Sudan: The Conquest Reappraised* (E. M. Spiers, ed., London: 1998).
2. See Vandervort, *Wars*, pp. 170–7.
3. See *Sudan*, pp. 69–70.
4. See A. N. Porter, *The Origins of the South African War* (Manchester: 1980).
5. Sir N. Lyttelton, *Eighty Years* (London: 1927), p. 212.
6. Also see E. M. Spiers, *The Late Victorian Army* (Manchester: 1992).
7. See D. M. Schurman, *The Education of a Navy: The Development of British Naval Strategic Thought, 1867–1914* (London: 1965).
8. See Gat, *Development*, pp. 173–204.
9. *Report of Chief Engineer J. W. King on European Ships of War…* (Washington: 1877), p. 175.
10. See L. C. Buhl, 'Maintaining an "American Navy", 1865–89' in *Peace and War: Interpretations of American Naval History* (K. J. Hagan, ed., Westport, CT: 1984), p. 148.
11. See S. Makarov, *Discussion of Questions in Naval Tactics* (Washington: 1898); Z. Montechant and H. Montechant, *Essai de Stratégie navale* (Paris: 1893).
12. G. W. Steevens, *With Kitchener to Khartoum* (Edinburgh: 1898), p. 22.
13. Quoted in D. Gillard, *The Struggle for Asia, 1828–1914* (London: 1977), p. 151.
14. Quoted in Gat, *op. cit.*, p. 59.
15. See Bury, p. 146.
16. *War Correspondents*, p. 168.
17. J. Kincaid, *Adventures in the Rifle Brigade and Random Shots* (Glasgow: abridged edn, 1981), p. 224.
18. Quoted in A. Brett James, *The Hundred Days* (Cambridge: 1989 edn), p. 162.
19. Quoted in Pakenham, *Boer War*, p. 76.

SELECT BIBLIOGRAPHY

(All titles published in London unless indicated otherwise.)

Alexander, R. S. *Bonapartism and Revolutionary Tradition in France* (Cambridge: 1991)
Bald, D. *Der Deutsche Generalstab, 1859–1939* (Munich: 1977)
Bartlett, C. J. *Defence and Diplomacy* (Manchester: 1993)
Beaumont, R. A. *Sword of the Raj* (Indianapolis: 1977)
Bond, B. *The Victorian Army and the Staff College, 1854–1914* (1972)
Broers, M. *Europe Under Napoleon* (1996)
Carr, W. *The Origins of The Wars of German Unification* (1991)
Chandler, D. G. *The Campaigns of Napoleon* (1966)
Charle, C. *A Social History of France in the Nineteenth Century* (Oxford: 1994)
Collins, B. *The Origins of America's Civil War* (1981)
Conacher, J. B. *Britain and The Crimea, 1855–56* (1987)
Conquest and Resistance to Colonialism in Africa (G. Maddox and T. K. Welliver, eds, New York: 1993)
Coppa, F. J. *Origins of the Italian Wars of Independence* (1992)
Cowburn, P. *The Warship in History* (1966)
Cunningham, A. *Eastern Questions in the Nineteenth Century* (1993)
Curtis, J. S. *The Russian Army under Nicholas I, 1825–55* (Durham, NC: 1965)
Droz, J. *Europe Between Revolutions, 1815–48* (1967)
Foote, S. *The Civil War* (3 vols, New York: 1958, 1963, 1974)
Gat, A. *The Development of Military Thought* (Oxford: 1992)
Gates, D. *The Napoleonic Wars* (1997)
Gates, D. *The British Light Infantry Arm* (1987)
Goldfrank, *The Origins of the Crimean War* (1994)
Gooch, B. D. *The New Bonapartist Generals in the Crimean War* (Den Hague: 1959)
Gooch, J. *Army, State and Society in Italy, 1870–1915* (1989)
Goutmann, A. *La Guerre de Crimée* (Paris: 1996)
Greenhill, B. *Steam, Politics and Patronage: The Transformation of the Royal Navy, 1815–54* (1994)
Grenville, J. A. S. *Europe Reshaped, 1848–78* (1976)
Hoppen, K. T. *The Mid-Victorian Generation, 1846–86* (Oxford: 1998)
Hougaard, W. *Modern History of Warships* (1920)
Howard, M. E. *The Franco-Prussian War* (1961)
Howes, P. *The Catalytic Wars* (1998)

Kennedy, P. M. *The Rise and Fall of British Naval Mastery* (1976)

Kinglake, A. W. *The Invasion of the Crimea* (8 vols, Edinburgh: 1863–87)

Kuropatkin, A. N. *The Russian Army and the Japanese War* (1909)

Lambert, A. D. *The Crimean War: British Grand Strategy, 1855–56* (Manchester: 1990)

Lone, S. *Japan's First Modern War: Army and Society in the Conflict with China, 1894–95* (1994)

The Making of Strategy (W. Murray, M. Knox and A. Bernstein, eds, Cambridge: 1994)

McPherson, J. M. *Battle Cry of Freedom: The Civil War Era* (New York and Oxford: 1988)

Meyer, J. et al., *Histoire de la France coloniale.* (Vol. II) *Des Origines à 1914* (Paris: 1991)

The Military in Imperial History: The French Connection (A. A. Heggoy and J. M. Haar, eds, New York: 1984)

Muir, R. *Tactics and Experience of Battle in the Age of Napoleon* (New Haven, CT: 1998)

Nish, I. *The Origins of The Russo-Japanese War* (1985)

Pakenham, T. *The Boer War* (1979)

Pakenham, T. *The Scramble for Africa* (1991)

Parish, P. J. *The American Civil War* (New York: 1975)

Peck, J. *War, the Army and Victorian Literature* (1998)

Pick, D. *War Machine: The Rationalisation of Slaughter in the Modern Age* (New Haven, CT: 1993)

Pilbeam, P. M. *Republicanism in Nineteenth-Century France, 1814–71* (1995)

Porch, D. *The March to the Marne: The French Army, 1871–1914* (Cambridge: 1981)

Porter, A. N. *European Imperialism, 1860–1914* (New York: 1996)

Pratt, E. *The Rise of Rail-power in War and Conquest, 1833–1914* (1915)

Ralston, D. B. *Importing the European Army* (Chicago: 1990)

Robinson R. et al., *Africa and the Victorians* (second edn, London: 1981)

Royle, T. *Crimea* (1999)

Smith, I. R. *The Origins of The South African War, 1899–1902* (1996)

Spiers, E. M. *The Army and Society, 1815–1914* (1980)

Spiers, E. M. *The Late Victorian Army, 1868–1902* (Manchester: 1992)

Stone, N. *Europe Transformed, 1878–1919* (1985)

Strachan, H. *From Waterloo to Balaclava: Tactics, Technology and the British Army* (1985)

Strachan, H. *The Politics of the British Army* (Oxford: 1997)

Trebilcock, C. *The Industrialization of the Great Powers, 1780–1914* (1981)

West African Resistance: The Military Response to Colonial Occupation (M. Crowder, ed., 1971)

INDEX